Event, Metaphor, Memory

Central Gorakhpur

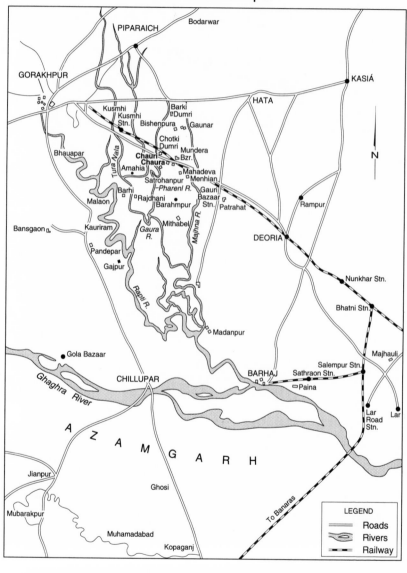

PIPARAICH
Bodarwar
GORAKHPUR
KASIÁ
Kusmhi
Barki
HATA
Kusmhi Dumri
Stn.
Bishenpura
Gaunar
Chotki
Dumri
Mundera
Bhauapar
Chauri
Bzr.
Chaura
Amahia
Mahadeva
Menhian
Satrohanpur
Pharenl R.
Barhi
Gauri
Malaon
Rajdhani
Bazaar
Rampur
Barahmpur
Stn.
Patrahat
Bansgaon
Mithabel
Kauriram
Gaura
DEORIA
R.
Pandepar
Gajpur
Nunkhar Stn.
Bhatni Stn.
Madanpur
Majhauli
Gola Bazaar
Salempur Stn.
BARHAJ
CHILLUPAR
Sathraon Stn.
Ghaghra River
Paina
Lar
Lar
Road
Stn.
A Z A M G A R H
Jianpur
Ghosi
Mubarakpur
To Banaras
LEGEND
Muhamadabad
Roads
Kopaganj
Rivers
Railway

Tura Nala
Rapti R.
Majhna R.

N

Event, Metaphor, Memory

Chauri Chaura 1922 - 1992

Shahid Amin

University of California Press (1995)
Berkeley   Los Angeles

University of California Press
Berkeley and Los Angeles, California

Published by arrangement with Oxford University Press

© Oxford University Press 1995

Library of Congress Cataloging-in-Publication Data

Amin, Shahid.
    Event, metaphor, memory : Chauri Chaura 1922-1992 / Shahid Amin.
        p.   cm.
    Includes bibliographical references and index.
    ISBN 0-520-08779-8. — ISBN 0-520-08780-1 (pbk.)
    1. Chauri Chaura (India) — Politics and government.   I. Title.
DS486.C464A45   1995
954'.2—dc20   94-737
                                                                                CIP

Typeset by Rastrixi, New Delhi, India
Printed in the United States of America
9 8 7 6 5 4 3 2 1

For
Ranajit Guha

Acknowledgements

I have worked intermittently on this book for the last fourteen years—a long enough period to accumulate numerous debts, some of them outstanding.

I should like to thank the President and Fellows of Trinity College, Oxford, for electing me to a Junior Research Fellowship (1979–82) and for supporting research in England and India. Travel grants from the British Academy and the Indian Council of Historical Research materially aided fieldwork. A short-term visiting fellowship at the Research School of Pacific Studies, Australian National University, Canberra, in the summer of 1987 gave me an opportunity to essay an outline of this work. The actual writing was done during 1990 and 1993 while I was a Fellow successively at the Stanford Humanities Center, Stanford University; the Shelby Cullom Davis Center for Historical Studies, Princeton University; and the Wissenschaftskolleg zu Berlin. I am much beholden to each of these remarkable institutions for their most generous support of this project. My special thanks to Bliss Cornachan and Charlie Junkerman at Stanford; Natalie Zemon Davis and Kari Hoover at Princeton; and Wolf Lepenies and Joachim Nettlebeck in Berlin. I am grateful to my home university in Delhi for granting me leave of absence for three years.

I wish to thank the librarian and archivists at the St Stephen's College Library, Ratan Tata Library, Nehru Memorial Museum and Library, and the National Archives of India, all in Delhi; the UP State Archives and the Secretariat Library in Lucknow; the India Office Library and Records, London (and Richard Bingle and Shabana Mahmud in particular); the Stanford and Princeton University library sytems; and Frau Bottomley and her colleagues at the Bibliothek at the Wissenschaftskolleg zu Berlin.

Heather Joshi, David Page, Dinesh Bhugra, Mr Ved Prakash, Alok Sinha, Rana and Ataullah Qureshi, Habib Ahmad, Ramchandra Dwivedi, Saad Saidullah and Professor Ramchandra Tiwari have helped me in various ways in London, Lucknow, Allahabad and Gorakhpur. My acquaintances and informants in Chauri Chaura, Chotki Dumri, Gaunar and Mundera have greatly affected the shape of this work.

Parts of this book were presented to seminars at universities and colleges at the following places: Stanford, Berkeley, Santa Cruz, Chicago, Ann Arbor, Charlottsville, Philadelphia and Oberlin in the United States; Toronto and York in Canada; and at the School of Oriental and African Studies in London. I am also grateful to the participants of the Friday Sociology Colloquium at the University of Delhi, and in particular to J.P.S. Uberoi, Veena Das, Deepak Mehta, Savyasachi, Roma Chatterji, and Rita Brara.

Several colleagues and friends helped with their comments on the manuscript as it took shape during 1990–1. I wish to thank Akhil and Purnima Gupta, Lata Mani, Julio Ramos, Margo Hendricks, Elizabeth Wood, Daniel Herwitz, Barbara and Tom Metcalf, Eugene Irschick, T.N. Pandey, Dilip Basu and Paul Kashap for their suggestions. Peter Brown, Christopher Hill, Natalie Davis, Bernard Cohn, Arcadio Diaz, David Boon, Gyan Prakash, Webb Keane, Nick Dirks, Pratap Mehta, John Kelly, Steven Fiereman, Zacharay Lockman, Richard Elphick, Leonard Blussé, David Ludden, Homi Bhabha, Arjun Appadurai, Prasenjit Duara, Gayatri Chakravorty Spivak, Upendra Baxi, Ashis Nandy, Lloyd and Susanne Rudolph, Carol Breckenridge, Una Chaudhuri and Luisa Passerini have all very kindly commented on a part or the whole of the manuscript.

My colleagues in the Subaltern Studies team: Partha Chatterjee, David Hardiman, Gautam Bhadra, David Arnold, Gyan

Pandey and Dipesh Chakrabarty have read successive drafts and offered much constructive advice. I also wish to thank Ravi Dayal for his valuable editorial comments. My editor at Oxford University Press has been, once again, remarkably helpful. I have also benefited from the comments and suggestions of Lynne Withey, Tom Laquer, and the two anonymous referees of the University of California Press.

And finally a big thank you to Bano and young Adil:

hāsil-i-husn-o-ishq bas itna
ādmi ādmi ko pahchāne

Delhi   SHAHID AMIN
23 August 1994

Contents

Illustrations *(between pp. 130 and 131)*

1   Rubber Stamp Impression of Mahatma Gandhi on the Register of Volunteers, Gorakhpur Congress Committee. A similar 'image' (*murti*), with customized name and address, was marketed in 1921 for a rather high Rs 3.50.
    Source: Exhibit 78, Chauri Chaura Records, Gorakhpur.

2   A 'Swadeshi commodity' of the time of the Khilafat-Non-Co-operation Movement. The names of Shaukat Ali and Mohammad Ali are engraved alongside Mahatma Gandhi's.
    Source: In author's possession.

3   Receipt for a one-rupee contribution to the Tilak Swaraj Fund, 1921.
    Source: Exhibit 453, Chauri Chaura Records.

4   A more elaborate receipt for contribution to the Khilafat Fund, 1920.
    Source: Exhibit 453, Chauri Chaura Records.

5   Cartoon in *Amrita Bazar Patrika*, Calcutta, 15 August 1947.
    Source: Album no. 129, photograph no. 4658, NMML, New Delhi.

6   Prefatory Note to the pictorial catalogue of the violence compiled by the Provincial Government.
    Source: CID File on Chauri Chaura, Lucknow.

7   The aftermath of the violence, from the official album on Chauri Chaura.
    Source: CID File on Chauri Chaura, Lucknow.

Prologue

When writing histories of the unlettered—workers or peasants who produce goods and services, not documents—it is now conventional to latch on to extraordinary events in the lives of such people.[1] Peasants do not write, they are written about. The speech of humble folk is not normally recorded for posterity, it is wrenched from them in courtrooms and inquisitorial trials. Historians have therefore learned to comb 'confessions' and 'testimonies' for their evidence, for this is where peasants cry out, dissimulate or indeed narrate. Like other members of my tribe, I have in this book attempted to interrogate the interrogators. In order not to write like the Judge, I have tried to find out how the Judge wrote.

This book studies one dramatic occurrence—the anti-police 'riot' of 4 February 1922 in a small market town in north India.[*] On this violent act hangs my tale of peasant politics and Gandhian nationalism.

This approach may seem perverse, for it involves unravelling a professedly non-violent polity by focusing on a murderous event. Yet my intention in doing this is not to give the lie to the self-image of Indian nationalism. For who if not India's peasants, with their adoration and regard for Gandhi, made him into a Mahatma? But precisely for this reason it is necessary to historicize an event which all Indians, when commemorating the nation, are obliged to remember—only in order to forget—as an 'error': the peasant-

---

[*] Subsequent uses of the word 'riot' will not show it within inverted commas, these should be taken as read.

rioters of 1922 who burnt the police precinct did so to the cry of 'Victory to Mahatma Gandhi!'

My book does not attempt a socio-psychological explanation of this act of peasant violence in colonial India.[2] Instead, I re-narrate a richly documented event in order to fathom the curiously 'Gandhian' politics of the peasants before they entered the record as 'rioters'. I also search out here the relationship between Gandhi and his peasant followers by correlating present-day oral accounts of 'those times' with what lies preserved in the judicial and nationalist record. This, I hope, will illustrate some of the problems and possibilities of doing 'historical fieldwork'.

The value of the riot of 4 February consists not just in the *matériel* it offers on peasant politics. This violent event, with its iconic status in the history of the Indian nation and Gandhi's career, equally affords insights into the ways of nationalist historiography. Most writings on Third World nationalism, in their preoccupation with social origins and politics, have tended to bypass the question of nationalist narratives. The ways in which the nation was talked about are considered an aspect of ideology; or, alternatively, writing the history of a particular national struggle itself becomes a part of an ongoing nationalist enterprise. This leaves virtually no space for the *interrogation* of narrative strategies by which a people get constructed into a nation.

The master saga of nationalist struggles is built around the retelling of certain well-known and memorable events. There is very often an exasperating and chronicle-like quality about such celebratory accounts, but the significance of nationalist narratives lies in their elaborate and heroic setting down, or 'figuring', the triumph of good over evil.[3] The story of Indian nationalism, for instance, is written up as a massive undoing of Colonial Wrongs by a non-violent and disciplined people.

The triumph of such histories lies not only in making people remember events from a shared past: the nationalist master narrative also induces a selective national amnesia in relation to specified events which would fit awkwardly, even seriously inconvenience, the neatly woven pattern.[4] These awkward events are recounted so as to embellish another, and rather more edifying, tale. The exclusion of such events and the marginalized references to them serve the purpose of distinguishing authentic popular protest from 'crime'. The organization, unity, discipline and morality of the nationalist public are thereby underscored.

The memorialization of the violence at Chauri Chaura—that being the name of the police station which the peasants burnt to a perfidious invocation of Gandhi—has been an obsessive concern within most accounts of Indian nationalism. Chauri Chaura, a place name, has since become a figure of speech, a trope for all manner of untrammelled peasant violence, specifically in opposition to disciplined non-violent mass satyagrahas. This book is a history of Chauri Chaura as both event and metaphor. I write about the riot as an event fixed in time (early 1922) and also as a metaphor gathering significances outside this time-frame. Simultaneously, I attempt to reveal the process by which the same occurrence is first excluded from the calendar of nationalist events and later allowed entry into the official record of the Nation by special pleading—as an instance of 'politics by other means'.

This double movement enables the nationalist mainstream—the Gandhian, in our case—to appear as both 'pure' and accommodating at different moments within the story of the nation: one represents the moment of the struggle, the other represents its appropriation by the nation-state. So my concern is with how nationalist history is made and remade. I hope also to uncover the strategies—narrative or otherwise—which go into its making.

Recovering the event from the judicial and nationalist record has not been easy: interpretations of the evidence, archival as well as oral, are a necessary part of the history of that event. The empirical content of the riot—the physical occurrence and the light it sheds on the structure and process of peasant politics—cannot be deduced entirely independently of the pronouncements of the Judge and the discourse of Gandhi, the Father of the Nation. The desire to discover in oral history an entirely different source from the archival offers a faint promise. But for me it was not a question of counterposing local remembrance against authorized accounts: the process by which historians gain access to pasts is richly problematic, as is the relationship between memory and record, and the possibilities of arriving at a more nuanced narrative, a thicker description, seem enhanced by putting the problems on display.

A large part of this book is based on fieldwork in and around Chauri Chaura in August 1988, February 1989 and July 1991. My major concern has been to try and give the event a pre-history. I attempt this by underlining local contexts, nationalist or other-wise, within which most retellings begin and assume form. This I hope will help take out the elements of both spontaneity and stereotypicality from this police–peasant encounter.

During my field trips I was not looking for particular inform-ants but for a very special group of people: relatives of the rioters. During my quest, armed with knowledge of the 'criminal' pasts of the ancestors of these relatives that I interviewed, I felt like a colonial policeman! I was of course different. I was welcomed in Chauri Chaura as an intellectual, the sort of fellow who travels halfway round the globe to talk to peasants of the neighbouring district. Among the village intelligentsia I was 'the visiting historian'; to my precious octogenarian informants I was the man from Delhi who was interested in their pasts.

Which differences between them and me, I asked myself, were erased through our affinity? Which remained? And which were created as we talked about the event, about Gandhi, and about much else besides? How would these affect the possibility of generating a different narrative of Chauri Chaura and Indian nationalism? My field encounters were very moving, but this book eschews excessive concern with my own 'subject position'. The irony of an old, low-caste woman using the same term—*sarkār*—for the colonial government and for me (in the latter case, an attention-seeking honorific) during our conversations was not lost upon my mind; nor was the use of *babu*, a term of endearment for children which verbally also designates members of a junior landed lineage, and more generally any male superior to the speaker. My familiarity with the local Bhojpuri dialect may paradoxically have accentuated the use of status-markers in our conversation; my desire to research a history of Chauri Chaura *in* Chauri Chaura may in turn have helped forge a community of purpose. Historical fieldwork and the narratives emerging out of it were seen by many to feed into a history. *'Kitāb nikri! Kitāb!'* (a book will come out of all this) was the cue used in the village to align memories into stories.

There remains the question of language and readership. How to make the dialect of my informants, which would anyway have to be reshaped into a standard Hindi or Urdu, intelligible in the words of this book? What linguistic and cultural communication must precede the work of the historian? How much translation and orientation is required to de-ghettoize Indian history such that a history of Chauri Chaura is read independent of India and Area Studies affiliations? In other words, what must readers know beforehand in order to empathize with this shifting tale of an obscure event with a long afterlife? I try to take such difficulties into account without necessarily setting out systematically to answer all these questions.[5]

Not each and every spoken word included here has been translated. While reporting local speech I have also retained some quotations in transliterated Bhojpuri; these are sometimes followed by a translation, on other occasions with only a paraphrase or a brief introductory comment. At several places, where it was necessary to linguistically underscore a point made in the text, I have reproduced the dialect in the Hindi script within the endnotes. Apart from making peasant speech available to the north Indian Hindi public, I hope this graphic device helps visualize the distance that this book straddles and falls short of.

What follows is a story of anonymous characters from a self-defining event of Gandhian nationalism. The peasant-actors who people this book are unknown in India. They belong to a well-known riot about which nothing much needs to be known. Many may find my account too deeply localized. But a narrative which seeks to interrogate official accounts with local memory can ill afford to wrap individual actors in prefabricated pasts within which the local is habitually forsaken in the supposed interests of a grand national.

No specialized knowledge of India is presumed. I hope those who know their nation will also discover something anew in this story of Chauri Chaura.

Part One

'You know this business about the *thana*—the burning etc.—all this leads back to him—to Gandhi Maharaj'.
                                    — Ramji Chamar, Chotki Dumri, 19.8.1991

'. . . Little reported activity preceded the massacre of the police at Chauri Chaura'.
                                    — Police Abstracts of Intelligence, U.P., 11.2.1922

Impressions

'And then an insignificant hamlet in the United Provinces, in a district whose Commissioner was proud to have used no special powers to keep the peace, wrote its name of Chauri Chaura into the record with the slaughter of twenty-two policemen by a maddened crowd.'

—Francis Watson, *The Trial of Mr Gandhi* (London, 1969), p. 49

'The Chauri Chaura occurrence which took place in the month of February 1922 is unique of its kind [*sic*] in the annals of the world.'

—Abhinandan Prasad, to Collector, Gorakhpur, 7.5.1923

'There is no parallel in the whole history of the British rule in India to the tragic event of Chauri Chaura . . . I see in it the beginning of a French Revolution in India.'

—'The Hero of Gorakhpur Tragedy' from a correspondent,
The Leader, 22.2.1922

'I must confess that I do not see the atmosphere for it [Civil Disobedience] today. I want to discover a formula whereby sufficient provision can be made for avoiding suspension by reason of Chauri Chaura.'

—Gandhi, early 1930, *CWMG*, xlii, pp. 376–7

' . . . there has been a second Chauri Chaura at a police station in Ghazipur district, the police station burnt and the staff murdered.'

—Governor, United Provinces, to Viceroy, 18.8.1942

'Babu! Apne dil se samajh leen! Ab kahwān le biyān kihal ja?' (Now Sir! Fathom it after your own heart! How much more can one narrate?)

—Naujadi, Chotki Dumri, 21.2.1989

1

The Riot and History

On 4 February 1922 a crowd of peasants burnt a police station at Chauri Chaura in Uttar Pradesh, killing twenty-three policemen. Gandhi's prompt condemnation of this 'crime' led to the relocation of this day within the life of the Indian nation.[1] To be a Gandhian in the spring of 1922, and for some time to come, was to share in an authoritative recollection of this anti-nationalist riot.

The unforgettable event was largely forgotten in nationalist lore; it came to be remembered only as the episode which forced Gandhi to call off his all-India movement of non-co-operation with the British. The 'true' significance of Chauri Chaura in Indian History lay outside the time and place of its occurrence. A spontaneous and mindless riot, it was quarantined within a consequentialist past: nationalist verse, political prose, and the memoirs of distinguished Indians all invoked the event only in order to explain the termination of a particular phase of our Freedom Struggle. Chauri Chaura became 'Chauri Chaura': the event, with all its distinctiveness and specificity and multiple peculiarities, was written out as it was recounted.

STOPPAGE OF THE NON-CO-OPERATION MOVEMENT OF 1921

This was the rubric under which a long demotic poem, published in 1931 to mobilize the nation, retailed the happenings of 4 February 1922. *Gandhi's War, or A History of Satyagraha*, to give this broadsheet its full title, had no place, being a 'proper' nationalist history, for an 'incensed "public" [that] burnt the police station'; Chauri Chaura was the place where that normal history was made to stop. So strong was this desire to immunize Indian nationalism from the violence of Chauri Chaura that, oblivious of chronology, the poem ends the Non-Co-operation Movement with the calendar year 1921, a month before the infamous event actually brought about its suspension.[2]

Nationalist prose of that time could be equally ungainly on the subject of Chauri Chaura. In a prefatory sketch of the Non-Co-operation Movement, the 'serious riots' of 'the month of February' are phrased with an emphasis on Gandhi's intentions and reactions. Babu Rajendra Prasad's awkward sentence, quoted below, illustrates the manner in which 'Chauri Chaura' was later recollected in nationalist historiography.

In the month of February, serious riots took place at a place called Chauri Chaura, in the district of Gorakhpur, and Mahatma Gandhi who had proceeded to Bardoli to lead a campaign of mass Civil Disobedience and had gone so far as to issue his message to the Viceroy and Government intimating his intention of mass Civil Disobedience had to suspend the campaign as a consequence.[3]

It would be tedious to recount exactly how ill this necessary footnote within Indian history has fared at the hands of professional historians and nationalist Indians. The former have sometimes even got the date wrong, and there has been some understandable confusion about the exact number of policemen killed.[4] I say this not as a disappointed local enthusiast who was born fifteen miles down the railway track from the scene of that bloody encounter. When historical significance is attached to an occurrence independent of the event, the facts of the case cease to matter. And where all subsequent accounts are parasitic on a prior memory, documentation seems almost unnecessary.

Indian schoolboys know of Chauri Chaura as that alliterative place-name which flits through their history books around the year 1922. Invariably, the riot is mentioned as a part of the activity of another subject, notably Mahatma Gandhi, and often the struggles of a nation. The number of policemen killed, Gandhi's torment, the suspension of an all-India movement because of localized violence—these are the images that school primers convey with their abbreviated allusion to the riot at Chauri Chaura.

I have no desire to memorialize the riot as if it were an *autonomous* event. Mine is neither a deliberately stark contrast against that narrative tradition, nor an attempt to celebrate some universalist notion—the encrusted economic interests of the peasantry, within the autarkically local—reduction of rents, opposition to landlordism, etc. The exclusion of *beliefs*—about the wondrous and the momentous, about Gandhi and the nation—would be equally distorting in the other direction. The interest of my story lies in its entanglement of a local affair with the affairs of Indian nationalism—as ideology, as practice, as history. To locate the rioters of Chauri Chaura outside this frame, to assign them agency only as genuine anti-Gandhians, is to write misleadingly; it is to be impervious to the paradoxes of political action and to be ignorant of the ways in which meanings get glued to events and the ways in which memory plays upon the certitude of facts. It is also to impoverish story-telling.

My story must begin with Gandhi, even though he disavowed himself from 'Chauri Chaura'. To begin any other way would be erroneous, because Gandhi is still the site upon which the contest over 'Chauri Chaura' takes place.

2

A Narrative of the Event

In late-1920 Gandhi was able to push through a radical programme of non-co-operation with British rule. Termed *asahyog*, this involved a boycott of the commodities and institutions through which England was able to rule India with the aid of Indians. Gandhi, the author of this movement, toured the country, campaigning for the boycott of foreign goods (especially machine-made cloth) as well as the legal, educational, and 'representative' institutions which had been newly introduced, while arguing also for a symbolic refusal by Indians to participate in the colonial system of rewards and honours. Two dramatic affirmations, swadeshi and ahimsa, were to accompany this quintet of Great Denials and presage in tandem the transition from Raj to Swaraj.*

The movement towards swaraj was made possible by the creation of a new nationalist-activist—the satyagrahi-volunteer. It has been suggested that Gandhi's ideas about the satyagrahi underwent a marked change after the violence which accompanied the first all-India mass campaign he organized against the Rowlatt Acts of 1919. There was in him 'little concern', till 1919, 'about the distinction between leader and satyagrahi and the masses . . . or about the organizational or normative safeguards against the inherent unpredictability of a negative consciousness playing itself out in the political battleground.'[5]

---

* *Swadeshi*: (campaign for) Indian-made goods; *Ahimsa*: non-violence; *Swaraj*: lit. self-rule; an ambiguous term which in the early 1920s meant 'freedom' of various sorts. A polysemic word, *Swaraj* was open to different interpretations and understandings.

Summing up the experiences of his triumphant train tours of 1920 Gandhi wrote: 'The Congress is a demonstration for the mob . . . Though organised by thoughtful men and women . . . our popular demonstrations are unquestionably mob-demonstrations.'[6] This nationalist manifestation of the people as a mob was now in need of an urgent disciplinary solution.[7] In September 1920 Gandhi put forward a twenty-point programme for controlling this 'mobocracy' of *darshan*-seeking crowds.* To overcome 'this mobocratic stage' of political development, it was obligatory for 'everyone to obey [the] volunteers' instructions without question'; 'It is no part of the *audience* to preserve order. They do so by keeping motionless and silent';[8] 'Before we can make real headway', Gandhi concluded, 'we must train these masses of men who have a heart of gold, who feel for the country, who want to be taught and led.' And then he added: 'But a few intelligent, sincere, local workers are needed, and the whole nation can be organised to act intelligently, and democracy can be evolved out of mobocracy.'[9]

Mobocracy—'an ugly word greased with loathing, a sign of craving for control and its frustration'[10]—required Gandhian volunteers to purge it of its originary, subaltern impurities. Volunteers, almost by definition, had to stand apart from demonstrators: they were to discipline nationalist exuberance by acting as the 'people's policemen'.[11]

By the winter of 1921 not 'a few' but many thousand volunteers had overrun the nationalist arena. In fact the numerical strength of these volunteers in a district (or its jail) came to be regarded as a manifestation of the nationalist spirit in a particular locality. The signing of a paper called the Pledge Form, which started after the various volunteer organizations had been outlawed in November 1921, was documentary proof of mass civil

* *Darshan* : Paying homage to a holy object or a saintly person by presenting oneself in the vicinity of the personage.

disobedience. These pledge forms were formidable three-part affi-
davits. They were constructed to function as a nationalist record
and had therefore to be filled out in triplicate: one copy to be
retained in the village, the other two to be lodged at the district
and provincial headquarters. People became volunteers by pledg-
ing 'in the name of God' to wear *khaddar*,* practice non-violence,
obey the 'orders of officers', 'oppose as a Hindu the evil of un-
touchability', uphold the principle of religious amity and unity in
a multi-religious society, suffer all manner of hardships (including
imprisonment), and refrain if arrested from asking for financial
support for kith and kin.[12]

In mid-January 1921 a village unit (*mandal*) of such volunteers was set up in Chotki Dumri, a village one mile west of the
Chauri Chaura police station.[13] A functionary of the Gorakhpur
District Congress and Khilafat Committees had been invited for
this purpose by one Lal Mohammad Sain of Chaura. Gandhi's
desire to fuse his campaign for non-co-operation with the Khilafat
Movement—launched by Indian Muslims in 1919 to prevent the
dismemberment of the Ottoman Empire and 'preserve intact the
spiritual and temporal authority of the Ottoman Sultan as the
Caliph of Islam'—was an organizational success in Gorakhpur.[14]
In the winter of 1921–2 the Khilafat and Congress Volunteer
Organizations were merged into a composite National Volunteer
Corps.[15]

Hakeem Arif, the man invited to Chauri Chaura from
Gorakhpur, gave a lecture on nationalism and Gandhian political
economy, appointed some 'officers', and took the evening train
back to his district headquarters. The peasant officers of Dumri
mandal then went about their business. Pledge forms were filled
out, subscriptions were collected, and, with a characteristic extension of the Gandhian message, meat, fish and liquor, rather than
retail outlets of foreign cloth, became the target of picketing.

* *Khaddar* : homespun, handwoven cloth.

The famous apocalyptic clash with the police had its roots in this mundane and vociferous attempt by local volunteers both to stop trade in these articles and to enforce a just price for meat and fish in the nearby Mundera bazaar. Some days before the main event, police officers beat back volunteers and also administered a salutary thrashing to one Bhagwan Ahir, a demobilized soldier from the Mesopotamia campaign (and therefore a government pensioner) who had no business to be so demonstratively disloyal to the Raj. The leaders of the Dumri mandal sent letters to other leaders in neighbouring villages, informing them of this oppression on the part of the local police.

Volunteers were urged to congregate at Dumri on Saturday, 4 February, a bazaar day at Mundera. Arrangements were made for this gathering at the village threshing-floor (*khalihān*): raw sugar was collected for refreshments, gunny cloth was spread on the floor, and garlands prepared to welcome the volunteer chiefs. The meeting was eventful: a debate on the best course of action took place, and 'influential persons' sent by the *thanedar* to dissuade the crowd were disregarded even as their bona-fides were questioned.* The 'real' leaders were garlanded. Nazar Ali, one such leader from Chotki Dumri, bound the crowd together by oath, and the volunteers marched in serried ranks to the thana to demand an explanation from the thanedar and then mass picket the nearby Mundera bazaar. It was this procession of volunteers which clashed with the police on the afternoon of 4 February 1922.

Gupteshar Singh, the thanedar, was expecting the crowd; additional policemen had been sent for from Gorakhpur. Eight armed guards arrived by the morning train and these, along with local constables and *goraits* and *chaukidars* (rural policemen) from neighbouring villages, were assembled in an intimidatory fashion

* *Thanedar*: station officer, in-charge of a police station, or *thana*. Also referred to as S.I. or Sub-Inspector (of Police); called *daroga* in indigenous parlance.

to dissuade the crowd from marching on to the bazaar. The symbolic display of force failed, however. Influential leaders had once again to be pressed into action to parley with the leaders (*māliks*) within the crowd.[16]

Allowed to pass unhindered in the direction of the bazaar, the crowd celebrated the ineffectiveness of the police with derisory claps and by shouting a common north-Indian abuse: the thanedar, and by extension the government (*sarkar*), it said, were 'shit scared'![17] The police officer sought to recover lost ground by firing in the air. This signal was disregarded. It was as if an amber light, a cautionary sign of 'danger ahead, retreat', was read as the precursor of green, 'go ahead'.

'Bullets have turned into water by the grace of Gandhiji' was the construction put by the crowd on the failure of the police's symbolic firing. The crowd then responded by rushing and brick-batting the police. This time, cornered, the police's firing was real; three of the crowd were killed and several injured. But the hail of stones which came in return from the adjacent railway track, where the furious peasants now stood, was overwhelming. The police-men retreated into the thana. The crowd locked them in and set fire to the building by sprinkling it with kerosene oil seized from the bazaar. Twenty-three policemen, including the station-officer, were battered and burnt to death.

The death of the policemen was not the end of this riot. Police property was systematically destroyed, rifles were smashed, and the bits of brass with which police *lathīs* were capped (to make them deadly weapons) were taken off.* Over three dozen chauki-dars managed to escape by throwing away their conspicuous red turbans and milling into the crowd. The police turbans (*pagrīs*) of these rural policemen were torn to shreds.

The crowd dispersed by nightfall. Many among it did not return to their homes but ran to relatives in distant locations. A

---

* *Lathi* : a stout bamboo stave.

violent inversion of the role assigned to volunteers came about with the 'abolition of the thana', which was proclaimed by them as a sign of the advent of 'Gandhi raj'. By the time reinforcements reached the smouldering thana, Dumri and the nearby villages were deserted. In police parlance 'the rioters had absconded'.

The repression was immediate. Chotki Dumri was raided early next morning. But the leaders were not at home, and the identity of the other rioters had to await the naming of names and the discovery of incriminating documents. The fact of having signed the pledge form was now documentary proof of being a volunteer and, by extension, of participation in the riot. Lists of volunteers were compiled from police and nationalist records, and where names tallied with an identification in a confessional or in an eyewitness account, the peasant found himself in the dock as a Chauri Chaura accused.[18]

The Gorakhpur nationalists moved quickly. Members of the District Congress, along with some other 'public men', were at the thana the next day. An emergency meeting on 9 February ordered the dismantling of volunteer groups in the villages around Chauri Chaura, and an end to aggressive nationalist activity in the district altogether.[19] Devdas Gandhi, Mahatma Gandhi's son, rushed to Gorakhpur and issued a statement on 11 February.[20] Mahatma Gandhi had already proposed a general suspension of 'mass civil disobedience'. Civil disobedience was suspended all over India on 12 February.[21]

In consultation with local leaders Devdas helped set up a Chauri Chaura Support Fund. Its immediate aim was to show 'genuine sympathy' and 'offer monetary help' to 'those in trying circumstances on both sides'; the ultimate objective was 'to atone (*prāyashchit*) for this sudden and inauspicious mishap'. While every district in the province was to raise up to Rs 2000 for this project, the guilty people of Gorakhpur were to contribute an almost punitive Rs 10,000.[22]

Gandhiji suspended the satyagraha movement. Branded with the stigma of violence, the people of the region endured all manner of suffering for years to come.[23]

So says the demi-official history of the freedom struggle in Gorakhpur district in 1972, fifty years after the event. It was not just some peasants who had rioted that day. The dead weight of collective guilt had fallen on an entire population—of Gorakhpur district in particular and the nation more generally.

Part Two

'Chaura, or Chaura Chauri, a village in tappa Keutali of pargana South Haveli, stands on the unmetalled Gorakhpur and Deoria road, sixteen miles south-east of the former place. It was in 1872 inhabited by 132 persons only. But Chaura has a third-class police station, a district post office, a small hostel (*sarāi*) for travellers, a cattle pound, and an elementary school'.

— *Statistical, Descriptive and Historical Account of the North-Western Provinces of India, vi* (1881)

3

Chauri Chaura-Dumri-Mundera

Chauri Chaura, the place name, owes its existence to the railways. It was the decision of a traffic manager to name the wayside rail station after two adjacent villages, Chaura and Chauri, which created this new site in January 1885. The warehouse and the sidings were located in the smaller of the two settlements, in Chaura, a place with 'so few grain dealers . . . that supplies must be brought a considerable distance', noted the *Gazetteer* in 1881.[1] The notional importance of the much larger village, Chauri, was retained in the order in which the alliterative place-name was written up. Peasants, following the local dialectal shift might invert the word order, as they do even today, but the inscription at the station had placed the weight where it was due.

Chauri Chaura was just a railway station; no such place existed outside the platform and the *mālgodām*.* The bazaar as it developed from the mid-1880s, and the police station that had been set up after the Rebellion of 1857, were both called simply Chaura. It was to Chaura police station that the peasants marched on the afternoon of 4 February 1922; it was the Chaura thana which was burnt that evening. As reinforcements and punitive expeditions arrived at the rail station, and as the riot gained a certain notoriety in nationalist and official writings, the name Chauri Chaura came to acquire a substantive presence. And when the burnt-out tiled-and-thatched thana was rebuilt in brick and mortar, incorporating a mock turret-tower to enable police marksmen a better view of

* The north-Indian term for the colonial-English 'godown'.

marching crowds, the new ground plan was called 'the Chauri Chaura type'.

It was the railways that made Chaura village a bazaar. Between 1872 and 1881 its population had increased by 85 (from 265 to 360), over the next ten years it jumped up by another 300. New dwellings sprang up on both sides of the unmetalled road, and a large *gola* or line of warehouses was constructed adjoining the station yard. There were sixty-seven houses in 1881, while another eighty dwellings—mostly shops and godowns in which the owners also lived—were set up over the next ten years. Eleven per cent of all inhabitants were Kalwars, a caste of distillers and petty merchants who had a dominant presence in Chaura and the nearby Mundera bazaar as well. One-third of the population was now non-agricultural, made up equally of traders, brokers and labourers. Hides and skins from the adjacent Bhopa bazaar, split lentils from the much bigger Mundera, wheat (some rice), linseed, and sugar (both refined and raw) were freighted out from Chaura; cotton cloth, kerosene oil, nails and matches were the main items of import.[2]

This pattern of trade already in evidence in 1890 was to continue substantially unchanged into the 1920s. Further development of railways in other parts of the District intercepted some of the traffic that had come down from the north to the Chaura railhead, but pulses, grain, raw sugar, and hides retained their importance in the regional economy.[3]

A novel development in twentieth-century Chaura was the introduction of steam engines for the manufacture of sugar, rapeseed oil and mustard oil. A small model sugar factory, exhibited at an industrial exhibition in 1911 and put up in partnership by Sardar Harcharan Singh, the supervisor of the bazaar, had been a failure.[4] The *baillot*, as the sugar boiler was called by the peasants, was inoperational in 1922, but there were a total of fifty-six ordinary oil-pressing *kolhus* attached to three steam engines in the bazaar. The wear-and-tear of these wooden oil-presses was such that they had to be replaced every two months, in some cases even earlier. One of the mills, owned by Sardar Umrao Singh, the landlord of Chaura, was leased out to a local Kalwar trader at a high rent of Rs 1380 per year; the biggest was owned by a Marwari merchant, and the third by Bisheshar Teli, an oil-presser by caste. Bisheshar doubled up as a carpenter and did the repairs himself; otherwise each of these mills had a specialist carpenter, an engine driver, a fireman, and four to six general labourers: in all twenty-eight persons were employed in Chaura in 1922 in running these oil mills. The local market for the left-over cakes as fodder was limited; with the last drop of oil squeezed out, these oil cakes, peasants argued, were now of little nutritive value to their cattle.[5]

Besides the oil mills there were several indigenous sugar-refining establishments in Chaura and Mundera. A fair amount of raw sugar (*gur*) was brought in from a ten-mile radius for local sale, or exported by rail to distant markets in eastern, western and central India. Some of the peasant produced gur was boiled down into sugar in the traditional manufactories, like the one owned by Lala Halwai and his two sons, across the road from the police station. Peasants were growing cane for sale in its natural form to the nearby Saraya factory (set up in 1920), and also converting it into gur. A complete dependence on the bigger sugar mills would come about only in the mid-1930s. Twelve miles to the north, the indigenous sugar refiners of Pipraich were still doing a brisk trade: the peasants of Chotki Dumri, near Chaura, converted a substantial portion of their cane crop into gur in fourteen cane kolhus, for which they were taxed Rs 1.25 per press by their landlord every year.[6]

Chaura bazaar in early 1922 had three oil mills, a couple of sugar manufactories, two large sugar and gur brokers, two small shops of cloth sellers, who stocked imported as well as Indian mill-made cloth, and a fair sprinkling of small Kalwar traders.

Distillers by traditional occupation, Kalwars like Bishunath, Bhagelu and Balli not only kept shop for grains and sundry merchandise, they also bid against each other or entered into partnership to get the lucrative contract for kerosene which had by now replaced vegetable oil as the source of light in peasant houses and shops alike.[7] Next to the rail goods-shed, the Burmah Shell Company had erected a medium-size storage tank for *matti-ka-tel* (kerosene oil).* The plundering of the tank is poignantly recounted in Chotki Dumri and Chaura even to this day. How and from where the oil was procured to set the thana afire is essential to any local account of that riot. Like many other key moments from a historic local event, matters of precision tend to get recollected variously.†

Apart from the larger commercial establishments tied to manufacturing and the export/import trade, there was a *gānja* and a country liquor shop. On Mondays and Fridays, the two days of the week when peddlers and peasants brought in additional stuff —grains (uncooked and parched), vegetables, fruits, condiments, handloom scarves and *angochās*—fresh catches of fish and goat meat were also on sale. It was on Mondays and Fridays that the peasants came to Chaura 'to do bazaar', as they say in north India. On these two days of the week the normal population of Chaura (1373 in 1921) would swell considerably.

On Saturdays the specialist mart for hides and skins at Bhopa, just beyond the rail godown, which was peopled principally by

---

* Locally so called from the fact that it comes out of *matti*, the earth, and not from a plant.

† Testimony tendered in the court indicates that it was castor oil and not kerosene which was seized from the bazaar to set the thana ablaze; local accounts, however, introduce the raid on the kerosene oil storage tank as an essential element in their recall of the riot. See CCR, II, p. 79; Sessions' Judgment, p. 123 and chapter 27, below.

Muslim traders and Chamar tanners, sprang up for that one day a week. About 300–400 persons came together to do business: the export of lightly cured hides from Chauri Chaura to the bigger leather marts of Kanpur and Calcutta was considerable. Most Muslim cultivators of the nearby villages dabbled in this trade at the Bhopa hides bazaar. Resident Chamars had rights over skinning the dead cattle of the village. For this, as for everything else, they had to pay the landlords a share of their take, which in this case was nearly half the price of the skin. This yielded a modest sum of Rs 11 for Chotki Dumri; in Chaura the contract for collecting the landlord's cess was auctioned annually to a leading Chamar for just under Rs 100 a year![8]

Over 50 per cent of the permanent residents of Bhopa were Chamars, some employed by the more substantial of the Muslim traders to handle bookings of their consignment at the Chaura railway station. Muslim dominance of Bhopa was underlined by a mosque which had come up opposite the bazaar; a Shiva temple constructed by a trader was quite some distance away, in the main Chaura market. Bhopa was not a pleasant place for doing bazaar; the stink of hides was enough to drive anyone except the committed trader away. *Halwāis* like Gobardhan from Chaura would set a temporary stall for sweets at Bhopa on the market day.[9] Sundar Kewat, a *palledār* (weighman) at Chaura, claimed that as a Hindu he would never go to Bhopa on a market day, yet Hindus did keep shop in grain and pulses at the hide market. Meghu Tiwari of Menhian village, who traded a little in split lentils within Chaura, also had a grain gola (shop) in Bhopa, in partnership with Abdullah Churihar. Both were active volunteers and were hanged for their part in the riot.[10]

Bhopa was almost an extension of Chaura bazaar, located at a distance because of its specialized leather business. Care had been taken to ensure that Saturday, the weekly day on which Bhopa came alive, was not a special bazaar day for Chaura.

Situated on an unmetalled road, fifteen miles due east from the town of Gorakhpur, Chaura had a certain importance which antedated the coming of the railways. A rudimentary armature of the state had been assembled at Chaura in the aftermath of the Great Rebellion of 1857–9. Perched at the edge of a large forested tract that spread virtually all the way to the outskirts of the district headquarters, Chaura was an apposite site for a new police station; for it was here that English authority had been badly mauled by the pillage and rebellion of the *ghadar* (rebellion) years. In 1880 it already boasted of a post office, a small resthouse for travellers, a 'cattle pound' and an elementary school.[11] It also figured as a minor dot on the proselytizing map of India. The house of a missionary, though deserted, was still habitable in 1922: the Deputy Magistrate who was sent from Gorakhpur to rope in prisoners and record their confessions the day after the riot, spent the first night at the padre's house, opposite the post office.[12]

Chaura also functioned as an outpost of the landed estate of Barki Dumri, confiscated in 1858 for rebellion and conferred as reward upon a loyalist Sikh family from Majitha in distant Punjab. Here were located a *kothi* (lit. mansion) and a *chāoni* (an outpost), and here lived Sardar Harcharan Singh, the supervisor of the bazaar, assisted by a high-caste subordinate. Four club-wielding peons were attached to his establishment. Each goon had his own beat of four or five villages within which to 'help' with the realization of rents, or round up the peasants for *hāziri* (personal attendance) and *begāri* (unpaid labour) at Barki Dumri and Chaura.[13]

The rival and bigger bazaar of Mundera lay across the railway track. It had a denser cluster of shops and commercial establishments, and specialized quarters for different trades and goods. While Chaura, in its layout, resembled an American Wild West town, with shops and dwellings lining a dirt road, Mundera was

an intricate maze of lanes branching out from the main cart track
that passed through the bazaar. It was an old market site where
'salt, rice and lentils (*dāl*)' were known to have been sold since
the early nineteenth century.[14] In 1891 Mundera housed 273
'agriculturists' who cultivated the 200-odd acres of land attached
to the bazaar. It had a slightly larger number of 'non-agricul-
turists', 282 in all, of which 91 were classed as traders, 150 as
labourers and 21 as artisans. Kalwars, the main local trading caste,
accounted here for 30 per cent of the total population. In 1921
3371 persons were enumerated in the bazaar, 2000 more than
were resident in Chaura.[15] Mundera grew as a bazaar continuously
from the 1880s; between 1891 and 1921 its population increased
fivefold.

Split lentils (dāl), gur (raw sugar) and rice were the main
commodities traded at Mundera. In fact the most important
activity here was the splitting of pulses into lentil. *Arhar* (*Cytisus
cajan*) was the only pulse split and cleaned, then exported in huge
quantities eastwards to Banaras and Calcutta—Arhar dāl being a
delicacy in eastern UP. A meal consisting of good quality rice and
arhar garnished with lime or *ghee** was considered the ultimate
culinary pleasure in Gorakhpur, its flavour preserved in rustic
poetry and proverbs even to this day. Arhar lentils were in fact a
standard complement to the rice-based meals of eastern India.
Gorakhpur did not specialize in arhar production; in 1921–2 only
80,000 maunds were produced in the district as a whole, while
Mundera bazaar itself exported 200,000 maunds of cleaned and
split lentils in that year. Local production was augmented considerably by imports from the neighbouring districts of Basti, Gonda
and Bahraich.

The dāl was purchased and stocked at Mundera for the entire
year, and the finished product was often held back to await a better

---

* *Ghee*: clarified butter, often used as a garnish for lentils, usually by frying
garlic in it.

turn in the distant markets. With one-tenth of its gross weight lost to husk and another 5 per cent wasted in drying and cleaning, 100 kg of arhar yielded 70 kg of split and cleaned dāl, and another 15 kg of large and small broken pieces. The Rs 62,000 profit accruing a year to the three major dāl dealers of Mundera was a substantial sum indeed: in 1922 it would have equalled the rental income from 90–100 villages in the locality.[16] A certain amount of the lentils produced were traded locally. Smaller Kalwars had set up shops which sold broken-up pieces of the dāl to the large number of peasants who could afford only these splintered bits.[17]

The most important aspect of dāl production in Mundera was that it was all done by human labour in a *chakki*, a traditional hand-grinding mill which was only slightly modified for large-scale production. Hundreds of men, women and children worked all day long in Mundera, grinding arhar dāl. 'Everybody ground dāl in Mundera', recalled old Nàujadi, wife of Nageshar Pasi, convicted for eight years for his part in the riot. A much larger number of women (of all ages) than men worked these chakkis. The labour of women, as of children, was priced in 1922 at only 2.5 annas a day, as against men's 4.4 annas, and this routine undervaluing of female labour resulted in a greater number of women workers within Mundera. Zahur of Chaura, who migrated periodically with his wife to Calcutta, left his old mother behind as a matter of course to grind dāl in Mundera.[18]

It was this dāl-splitting by women and children that tied the nearby villages, such as Chotki Dumri, much more securely to Mundera than to Chaura, where, in contrast, the mechanized manufacture of vegetable oil required considerably less manpower. The dāl-splitting chakkis of Mundera were designed to spin rapidly and lightly by the attachment of an iron ring in between the upper and the lower stones; only light pressure was required, for unlike corn the pulse had to be split and not ground into flour. Still, it required two women to each chakki, though often a child took the place of the second woman.

Not only were these dāl factories considerable establishments, even the shops in Mundera—whether for cloth, provisions, liquor, opium, ganja, or goat meat—were also much larger. The butchers of Mundera, for instance, had a regular slaughterhouse at the far end of the bazaar, opposite the fish market; no such specialized enclosure existed in Chaura. Mundera is the real bazaar *(Asli Bazaar Mundera hi hai)*, said a local trader to me, emphasizing the word 'real' for the record. It was merely the railway station which had conferred an undue, technical importance upon the wayside Chaura bazaar.

So it was at Mundera that the *barki*—local parlance for 'big bazaar'—was held every Saturday. On one such Saturday, 4 February 1922, the leather-trading crowd spilled over the railway level-crossing from Bhopa into Mundera bazaar, as it did every week. All kinds of things were sold in Mundera on these market Saturdays. Bishunath Kalwar, son of Narayan, would come over from Chaura to sell brassieres: 'He sells bodices there . . . bodices and caps. He does not sell anything else.'[19] Bishunath Kalwar was sentenced to death by the lower court.

The staggering of market days between the two bazaars allowed many other small traders to operate in both Chaura and Mundera. However, tension arose when the bigger merchants, such as the cloth traders, moved shop. In 1903 the move of the two big Marwari clothiers, Shiv Dat Rai-Badri Das and Hardat Rai-Kanhaiya Lal, from Chaura to Mundera led to criminal proceedings involving the owners of the two bazaars.[20]

There could be similar disputes between leading landholders over the income from major fairs in the locality. The most important of such gatherings was held for ten days every year in the month of Chait (March–April) at Tarkulha, three miles west of Chaura. Located in the middle of a jungle, the site *(thān)* of Tarkulha Debi fell mostly on the lands assigned to the Dumri estate, but the fair would spill over on to the domain of Raja Motichand of Azmatgarh. Apart from a levy on every head of cattle sacrificed to the goddess and a fee charged from barbers on every tonsure, the fair also generated a considerable income from the sale of utensils and food. In 1910 the two estates fought a court battle about their respective shares from the Tarkulha fair.[21]

Unlike Chaura which was owned singly by Sardar Umrao Singh of Barki Dumri estate, Mundera was the joint property of four 'owners' belonging to the Sirnet Rajput house of Bishenpura.[22] But such was the power of the leading shareholder, Sant Baksh Singh, that it was customary then, as it is now, to speak of Mundera as Sant Baksh Singh's bazaar. Mundera also had a *chāoni* staffed by a manager, a *zilādār*, a *munshi*, peons and *bayās* (intermediaries) who supervised the sale of gur, grain and pulses, and who collected a tax on sales and exports out of the bazaar. Grain was collected by taxing carts which brought in rice and pulses, and this taxed grain too was sold in the bazaar. The cash proceeds—some of it in the regionally minted copper coinage or *kaccha paisa*—was then carted off to the estate headquarters, six miles north of Mundera.

Liquor, toddy, meat and fish shops were taxed at a sliding rate of Rs 3, Rs 2 and Re 1. '*Zamindar kauri tahsīl karen*', said Sita Ahir of Chotki Dumri, using the term 'cowrie' to mean collections of tax in small coins, a wide range of which (*adhela*, *dokra* and other regionally minted bits of copper) circulated under the expressive name of kaccha (i.e. not quite proper) paisa. From the bigger shopkeepers, such as the cloth merchants, Rs 2–4 were collected each year; the estate also claimed a 25 per cent share on all property transactions in Mundera.[23] Income from bazaar levies was estimated at Rs 3700 for 1915 in revenue papers of the day.[24]

The money raked in by Sant Baksh Singh was considerable. Babu Saheb, as he is known locally, is still remembered in Mundera and Chotki Dumri for his heavy-handed paternalism. 'He would tax the bazaar heavily' (*Babu Saheb kauri bahut lete the*) said a trader from Mundera, 'but he also tended it like a garden', he added for good measure. 'Now! Babu Saheb was quite

something!', says Naujadi, a *praja* (subject) of the rival parvenu
Sikh landlord of Barki Dumri estate—after which her village,
Chotki Dumri (lit. Little Dumri), won over from the forest in the
1870s, had been dimunitively named.

'Little Dumri' had been carved out of a jungle tract which belonged to the locally dominant landed lineage based in the two
adjacent founding settlements of Barki (i.e. Big) Dumri and
Bishenpura. It was the babus of Dumri and Bishenpura, cadet
branch of a powerful pre-colonial local kingdom, who dominated
a large tract, 15 miles long, 8–10 miles wide between the Pharend
and the Majhna rivers in the sprawling central *pargana* of Haveli
Gorakhpur.[25] The babus of Dumri were punished with death and
confiscation of property for their rebellion during 1857–9: they
lost all thirty-four of their villages as well as a tract of jungle which,
when cleared and settled, gave rise by the 1870s to 19 (or perhaps
25) new villages, including Chotki Dumri. The new owner of the
Dumri estate was a Sikh loyalist from Punjab. The other branch
of Sirnet Rajputs, based at Bishenpura, survived with its share of
land, and of a similar though smaller 'jungle grant' intact: Babu
Saheb Sant Baksh Singh, the tough and admirable 'owner' of
Mundera bazaar and thirty-three other villages, belonged to this
house.[26]

The result of this major property revolution in and around
Chaura was to create a chequered pattern of land ownership.
Whereas it had been remarked earlier that no raja or zamindar in
the district could hold his own against the quondom proprietors
with whom the tenantry sympathized during the Rebellion,[27] now,
in 1922, settlements from the domain of a locally dominant
lineage were positioned cheek and jowl with those awarded to the
Sikh loyalists from Punjab. It was thus that Chaura fell to the lot
of the Sikhs of Barki Dumri, while the adjacent Mundera bazaar
remained in the family of Babu Sant Baksh Singh.

There were a few other nearby settlements, like the adjacent village of Chauri, which did not belong to big landed estates. But the historical tendency, in both pre-colonial and colonial times, had been towards the creation of large properties in this forested tract.[28] North-west from Chaura, between the Pharend and Tura rivers, was a compact estate of 15 villages assigned by the Nawab of Awadh in 1790 to a Muslim divine: this central village of Kusmhi, with half a dozen daughter settlements or *tolās*, had come up in the large forest of that name; south of the road from Chaura was a cluster of five villages, collectively known as Rampur Raqba, carved out of another jungle grant by an important merchant-banker family which had its base in Banaras and neighbouring Azamgarh district. Yet further south was another compact estate of twenty-nine villages owned by the Dube Brahmins of Barhampur and Mithabel, which they had held since the sixteenth century.

Each of these large agrarian properties had their own bazaars. Mian Saheb, Gorakhpur's pre-eminent Muslim divine, owned the important sugar refining town of Pipraich, twelve miles to the north of Chaura; the Dubes of Barhampur controlled an important market in Barhampur itself, and then there were the contiguous bazaars of Chaura and Mundera, adjacent to the village of Chotki Dumri.[29]

Little Dumri was a relatively new village, just about fifty years old in 1922, but that did not mean it was sparsely or indifferently cultivated. Its western boundary had been secured against the depredations of wild animals by the construction of a ditch in the late 1880s, and its thirteen ponds, four masonry wells and numerous shallow watering holes, operated singlehandedly with a *dhenkul* (the characteristic lever-and-bucket), provided sufficient irrigation. Its lands fell just within the heavy alluvial *bāngar* soil which produced both wheat and rice, and, as the demand rose, a fair amount of sugarcane as well. The average in 1917 for a tract of this particular soil-type was for 60 per cent *rabi* winter crop and 75 per cent *kharif* or autumn crop; around 40 per cent of the area grew two crops a year. The fairly complete crop statistics for Chotki Dumri for 1885 show a much higher proportion of irrigated spring harvest to the monsoon-fed autumn crop: 89 per cent rabi, 60 per cent kharif, and roughly half the total area under *do fasli* (two crops a year). Out of a total cultivated area of 345 acres, 165 acres (or 47 per cent) was under broadcast rice, and a similar area (144 acres or 41.7 per cent) under wheat, barley, and wheat and barley mixed together. Winter peas (105 acres, or 24 per cent) were another major crop.[30]

The cultivated area had increased, on a rough count, by 16 per cent between 1885 and 1917; however, there were no major changes in the cropping pattern, except that the 47 acres under linseed had been replaced by an extended acreage under cane: in 1917 Chotki Dumri had fourteen iron cane crushers to the two wooden ones recorded in 1885.[31] Old residents of the village are categorical about the crops grown in the early 1920s: wheat, barley, broadcast rice and sugarcane. On the distant fields across the railway track, which had sliced through the village lands in 1885 and given rise to the new residential site of Piprahiya *tola* on the other side of the raised embankment, there was only rice. The separate Chamar quarters, though at the requisite distance from the village proper, were still on the right side of the railway track.

Chamars formed the single largest caste cluster in Chotki Dumri. In 1891 roughly one-third (29 per cent) of the population of the village (233/796) was returned as Chamars. If we assume a growth rate among them similar to the rest of the village population, there would have been 371 Chamars among the 1280 persons who lived in Chotki Dumri in 1921. Roughly half the tenanted land (151.2 acres out of a total of 345 acres) was held by Sainthwars, the preponderant peasant caste of the region;[*] the

---

[*] Sainthwar: a middle-ranking caste of 'industrious' peasants, closely related to the Kurmi.

thirty-five Sainthwar peasant households held on an average 4.32 acres, each of which was one-and-a half times the average tenant holding for the village. Thirty Chamars were recorded in 1885 to have held 60.37 acres among them, at an average 2 acres per head, well below the 3 acres which was the average for the village as a whole. Chamars might have been numerous, but the peasants who counted in Chotki Dumri were the Sainthwars. 'Dumri was a village of Sainthwars' is how Sita Ahir, the oldest resident, put it to me. 'The Chamars did not hold any land, they only ploughed for the Sainthwars', added Sita. The small holdings of the Chamars, in distant and unfertile corners of the village, had probably receded beyond the pale of Sita's memory, or perhaps the forty years after 1885, marked by price rise and rising rents, had seen the Chamars of Dumri dispossessed by their Sikh land-lords. Among the high castes the Brahmins, and within the middle order the Ahirs, were both relatively unimportant.[32]

It was the twenty-odd houses of Musalmans, though well under 7 per cent of the total population, which seem to have pulled considerable weight in the village. There were several reasons for this uncharacteristic dominance of Musalmans in Chotki Dumri. The village was new, and therefore unencumbered by the regionally dominant Rajput landed elite. The three Brah-mins entered in the 1885 revenue papers as tenants had an insigni-ficant combined cultivation of 5.41 acres among themselves. The Sikh landlords lived six miles away and seem to have purposely settled a few Musalman families in the village on favourable terms.

The evidence on social relations in Dumri, especially between the locally powerful Musalmans and the middle castes (Sainthwars and Ahirs) and Untouchables (Pasis and Chamars), is scanty but interesting. The village *akhāra* (wrestling pit) was run by a Musal-man guru who had Ahir lads as his apprentices. The Musalmans had their drinking-water well separate from the one drawn on by caste Hindus, but a large number of Untouchable Chamars used this 'Muslim' well. A quarrel in early 1921—over the entry of a sacrificial pig from the Chamar quarters into a Musalman's house—had ended this social proximity. The Chamars had then dug their own well. Even this had not created an unbridgible gulf between the two communities. Both shared in the leather trade at Bhopa, and when Nazar Ali and Shikari (two Muslims who figure prominently in our story) began enrolling volunteers in early 1922, they were able to recruit a fair number in the Chamrauti or the segregated Chamar quarters.[33]

Muslim peasant holdings were relatively large. In 1885 the three recorded Muslim tenants of Dumri cultivated on an average 4.57 acres each, a farm size which was even higher than the one held on average by the Sainthwars.[34] In 1922 Mir Shikari, son of Mir Qurban, paid Rs 37 per year in rent, which even at a high rate of Rs 4–5 per acre meant a very considerable cultivation indeed. However, it was not just large holdings but trade in skins and hides at the nearby Bhopa bazaar that made the tightly knit Muslim male adults of Dumri important actors in the local economy, and, as it turns out, in peasant politics. Shikari traded in hides; Ghaus Ali, the father of Shikari's son-in-law, was a substantial purchaser of skins: on 4 February 1922 he had bought eleven skins in Bhopa; Abdul Karim, Shikari's uncle, also traded in leather at the same bazaar.[35]

Two outsiders, Nazar Ali and Abdullah, lent their weight to this dominant Muslim family of Dumri in the early 1920s. Both were *churihārs* (banglesellers) from two distant villages, a good 15–20 miles south of Dumri, but regular visitors to Dumri, Mundera and Chauri Chaura. Both had left their traditional calling to become tailors. Abdullah had retained his tailoring shop in his natal village, Rajdhani. Nazar Ali had taken a circuitous route; he had left his village in the precarious tract in the flood line of the Rapti river, migrated for a few years to Rangoon, and upon his return had set up house in Dumri and a tailoring shop in Mundera bazaar.[36]

Nazar Ali was not the only migrant to Chotki Dumri from

the densely populated and precarious villages south of the river Rapti. A certain margin of cultivation, and proximity to the two bazaars of Chaura and Mundera where work was at hand, attracted many families to Chotki Dumri. Thus, Sita Ahir's father Sivcharan Ahir, from the overpopulated Bansgaon tract, on his marriage to a Dumri girl in late-nineteenth century, decided, contrary to convention, to settle down in his wife's natal village.[37] And then there were others—pandits and preachers—who would regularly traverse a distance of 10–12 miles from old established villages within the loop of the Rapti river, south-west of Dumri, to hobnob with the station officer at Chaura or popularize the intricacies of Sanatan Dharma Hinduism in Mundera bazaar.

One such regular visitor was Pandit Jagat Narain Pandey from Malaon, home to the Sankritya sept of the prestigious Saryupāri Brahmins of eastern Uttar Pradesh. Malaon-Pandey, in his own words 'a follower of Mr Gandhi', was present at each of the major developments leading up to the riot on 4 February 1922: he tried to dissuade Nazar Ali and party from picketing Mundera bazaar on 1 February, he was with the sub-inspector when volunteer and ex-soldier Bhagwan Ahir was thrashed for his misdemeanour, and he arrived at Chotki Dumri on the morning of 4 February to persuade Nazar Ali, Shikari, and the volunteer-crowd from marching on to the thana.[38]

If people moved into Dumri, Mundera and Chaura for various reasons, they also went out in search of work. 'Assam, Burma and Rangoon, mostly to Rangoon', were the places to which people from Dumri and adjoining villages migrated.[39] The regional migration to Burma was considerable. An indirect index of this seems significant: no fewer than fifty-one new subscriptions were taken out in 1921 to the district nationalist weekly *Swadesh* by Gorakhpuri migrants resident in Burma in that year. Two of Bihari Pasi's sons had gone to Rangoon from Chotki Dumri; the secretary of the nearby volunteer unit of Barhampur had to be replaced in early 1922 as he had decided to leave for Burma.[40]

The Rangoon-goers returned with cash, but their absence caused significant developments in the natal village. Wives had to sustain themselves through prolonged periods of separation and mental torture at the hands of sisters- and-mothers-in-law: Such bereft wives would also have had to cajole someone or the other, very likely a semi-literate village boy, to scribble a few ritualized 'wishing you well' lines on the self-addressed 'return' or *jawabi* half of the double postcard that came attached to the original missive from Burma. Postage was not at hand in villages, and postcards were printed in India, then as now, in batches of two.[41]

Migrants also made the villagers familiar with the magic of the money order, as the nearby postal offices became conduits for transferring long-distance cash into peasant homes. It was this dependence on cash flow which elevated the village postman to a position just below the policeman's! Officiously known as Chitthirasa Sahab (from *chitthi* or letter), the postman, with his 'red turban, leggings, and leather shoulder bag', cuts an impressive figure in a novel called *Ram Lal* set in rural Gorakhpur (*c.* 1916), exacting a high price for undoing the straps of his money-order bag. 'This is no ordinary bag', the novel's narrator sardonically remarks, describing the eagerly awaited weekly visit of the postman, for 'it encapsulates the hopes and despair' of the parents and wives of migrants.[42]

Since 1886, the government had given peasants the option to remit their rents to landlords by money order. In neighbouring Azamgarh district, for which we have figures, the offer was taken up with alacrity. Money order rents rose immediately to a high 20 per cent of all rents received. Peasants from the migrant zone of north India, familiar with the money order, were now asserting their legal right to get receipts for rent and demeaning their landlords by refusing to pay rent in person; it made better sense to despatch a money order instead from a safely distant post office.[43] Landlords soon got the better of this novelty: duly stamped rental money orders were refused,[44] and in parts of Gorakhpur district, where recorded rents were invariably lower than what was paid, 'the money order system of payment of rent' was 'utilized as a device for concealing concealment'! In one estate, a record of rents received by post was maintained for government officials, but peasants were made to pay double or treble that amount to the landlord's office in person.[45]

In Dumri and neighbouring villages, where personal attendance at the landlord's house was required several times a year, and the zamindar riding through the village was entitled to a proper salutation with a cash 'offering', remitting rent by post was an act of collective protest requiring resolve and deliberation.[46] When Kallu, peon from the chāoni at Chaura broke Sidhari's wrist because he was not prompt in marching to Chaura for begār (unpaid labour) at the call of Sardar Harcharan Singh, 'the whole village' came together in the evening and resolved to send rent from Chotki Dumri by money order. In nearby Rampur Raqba, across the road from Dumri, an attempt by the estate to raise rents to pay for better irrigation facilities was similarly met by village gatherings demanding the despatch of rent by money order.[47]

There was one further experience, apart from beholding Gandhi in person, which was to prove instrumental in loosening the bonds of deference in north Indian villages during 1920–2. This was the experience of war in the trenches of Flanders and Mesopotamia. Recruitment for the Great War from Gorakhpur and the Awadh districts might not have been massive, as it was from Punjab, but it had a novel political impact on the peasantry. The figure of the returned soldier in pro-recruitment literature suggests someone who was feted by the landed elite yet wore his uniform lightly, remaining deferential and peasant-like. This image symbolizes the real danger which the experience of war, and the reward of state-sponsored tenancies, were thought to pose to rural peace.[48] Demobilized soldiers in uniform, flaunting their war ribbons, figured prominently in many anti-police and anti-landlord battles during the course of a prolonged peasant movement in the nearby Awadh districts.[49]

Gorakhpur district yielded more cash than men to the War,[50] but people who had done their stint for King and Country were not unknown in and around Chauri Chaura. Mangru Kewat of Barhampur was employed as a servant to a Captain in Basra; Ram Saran was rewarded on his return with a small grant of land in his native village, Bilari.[51] And then there was Bhagwan Ahir of Chaura, who claimed that Sardar Harcharan, supervisor of the bazaar, 'wanted to sell him as a recruit to a Punjabi'; but he refused. Bhagwan went as a non-combatant to Basra instead.[52] On his return after two years he received a monthly pension for his services during the Great War. When a unit of nationalist volunteers was set up in Chotki Dumri village in early 1922, Bhagwan, the returned soldier, was chosen to act as a drill-master to peasants recruited for the nationalist cause.

Bhagwan Ahir, sporting his khaki uniform, was to be a prominent figure in the events leading up to the clash with the police. He drilled the volunteers in Chaura bazaar within earshot of the local thana, he participated in the bigger nationalist meetings, he tried picketing Mundera bazaar, and when rebuked by the sub-inspector came back with a stunning 'Lund-se' (Fuck You) whiplash to the head of the police station. Not surprisingly, this resulted in his being beaten up by the inspector, and it was the beating of Bhagwan Ahir by the police that subsequently forced the pace of events. The Dumri leaders flared into heat. They were in a mood to show the station officer that individual volunteers could no longer be thrashed at will. It was this clash, between a disciplined crowd nursing a grievance and a police force armed but vulnerable, that resulted, through a set of moves and counter-moves, in the burning down of that thana to the cruel cry of 'Long Live Mahatma Gandhi!'

Part Three

'Dil ko to adāb-i-bandagi bhi na āi, kar gaye log hukmarāni bhi'.
— Firaq Gorakhpuri

4

Fraudulent Reports

As the national leadership debated the 'Crime of Chauri Chaura', this being the name of Gandhi's authoritative essay, talk of *what had indeed happened* was already in the air. Another nationalist narrative, as yet untouched by guilt, penance and prāyashchit (atonement) briefly raised its head in the weeks following the clash with the police.

It was heard in Azamgarh that 'the police had fired in the air out of sympathy for the rioters'; at another place 'the murder of 8 or 9 Europeans' was added to the list of Indian policemen dead; from Saharanpur, 700 miles distant, came a sober 'regret that the murdered police did not include a European officer'.[1]

These oral reports—whispers (*bhunkars*) and rumours (*gogās*)—of popular parlance, were quick to assume graphic forms. An *uranghai*, (fraudulent report; lit. 'flying through the air'[2]), was found pasted on a notice board in Fatehpur, 250 miles south-east of the burnt thana. Functioning as a reporter of nationalist rumours, several of these boards at Phatak Hazari *mohalla** had been impounded and their editor arrested in May 1922. With both author and tablets in custody, the police were all set to delete these 'actionable inscriptions' if 'recourse is had to walls', but the notices persisted into the summer.[3]

The notice board was full of unauthorized news in early 1922. On 12 February, the day Congress suspended Civil Disobedience, it wrote up its account of Chauri Chaura—

* *Mohalla*: a neighbourhood

alleging that the police used to beat non-co-operators till the flesh was raw and then rub in salt; that on the day of the event the police used up all their ammunition on the crowd which was going away as ordered, killing 200 people whose bodies were then concealed; that the local leaders who went to investigate were arrested and threatened by the Superintendent of Police who said he would shoot them if they went near the prisoners, the Congress people who went to investigate were arrested, kept hungry and thirsty and abused.[4]

Not all this was hot air. On reaching the site of the smouldering thana, the President and the Secretary of the District Congress Committee 'were taken into custody'. 'When we got off the train' the next day, 'at once police made us sit down and said we could not go anywhere', the Secretary stated in court.[5]

On 23 February the notice board announced that one 'Swami Satdeo had described the Gorakhpur affair as "very ordinary", and not the deadly event that Gandhi was making it out to be.'[6] Reports came in from parts of the district of 'activity by low-caste volunteers who said that Gandhiji has been replaced by Andhiji and that Holi this year will be celebrated with blood.'[7] The pun on Gandhi's name was here made to yield the north-Indian word for whirlwind, which, set in motion by the burning of the Chaura thana, would sweep everything before it. Even more ominous was the declaration that bloodletting, and not the customary sprinkling of coloured water, would mark the celebration of Holi that year.

At about the same time 'a gang of some 20 volunteers of Saran', from neighbouring Bihar, crossed the Ghaghra river into Gorakhpur district. 'They were headed by a *sadhu* with a flag, and said that they were proceeding to Chauri Chaura where Gandhi raj had been established.'[8]

The peasants who had returned home that evening, crying out that 'they had burnt and thrown away and Swaraj had come', were now in hiding, trying to save their lives'[9]. The army was route-marching across the district, putting the fear of the *angrej*[*] into the peasantry: landlords were to provision the troops; mounted police were cantering from the burnt-out thana, laying siege to entire villages, imprinting peasant memories with the echoes of their metallic clatter.[10] At this same time, but at a remove from Chotki Dumri and Mundera, a nationalist narrative of Chauri Chaura was taking shape. The nature of the violence required that nationalists act and write on it in the immediate present. Reflection on the riot had to be instantaneous. All history was subject to the rule of nationalist non-violence.

5

The Lessons of the Riot

Five days after the 'Grave Riot', an editorial in the Hindi *Aaj* agonized over the factors that *could be said* to lie behind the event.[11] The need of the hour, it said, was that Indians pay heed to 'the lessons of the riot' and to nothing else. It interpreted the violence of that day in terms of a local context and parallelisms from world history.

The local context was that the people of Chauri Chaura were 'greatly perturbed by the improper behaviour of the police': they may well have 'gone out of control because of oppression by individual policemen'. In fact, 'the dead daroga's attitude towards "the public" was nothing short of deplorable'.[12] 'Whatever the cause'—and here we enter the tragic terrain of responsibility—

---

* *Angrej*: the English.

Whether the police fired first, or not; whether the crowd was in fact a procession merely going past the thana or had marched there on purpose; how many from among the crowd, for sure, were shot dead . . . ; who should take the initial blame; how to apportion responsibility—*this is not the time to ponder over such questions.*[13]

Nor, it said, was this the occasion

for us to cry out that rogues [*badmāsh*] there will always be in every society, that no campaign can be immune from such creatures, who commit the foulest deeds in the name of the noblest ideals. The pages of European history are stained red with crimes committed in the name of Christianity—the religion of love and toleration. *This is not the occasion for making such points.*

The occasion (*samay, avsar, avkāsh*) allows us only this much: 'that we realize a crowd of peasants burnt down the thana of Chauri Chaura in Gorakhpur District and killed a large number of policemen'. We cannot hold Mahatma Gandhi responsible for the 'evil deeds of these rogues—these so-called followers'—though Gandhiji no doubt will take the blame upon himself. What does this horrid mishap prove? '[It shows that] our people have learnt inadequately the lesson of non-violence, that our people willingly take rogues for leaders, that violence and revenge are extracted in the most brutal ways.'

From this point, nationalist prose would memorialize the event by place and policemen killed. Forever a lesson to be learnt, the 'riot' could no longer be accorded a narrative past. It could, at most, refer to past imperfection: in the Congress as an organization, in the nationalist public more generally.

6

The Crime of Chauri Chaura

Elements of this nationalist narration are present in Gandhi's celebrated essay, written soon after the event.[14] Gandhi starts this off by listing the long-standing and immediate provocations behind the riot. In this 'most extraordinary human document . . . his *mea culpa*, his public confession', Gandhi 'thanks God for having humbled him'.[15]

God has been abundantly kind to me. He has warned me the third time that there is not yet in India that truthful and non-violent atmosphere which and which alone can justify mass disobedience which can be described as civil which means gentle, truthful, humble, knowing, wilful yet loving, never criminal and hateful.

He warned me in 1919 when the Rowlatt Act agitation was started . . .

Madras did give the warning, but I heeded it not. But God spoke clearly through Chauri Chaura.[16]

Gandhi then comes to the possible pretexts which, in his judgement, could well lie behind the violence at Chauri Chaura:

I understand that the constables who were so brutally hacked to death had given much provocation. They had even gone back upon the word just given by the Inspector that they would not be molested, but when the procession had passed the stragglers were interfered with and abused by the constables. The former cried out for help. The mob returned. The constables opened fire. The little ammunition they had was exhausted and they retired to the thana for safety.[17]

Note the number of incitements which finally result in the riot. The police give much provocation; peasants who get cut off from the body of the crowd are interfered with and abused; the mob returns in response to the stragglers' cry for help. Faced with an entire mob, the constables open fire, retreating only after their ammunition is expended. All of this seems to be purposefully directed to a virtual explanation for the burning and the killing at the police station: 'the mob, *my informant* tells me, *therefore set fire to the Thana*'.

Gandhi's informant was his son Devdas. He was in Gorakhpur to investigate the riot but being denied access to Chauri Chaura, confined himself to collecting depositions at the District headquarters. SEND FULL ACCURATE REPORTS. KEEP PEOPLE NON-VIOLENT. GET ALL INFORMATION was what Gandhi expected of him in Gorakhpur. But who was to depose, and with what relation to the riot? At least one participant-deponent came to see Debidas (i.e. Devadas). Another, the luckless Raghubir Kewat, seriously injured by the police firing of 4 February, braved a ten-mile *ekka** ride from his village to the house of the district Congress president, in order, as he told the court, 'to get myself arrested and sent to hospital'! Maulvi Subhanullah, the president of the District Congress Committee, personally reported the 'rioter's' presence to the District Collector, but only after his deposition had been recorded 'by Devdas Gandhi and others'. The police let Devdas retain the document, but took custody of Raghubir Kewat.[18] Direct information about the reasons for the riot was provided by Raghubir on his way to the district jail.

Much like the *Aaj* editorial of a week earlier, Gandhi proceeds to list the long-term provocations which lie behind the attack: this is, after all, colonial India. The mob was in effect retaliating at Chauri Chaura to the district-wise 'high-handed tyranny of the police'. There was indeed a background to the riot; not that this could mean nationalists should ever condone the violence: there

---

* *Ekka* : a two-wheel light trap, drawn by a pony.

was no room for retaliation in satyagraha. Indeed 'no provocation', no amount of immediate and proximate causes, 'can possibly justify' this merciless act of nationalist indiscipline. What then were the practical lessons of the riot? These, according to Gandhi, relate to the question of disciplining both the satyagrahis and the 'hooligans of India'.

Non-violent non-co-operators can only succeed when they have succeeded in attaining control over the hooligans of India, in other words, *when the latter also have learnt patriotically or religiously to refrain from their violent activities at least while the campaign for non-co-operation is going on. The tragedy of Chauri Chaura therefore roused me thoroughly.*[19]

For all its listing of attenuating circumstances, the killing of the policemen remains *murder.* Further, the murder has to be attributed not to a mob, but to culpable peasants constituting that specific mob, to 'Congress . . . sympathizers [even] if not [people] actually connected with it'; these peasants may have killed 'with my name on their lips'. One part of the nationalist Gandhi 'cannot even wish them to be arrested', but suffer they must, as Gandhi 'would himself suffer for their breach of the Congress creed'.[20] He is morally unambiguous:

I would advise those who feel guilty and repentant to hand themselves voluntarily to the Government for punishment and make a clean confession. I hope that the workers in the Gorakhpur district will leave no stone unturned to find out the evil-doers and urge them to deliver themselves into custody.[21]

It was not just the violence but its political nature which condemned these 'evil-doers' of Chauri Chaura in the eyes of nationalists. 'It is not every kind of violence that will stop civil disobedience', Gandhi noted a month after the event. Family feuds, 'even though sanguinary', will leave him undismayed. Nor will 'the violence of robbers', much as it may indicate 'the absence of general purification'. 'It is *political violence* which *must* stop [the] civil disobedience [movement]'. Chauri Chaura was an instance of such political violence: 'It was a politically minded crowd', an 'infuriated mob . . . in sympathy with non-co-operation'. The 'ugly outbreak on the part of professing Congressmen at Chauri Chaura' was 'not individual' in nature, arising from 'any private wrong'; it was rooted in 'a *vague sense of political wrong*'. The 'violence broke out in connection with a *nationalist activity*'—the picketing of a bazaar selling foreign and intoxicating goods.[22]

The political and nationalist aspects of the violence distinguished Chauri Chaura from a series of other violent acts—from, say, the 'organized and sustained violence offered by the Moplahs' in Malabar who attacked not just the colonial state, but also their Hindu landlords and Hindus in general.

I can still distinguish between Malabar and Gorakhpur. The Moplahs *themselves* had not been touched by the non-co-operation spirit. They are not like the other Indians nor even like the other Mussulmans . . . The Moplah revolt was *so different in kind* that it did not affect other parts of India, *whereas Gorakhpur was typical*, and therefore, if we had not taken energetic steps, the *infection* might easily have spread to other parts of India.[23]

Gorakhpur was typical in the sense that the riot of 4 February was an act of nationalist indiscipline, caused by the absence of proper Congress organization: 'The incident at Chauri Chaura would have been impossible if the Congress and the Khilafat organizations were perfect. *It is all a question of perfecting the Congress organization . . .*'. [24]

7

Nationalizing the Riot

Within Gandhi's disciplinary prose there can be no ex-culpation for the peasant-murderers of Chauri Chaura: fellow-Indians, whom Gandhi would otherwise not even wish to be arrested, they must all the same now own up, confess, and accept punishment.

Post-colonial local histories, of which one example is a directory of accredited freedom fighters called 'History of Freedom Struggle in the Gorakhpur District', (1972), on the other hand, always exculpate the martyrs of Chauri Chaura. In these the provocation which Gandhi listed even while rejecting them are regarded as grave and gratuitous—in other words, such incitements to violence are seen as being typical of colonial rule. They serve to explain, as well as explain away, the murder. 'Chauri Chaura', then, is not the work of culpable individuals; it is caused by reflex action. The grave riot (*bhīshan upadrava*) of contemporary nationalist prose becomes the 'Chauri Chaura *kānd*' of the post-colonial directory of accredited freedom fighters. A violent event, but no longer an episode, it is now literally a chapter in the 'History of Freedom Struggle in the Gorakhpur District', and by extension of the Nation.[25]

Further, and paradoxically, this extreme reflex action is seen to stem from the *swayam sevaks'** disciplined disposition! The extreme consequence (*bhayankar parinām*), i.e. the murder of twenty-three policemen, is preceded in time, both immediate and historical, by police repression, by the characteristic though in this

---

* *Swayam sevak*: lit. 'servant by choice'; chaste Hindi for 'volunteer'.

case exceptionally fierce lathi and cavalry charge, and the firing which the disciplined satyagrahis withstood for a long time. They had come prepared to get 'beaten up in small batches'. *It was because they were disciplined for a long time that they finally lost their heads.*

Now, this crowd is seen as a nationalist crowd, much as Gandhi had stressed it was. But, with due respect to Gandhi, the Chauri Chaura volunteers are not indisciplined 'hooligans',[26] nor the 'rogues' (*dusht*) of all times and ages, 'who twist even the best of doctrines in ways so as to create disorder [*utpāt*] for their own selfish ends'.[27] In the 1972 District Account they figure as straight-forward satyagrahis.

'Before the Chauri Chaura kānd', the official directory of the Gorakhpur Freedom Fighters tells us, 'the local satyagrahis had given a good account of their organization and confidence'. In fact Gorakhpur was 'the only district [in the province] where the Congress organization was well-entrenched, from top to bottom', including of course in the villages around Chauri Chaura. The magical words that Gandhi uttered at the district headquarters: 'boycott foreign cloth, give up English education, spin yarn, weave and wear khaddar and the English will have to quit India real soon . . . ' were still ringing in the ears of the local satyagrahis in the winter of 1921–2.[28]

The politics of nationalism having been properly traced to Gandhi and the Congress organization, space is created for a standardized description. A dense detailing of nationalist facts ensues. This enables the Indian reader to appreciate the general colonial context of the violence at a specific police station. The retailing of 'nationalist facts' is organized around accounts of picketing and police oppression. Both these are marked by an excess of stereotypical description. This is characteristic, for na-tionalist narratives, when incorporating events into history, are seldom marked by economy of fact. It is this excess which allows the contribution (*yogdān*) of India's constituent units—province, district, locality, village—to be accounted for. As for the yogdān, it is elicited by nationalist exhortation and organization.

In 1921 then, the Congress organization had struck deep roots in Gorakhpur district. 'There were Congress committees even at the tahsil and mandal levels'* and satyagraha had commenced in the 'prescribed (vidhivat) manner at toddy, liquor and foreign-cloth shops'. As Chauri Chaura was 'at that time a big market of foreign cloth, it was natural to start satyagraha there in real earnest'.

Once set in motion by the district organization, serious dharna at Chaura bazaar goes on for a full two months. The names, activities and decisions of the Dumri volunteers find no mention in this account but toddy and liquor outlets as well as foreign cloth shops, are picketed by these unnamed workers. 'And during this entire two-month period, the police, with the help of land-lords (zamindars), kept raining lathis at the satyagrahis,' says the District Account. The 'satyagrahis were grievously hurt, but they stood their ground'.

State repression now shifts into another gear. The cavalry is summoned and sowārs are let loose on satyagrahis. 'The satyagrahis refused to be terrorized; they faced this onslaught with courage and equanimity.'[29] Hundreds are seriously hurt. It is feared that the batches of satyagrahis in readiness for 'next Saturday's picket-ing might be weakened'. Pandit Motilal Nehru, the 'impresario [sutradhār] of satyagraha of this area', is approached. He advises that volunteers be sent out in small successive batches, with the second contingent moving in only after the first had received its share of the beating. This procedure is followed for two subsequent Saturdays. A 'revised strategy' is devised with the help of the District Congress Committee.[30]

Special preparations are made for sending out contingents for

* Tahsil: a sub-division within a district; mandal: a unit, of one or more villages.

4 February, the third Saturday. The volunteers are determined not to retreat before police oppression; 400 gather from far and near, and are split, as instructed, into smaller groups. 'They marched from the Congress office in Barhampur to Chauri Chaura', four miles due north. The first batch is 'pounced upon by the sepoys, armed guards, horsemen and chaukidars', but it continues its forward march. The second contingent, as it approaches the thana, is even more brutally attacked. So vicious is this armed offensive that they are forced to sound the alarm signal (*khatre-ki-seeti*).[31] The volunteers rally back; the police starts firing into the crowd: 'Hundreds were injured and many satyagrahis were killed in that day's firing'. The sound of rifle shots and the cries of the injured together creates an 'insufferable situation'. (*Isi beech pulis ne goliyān chalāni shuru keen aur goliyon ki āwāz aur ghayalon ki karāh ne miljul kar ek asahya vātāvaran ki srishti kar di.*[32])

Under the circumstances even the most disciplined *yogi* would have lost his balance. Seeing their comrades fall to police bullets, the volunteers flared up. It was as if a prairie fire had been lit in their collective bosoms. (*Aise māhol mein kitna hi sajag yogi ho uska santulan bigar jāega. Apne sāthiyon ko marta dekh kar swayam sevak bharak uthe aur unka krodh prachand dāvagni ke roop mein bharak para.*[33])

The police run out of bullets and lock themselves inside the police station. '*Someone set fire to the thana with kerosene oil. In no time the thana, the daroga and his men were reduced to ashes*'.[34]

In this retelling the violence of the volunteers is overshadowed by a stereotypical recall of the common fate of all satyagrahis. The assent of the Indian reader is sought by portraying an insufferable scenario, an extreme instance of the oppression felt by all nationalists under foreign rule. It was this particularly gruesome violence which finally managed to overturn the non-violent resolve of hardened satyagrahis. *On that day, even a saint would have lost his head.*

The Chauri Chaura 'rioters' are here made to stand for all Indians under colonial rule. *They* did not do it; it got done by them. Whereas Gandhi had condemned the rioters ('Congress sympathizers' they may well have been) as anti-nationalist because they were responsible for their 'evil deeds', the 1972 District Account transforms them into nationalists by taking all distinctive responsibility away from them. Nationalist violence is thereby justified, forgiven and made to seem normal by an inflated rhetoric of heroism within the description, and by a denial of agency.

Let us go back briefly to the initial moment of encounter. The first batch of satyagrahis has just reached the thana. Straightaway, an amalgam of 'sepoys, armed guards, horsemen and chaukidars pounce on them'. Sipahis, armed police and chaukidars there certainly were at the thana that day, but the cavalry was to be trotted out only after the event. It then galloped around the countryside for several weeks, rounding up 'absconders' and intimidating relatives into handing over 'their men'.[35] Mounted police in the District Account, however, form the necessary Aristotelian middle in the story—an ascending trio of lathi charge–cavalry charge–firing; they are in Chauri Chaura well before they are summoned. Peasants in Dumri vividly recall the clatter of horses (*kham-kham-kham-kham*) from after the riot, even if they have extraordinary memories about how the people survived the combined wrath of that avenging *forus* (force). In the District Account the police's oppression, *before* and *after* the event, is combined into a common condition.

If the horses arrive before their time, so do the armed guards who fire on the crowd. In the one-line summary of the event with which the chapter on the Chauri Chaura kānd opens, the riot is caused by an incensed group of satyagrahis who have assembled at the thana to 'commemorate the martyrdom of activists [already] killed in police firing'. The nationalist telescoping of chronology here reaches its temporal limit. A crowd which lost at least three of its members to the police firing of 4 February is here assembled to protest an incident which is yet to happen![36]

It is not just time that gets tossed about, nationalist prose

mixes up people, places, and things as well. The most notable
displacement is caused by the name Chauri Chaura itself. No
other place-name is mentioned in the District Handbook, apart
from a fleeting allusion to the 'Congress office' at Barhampur.
Chauri Chaura stands for all places and for all things. It envelops
the key village of Chotki Dumri, one mile to the west, whose
volunteers had organized the march on the thana; it replaces the
important bazaar of Mundera which, though on the wrong side
of the railway track, was three times the size of Chaura and the
object of picketing by the Dumri activists. The site of 'two very
small cloth sellers shops' in 1922, Chauri Chaura gets portrayed
in the 1972 Account as 'a major depot of imported cloth'.[37]

It is this cloth-retailing character of the bazaar which marks
it out for special attention. The partiality shown the Chaura bazaar
in nationalist prose has several results for the narrative of the event.
It displaces the object of local volunteers' picketing—liquor, meat
and fish—and places in its stead an organized resolve to wage
satyagraha at 'the premier cloth mart of the district'. The
Gandhian symbolism of impure foreign cloth/pure khadi stands
valorized. And it leaves no room for the diverse ways in which
Gandhi's message of self-purification was understood in the villages of Gorakhpur, including those surrounding the Chauri
Chaura police station.[38] A slow accretion of meaning has by now
formed around the event, like a cell inexorably multiplying.

If the village of Chotki Dumri goes unnamed, so does its
mandal functionary Nazar Ali, who masterminded the boycott
and picketing of *dāru*-karia-*machri* in Mundera bazaar in late
January 1921.[39] Arrested on 4 March with the incriminating
whistle[*] with which he 'ordered' the volunteers a month earlier,
Nazar Ali was convicted and hanged in July 1923.[40]

---

[*] *Pace* Gandhi: 'At meetings volunteers should be dispersed among the
crowd. They should learn flag and *whistle signalling* in order to pass instructions
from one to another when it is impossible for the voice to carry', *CWMG*, xviii,
p. 244.

In the 1972 District History the names of the Dumri activists are altogether absent from the narrative of the event; Nazar Ali and associates are listed outside the narrative, at the beginning of the Directory of accredited nationalists where they top the list of 'Gorakhpur Martyrs'. Economical of local names, the narrative of the kānd mentions two prominent nationalists: Madan Mohan Malaviya, who 'appealed against the [District] Court's judgment at the superior court' (and saved 152 convicted from the death penalty) and Motilal Nehru, 'the *sutradhār* of satyagraha of this area', a distinguished nationalist no doubt, but one who is clearly absent from all other accounts, judicial and familial, of the event. In the 'History of the Martyrs of Chauri Chaura', inscribed at the site of a new nationalist memorial in August 1991, Motilal Nehru, the lawyer, makes another appearance. This time he is credited with fighting the Chauri Chaura case at the High Court.

8

The Case for Punishment and Justice

The conscription of a nationalist elder as advocate for the accused, though unrelated to fact,[41] is not without significance: it indicates a shift in the nationalist narrative on 'Chauri Chaura'.

Recall that Gandhi, while not even wishing the rioters to be arrested, had advised the repentant to hand themselves over voluntarily for punishment. Others were to be identified by local nationalists and urged 'to deliver themselves into custody'. Surrender and punishment was the recompense that a few 'evil doers' were to pay the nation as a whole. Underscoring this embarrassing affinity between *dusht* and *deshvāsis*—rogues and countrymen— the *Aaj* of 9 February wondered aloud: What must *we* do now? '*Our* first obligation is that the perpetrators of the crime—those who have burnt and killed—should surrender immediately, repent and accept punishment.' But these perpetrators, even when told expressly to 'surrender to Government according to Mr Gandhi's principles and to submit to punishment', were unwilling to do so. At least one of them, Dwarka Pandey, the leader of the Bar- hampur mandal, maintained that 'the Government was satanic and deserved it'. An unrepentant Dwarka was handed over to the city police by a Congress sympathizer.[42] Family members did produce individual absconders, but it is unlikely that they did so out of any obligation to the nation.

The plea for surrender, made in good taste immediately after the event, soon turned sour at what was considered to be the exemplary meanness of colonial justice. The death sentence passed by H.E. Holmes, the Sessions Judge of Gorakhpur, on *each and every* proven member of the violent crowd was met with a volley of protest in the nationalist press. 'The Chauri Chaura case was no doubt horrible but the judgment in that case is even more so', wrote the *Abhyuday* of Allahabad. 'This is not justice, it is the murder of justice', wrote another Hindi nationalist paper citing the Sessions Judge's decision to recommend the death penalty for 172 persons. Justice entailed keeping punishment untainted by vindictiveness, and this even the High Court at Allahabad had failed to do: its decision to uphold the hanging of 19 ringleaders and the transportation for life of another 110 was still excessive.[43] Nationalists and colonialists both started by labelling the violence a crime, but they had differing notions about the relationship between the burden of guilt and the infliction of punishment.

Routine reviews of punishment were strongly opposed by police officials. In a long-winded column called 'Superintendent of Police's remarks as to the prisoner's history previous to con- viction with special reference to the probability of his home environment leading to a relapse into crime', the convict was invariably put down as a felon from before the riot, and the Chauri Chaura locality was, in such documents, made 'to abound in criminals'. The demands of justice, police officials asserted, had *already* been met by the state having spared them their lives. The Chauri Chaura prisoners could not, in any eventuality, be let off before the expiry of their full term. When a clerk noted in a faltering hand that 'there is no objection in [*sic*] this man's [Ganesh Kalwar] release before the expiry of his sentence', a superior crossed out the babu's phrase and scrawled over it the cryptic order: 'Chauri Chaura case. Release not recommended'.[44] Chauri Chaura is here synonymous with heinous crime: it suffices to say 'Chauri Chaura' for the heinousness to be understood.

Nationalist lawyers advocated a different line of reasoning. Anticipating a legal occasion—the review of a life sentence after fourteen years of imprisonment—Madan Mohan Malaviya petitioned the governor on behalf of 'certain unfortunate persons . . . convicted in the most regrettable Chauri Chaura case . . . The demands of justice have perhaps been met, it may well be tempered now [1935] with mercy', wrote this eminent lawyer, who had defended the accused in 1923.[45] In the opinion of a high official, 'a crime of this sort' deserved twenty-five years' hard labour; mercy had in fact been shown, for all the perpetrators of this 'particularly serious crime . . . might easily have been hanged'; all of them were not.[46]

The question was not whether the requirements of justice had been met, for to argue that they had would be to persuade a coercive state towards individualized leniency. This was unlikely to mean much. The colonial state had to think of others it had imprisoned, besides the Chauri Chaura prisoners. Releasing the six remaining Chauri Chaura convicts *now*, after *only* sixteen years, would give the wrong signal to the troublemakers of Gorakhpur. 'Conditions in [the home district are] . . . becoming similar to those obtaining before the Chauri Chaura outrage'. An act of discretion, premature release may suggest that the government is taking 'a lenient view towards a striking manifestation of mob violence'.[47]

Seven months, a new governor, and a constitutional crisis later[48] the Congress government was able to arrange the release of five of the six prisoners. The grounds for this action and the exclusion of the most determined of the convicts allow us entrée into the ways of nationalist discourse.

The chief minister of the province maintained that Chauri Chaura was one of the political cases to which 'our attention was . . . prominently drawn when we assumed office'. The cabinet had agreed to release certain prisoners, but unfortunately that decision could not be implemented for a full year. Not content to simply assert that the political situation in Gorakhpur district and the province as a whole was unlikely to be affected by the five being set free, the minister went on to offer a sketchy but significant account of the case:

It was no doubt a case of mob frenzy in which *peaceful citizens* lost their heads under excitement and in consequence most deplorable acts of brutality were committed.

The offence of these prisoners, however grave it be, was due to *momentary insanity* and they do not belong to the class of *habitual criminals*.[49]

We are back here to the trope of the unintended act which permits the subsequent insertion of the kānd into a nationalist narrative. But if it could be said in their defence that they were not habitual criminals—a category which had begun to be created by nationalists to replace the demeaning colonial stereotype of criminal castes—they could not be regarded as political creatures either.[50] Mere peaceful citizens unconcerned with politics, they had already suffered punishment enough for their momentary insanity. It was time to let them go.

'They will be *asked* to go back to their villages and to apply themselves *quietly* to their normal avocations. I have no doubt that they will agree to *these terms* as they have *no interest in politics or matters political*.[51] Before their release the five prisoners were to be assembled in a jail near the provincial capital and '*warned not to take part in any demonstration or reception*'.[52] The Chauri Chaura convicts were in effect to give an undertaking of good behaviour. Ironically, this was something which Govind Ballabh Pant in UP and Mahatma Gandhi in Bengal refused to demand of 'educated' and 'sensitive youth' convicted of terrorist attacks on treasuries and armouries.[53]

9

Dwarka Gosain's Complaint

There was to be no immediate reprieve for Dwarka Gosain.[54] One of four brothers, with only two acres of tenancy, Dwarka had taken to part-time priesthood in Chauri Chaura in the early 1920s.* In an English petition addressed to the chief minister from Agra jail in April 1938, Dwarka presented himself and the case in a forthright manner:

Most humbly and respectfully I beg to say that I, Dwarka Prasad prisoner no. 9765, was convicted on the 9th of January 1923 in Chori Chora case *which was a political case beyond doubt. Since 1921, I dedicated my life to the service of the mother land with a large number of volunteers. In 1922 I collected Rs 700/- and paid to the Congress Committee Gorakhpur* for the Angora Fund which was started by the All India Congress

---

* 'I am a *pujari* [worshipper] in the temple of Hira Lal, resident of Chaura. I used to come daily from my village and remain in the temple till noon, then . . . go home in order to take my food and come back at 2 or 3 o'clock . . .'. Confession of Dwarka Gosain, 1 March 1922, CCR.

Committee. By this time, we prisoners of Chori Chora case have served about 16 years in the jail. Major part of our sentence is done. The Congress Government took up the cases of all political prisoners for considering their release but still no attention has been paid towards us.

Now I pray to your Government to *kindly consider the question of our release also together with other political prisoners* whose release is at present under the consideration of the Government, and thus *grant us an opportunity of doing our bit for the motherland during the rest of our lives.*

Kindly consider the question of recalling Shiv Dhar and Shankar prisoners of this case also who are serving their sentence in the Andmans.[55]

The officialese of this petition fails to capture the pugnacious character of Dwarka. Forty years old, and in his fifteenth year of jail life, with thirty-seven disciplinary hearings and sixteen months' remission forfeited, Dwarka had in September 1937 addressed a missive to 'My Prime Minister' in the vernacular.[56] Stretching a High Hindi style to its limits, the letter—no petition this—is a formidable indictment of the Congress discourse on 'Chauri Chaura'. The breathless opening sets the tone for the rest of this political statement:

Newspaper reports, by portraying the assumption of power by 'our' Congress government as a sign of the impending release of political prisoners throughout the country, have given a renewed sense of life to all of us drowning in the deep blue sea (of incarceration)—and for this glimmer of hope we shall eternally be grateful.

(*Hamāri Kangres sarkār ke hāth mein shāsan ka bagdōr āte hi samāchār-patron ne dēsh ke pratēk kone mein rajbandiyon ke muktārth sandēsh panhuncha kar rājbandiyon ko agādh samundra se dūbte ko tatasthta ka gyān kara kar mahān upkār kiya.*[57])

Were newspaper reports about the impending release of political prisoners by the Congress Government 'real news' or a mirage, asks Dwarka. 'My *sarkār* has done a great job of releasing the "Kakori" political prisoners,[58] but it saddens our hearts that it is still keeping mum about the rest of us.' In a passage marked equally by pride and pathos, Dwarka reminds the minister of 'an old case—well known to all political workers—and world famous as Chauri Chaura'.

'It was an unexpected event, caused by police excess during the conduct of the satyagraha campaign.' On an impartial view 'our government' should have released the Chauri Chaura prisoners first: the train robbery at Kakori by the well-known nationalist terrorists took place much later. 'By not doing so our government has hurt us, nay, even wronged us.'

(*Kintu aisa na karke uprōkt ghatna se pānch sāl pīche ke bandi riha kiya gaya isliye hamāre hriday par ek prakār ka aghāt hua aur annyāy ka roop bhi diya jāta hai.*)

'It is not my contention that the "Kakori" prisoners should not have been released.' 'I plead for the release of all political prisoners.' 'Irrespective of party affiliation, whoever fought against Imperialism and for swaraj, be he right or wrong, violent or non-violent, the goal is the same.' Using an interrogatory mode, Dwarka now demands an explanation from 'his' government.

Why have the rest of the political prisoners not been released? What is the reason for this? . . . Are we not political prisoners? Is the government willing to proclaim us remaining prisoners "criminals"? If that's how it is, then let it come out and say so openly. Let the government state that there aren't any political prisoners in our jails.

(*Shesh bandiyon ko abhi tak na riha karne ka kya kāran hai? . . . Kya ham log rājbandi nahīn hain? Sarkār shesh bandiyon ko (criminal) ghoshit karne ko taiyyār hai? Yadi aisa hi sarkār ka vichār hai to spasht kah diya jāi ki ab jailon mein koi rājbandi nahīn hain.*)

This extraordinary rebuke addressed to the provincial chief minister ends on a clichéd note of supplication—the ritual clasping of a superior's feet, but one which threatens to drag the august body into the dust.

I am not writing all this as criticism, merely craving your indulgence as a wretched supplicant. *Please, I must* receive a favourable reply by 30.9.1937, or I will have no option but to seek the [deadly] embrace of mother nature. The poor quality of paper on which I write should give you some idea of my situation and the considerate attitude of the prison officials. *At your service—and herewith this letter.*

(*Main kisi samālochak drishti se nahīn likh raha hoon, kintu deen-dukhi va prārthi ke roop mein prārthna kar raha hoon . . . Kripya āshvāsan-poorvak patrōttar 30/9/37 tak mil jāna chāhiye . . . kintu avashya hi mujhko prakriti devi ki sharan leni pare gi.*

In birange aur dhabbedār kāgaz se hi āp meri paristhiti aur kar-machāriyon kī sadbhāvnāon ka anumān laga sakte hain. Āp ki seva mein—aur yeh kāgaz.)

The supplicant, who hailed from the village of Mahadeva, had since his arrest in a nearby temple on 28 February 1922 for sixteen years 'ground corn'—a colloquialism for enduring rigorous imprisonment. The years he spent in prison had strengthened his keen 'interest in matters political' (*pace* Pant). The UP Governor expressed reservations about Gosain: 'his release', Sir Maurice Hallett argued, 'should wait till we have seen what effect the release of [the five others] has on the district'. Dwarka, recently convicted under the Prisons Act for his political hunger strike, had in any case an additional four months of corn grinding ahead of him.[59] 'Dwarka Prasad's release may follow later', chief minister Pant ordered blandly on the file.

The provincial bureaucracy had set 30 December 1944 as the date of Dwarka's 'probable release'. Dwarka Gosain was let out before that, just in time to be imprisoned for another year during the individual satyagraha campaign that Gandhi had launched in 1941 to protest against India's enrolment in the Second World War. The last of the Chauri Chaura prisoners to be released, he spent the next two years of the Quit India Movement (1942–4) also in jail. But it was another Dwarka who was 'honoured on 15 August 1972 by the Indian Government' as a Freedom Fighter.[60] Perhaps the last of the Chauri Chaura prisoners was no longer alive.

There is no room in nationalist narratives for the names of the Chauri Chaura actors. They can be named outside the narrative—in a directory, an appendix, or even on a granite column—but not as *a part* of the nationalist retelling. It is as if branding the event a 'mindless crime' absolved nationalists of having to take account of these 'criminals' as responsible agents.

That was to be the business of the police and the judge.

Part Four

'While on the one hand, few crimes in India are committed single-handed, on the other, a large number can only be proved by an approver'.

— Sir Cecil Walsh, *Indian Village Crimes: With an Introduction on Police Investigation and Confession* (London, 1929)

10

Violence and Counterinsurgency

What the police faced that day at Chauri Chaura was a violence that was contingent, discriminatory and total.[1] The Dumri meeting had been called to publicly confront the station officer, who had beaten the volunteers a few days earlier. The crowd did not merely attack the police station: its leaders first parleyed with emissaries and argued with the *daroga*.* Forcing him to apologize and give way, the procession jeered at the police functionary and marched towards Mundera to accomplish the unfinished task of picketing liquor, meat and fish shops. It was the subsequent tussle between some policemen and a section of the crowd, and the firing in the air, that 'started the riot'. It was only from this point that the police and everything connected with it came under systematic attack.

A few hours earlier, at the Dumri sabha, local dignitaries and minions of the daroga were either worsted in public argument, symbolically humiliated, or simply ignored. Jagat Pandey, alias Malaon Pandit, an eccentric (*ramta jogi*) itinerant preacher and a non-co-operator who frequented both the thana and the landlord's establishment at Mundera, was at first accorded a ceremonial welcome to the sabha, befitting his rank. He was garlanded and listened to when he began discoursing on Gandhian non-violence. The moment he started to dissuade the volunteers from marching to the thana, he met heated resistance from his listeners. His plea

---

* *Daroga*: A Sub-Inspector of Police, in charge of a *thāna* or police station.

that 'sepoys and guns' were in readiness, and that therefore the meeting better disperse, was rebutted by Nazar Ali, who suggested that 'the Pandit was in the secret service' (the CID), else 'he would not have laughed when 3 volunteers were beaten' in the bazaar. The Pandit's assertion that the Dumri activists 'were [spiritually] not yet fit to face guns and cannons' elicited a similar retort: this 'detective Pandit should be seized by the ear and turned out'.[2]

They clapped their hands at my name and turned me out. I entreated them again and lay down before them . . . I said if they insisted on going, they must make a bridge of my body. This entreaty had no effect whatsoever. The assembly was going on crying out 'jai'. When the mob threw the dust from their shoes on to me and walked past me, I went back. And so I went to Mundera Bazaar . . .[3]

The chaukidar of Chotki Dumri kept shuttling between the village and the thana, providing a running commentary on the day's events, without coming to any harm from the assembled volunteers. However, later in the day the mere suspicion of being a watchman could mean a merciless clubbing, if not death. Even now the violence was not indiscriminate. Petty landlords or agents of the powerful Dumri estate were not sought out, nor was either Chaura or Mundera bazaar looted.

The violence against the police was total: everything connected with the thana was attacked. Telegraph and railway equipment was destroyed to delay the arrival of reinforcements to the thana which had been gutted, a large number of its functionaries killed. When additional police arrived from Gorakhpur that night, the special train had to make an unscheduled stop: the track had been torn apart, the wooden sleepers removed, some even burnt; the Collector's party had to walk the last mile from Chotki Dumri to the police station. 'All the paraphernalia of the thana were found . . . scattered about . . . in a burnt condition.' 'No rupees or pice or article of value or paper of [the] thana was to be found. No private property of the police such as money or clothes was found'.[4] The treasury had been ransacked; the iron gate of the police station smashed. Padlocks were prized out from doors. Telegraph wires at the nearby post office were plucked out; signalling devices on the railway dismantled. The tattered remains of police turbans lay strewn all over the precinct.

Nothing in the daroga's house was spared. 'Rupees and pice' had been removed from the cash box; ornaments of the *darogāin*[*] and her daughters were snatched away. 'There was rice, dāl, ghī to eat, and clothes; these people took them. The clothes were in a box. They broke it open with spears'.[5] The widow and her two girls were turned out of the house, threatened with death but eventually spared.

And there was no one to be found. Chaura bazaar was deserted; only three functionaries of the loyalist Sikh landlord dared stay back that night.[6] Chotki Dumri, a village of 1300 to which another thousand had converged that day, was without a soul: 'not even a sparrow chirped in Dumri the next morning'.[7]

Search and capture had to start from scratch. Villages in the neighbourhood of the burnt thana were raided early in the morning. For a full week, the Superintendent of Police 'did not sleep in a bed'. Every night he was out chasing suspects: 'Up to the 11th I had no opportunity of taking off my clothes.' Stanley Mayers, the police chief, fell ill. He remained 'ill after going back to Gorakhpur'.[8] The memory of such early morning raids still lingers in Chotki Dumri, the village worst affected; for the rest we have the testimony of policemen in court.

The 50 persons whom I brought away with me from Chaura on 5th February were brought in order that I [Inspector Piare Lal] might question them as to the occurrence.

People of Bale, Bhartolia, Chaura and Mundera go out into the open to relieve nature; as they came they were caught and brought in. There were among them men, women, boys and girls.[9]

* * *

* *Darogāin*: the wife of a daroga.

Barhampur, five miles south of Chaura, was targeted for 4 o'clock in the morning; the purpose once again was to 'question the villagers', not to 'arrest any particular accused'. The settlement had to be surrounded, 'otherwise the villagers would have run away'.[10] Jaddu Chamar, one of the persons arrested, recounted that experience for the judge.

Five days after the burning of the thana there was a raid in Barhampur. Everyone was collected at the zamindar's door. The daroga asked which of them was a volunteer; the gorait* said so and so. The three of us were brought under arrest . . .

The daroga beat us much . . . He said we knew the volunteers. I said I did not know, but people were volunteers.[11]

Not only was Jaddu arrested, he was made to yield an incriminating document—his volunteer Pledge Form. Such pledge forms were recovered from many of those arrested soon after the riot. In several cases, 'pledges were found in their houses'. At least 'one wounded lad' came to the investigating officer and produced the volunteer form of his brother, Bihari Pasi of Chotki Dumri. In Jaddu's case a counterfoil of his 'paper' was ferreted out of the 3000 such forms impounded from the Congress office at Gorakhpur; the handwriting of the recruiter who filled in Jaddu's pledge was authenticated in court. Jaddu Chamar admitted being a volunteer but denied everything else that he was charged with. Jaddu was fortunate: the evidence of his rioting was limited, and though two parts of the tell-tale pledge had been filed in the court, the judge chose to believe his story.[12]

Confronted with similar pledge forms, others tried to distance themselves from their thumb impressions. 'I am not a volunteer', asserted the accused Aklu before the magistrate. Faced with Exhibit 37, his pledge form, Aklu responded: 'I did get my volunteer form filled but I don't remember if I thumbmarked it.'[13] 'I am not a volunteer. The whole world paid 4 annas [as subscription].

* *Gorait*: a village watchman.

I also paid 4 annas, and I also signed a paper but I don't know if it was a volunteer form.' 'I am not a volunteer. Babu Sant Baksh Singh [the landlord] may have got my name registered in the Congress office.' 'I am a volunteer but I did not work as a volunteer.'

The ambiguity of these denials rests on a fine distinction between intention and fact: 'I do not know if I became a volunteer'; 'I am not a registered volunteer, but people called me a volunteer'.[14] All these volunteers were not as fortunate as Jaddu of Barhampur; they were sentenced to between three to eight years' rigorous imprisonment.

The 225 accused of joint crimes were unfortunate in yet another respect. They tried desperately not to incriminate themselves in court—they were 'as economical of the truth as they dared'.[15] But colonial law had its own ways of unstitching silence. All it needed was to target and segregate one or two from the collectivity on trial, then offer these suspect legal creatures the freedom to 'sing for their lives'. The crime had to be framed for the court in more ways than one. Not that every trial in India required such a witness for the prosecution, a criminal turned King's Evidence, an Approver, as he was (and still is) called in the subcontinent. However, it was common practice that 'in every *big case* an approver . . . [be] put up'. Chauri Chaura was a case bigger than most. And 'therefore, after the statements of Ramrup Barai, Bhagwan Ahir and Shikari had been taken . . . [the DSP] and the DIG consulted as to who should be made approver out of the three; at last it was decided that Shikari be made approver . . .'[16]

11

The Making of the Approver

'An approver should be examined first and not after all the witnesses who are supposed to corroborate his evidence are examined.' It is thus that a certain priority is accorded to the approver's testimony in the latest edition of the classic Indian handbook on the law of evidence.[17] True to this form, Mir Shikari, a twenty-seven-year-old 'cultivator and hideseller' from Chotki Dumri, was ushered in as Prosecution Witness No 1 in the Chauri Chaura case.

In the course of his approver's testimony—an insider's recall of the crime in which the key distinction is the promise of personal freedom after the trial—Shikari covered considerable ground. The events he etched and elaborated included the formation of a local unit at Chotki Dumri; the enrolment of volunteers; the organizational network and channels of communication in *tappa* Keotali and the surrounding Hata *tahsīl*;* the participation of local volunteers in bigger Khilafat-non-co-operation meetings; the decision to picket liquor, meat and fish shops; the altercation with the thanedar of Chaura; the deliberations to assert volunteer strength at the thana and the bazaar; the organization and proceedings of the meeting preparatory to the march to the thana; the clash with the police and the burning and killing at the precinct. Indeed, a very large portion of what we now know about the momentous event at Chauri Chaura is a consequence of Approver Shikari's prodigious outpouring in the trial court.

As he took the stand, Shikari was conscious of the fact that

---

* *Tappa*: a sub-division within a tahsīl; *tahsīl*: a sub-division within a district.

he was now to relate the 'crime' *for the prosecution.* Recalled by the magistrate to add another name to the long list of peasants being committed to a full trial, Mir Shikari presented himself and the accused in a legally correct manner.

I am an approver in this case.
  I mentioned many men as being joint with me in the crime.
  I identified one of my accomplices today.
  This is Kalu or Lalu Chamar. He was with us in the sabha; . . . He accompanied us up to Chaura; . . . and he dismantled the thana tiles in the course of the riot. He lives in Rakba.[18]

On the run for six weeks, Shikari of Dumri was pardoned soon after his surrender. The price extracted for this pardon was a high one—material help in the conviction of fellow-rioters: a price which was to be paid by others. And so begins the donning of a shadowy mantle which was first created to incriminate the Thugs—the most 'Indian' of all criminals. Approver Shikari was to save his own skin and sacrifice those of his colleagues by his story-telling. His stories had to be demonstrably true, and Shikari, to ensure his own future, had to be an important character in them. His role in the theatre of colonial legality had been historically prepared; he was the latest *dramatis persona* in a long-running play.

Created in the 1830s by Henry Sleeman, the legendary Thug-catcher of the British Raj, approvers were to be employed by the Thagi and Dakaiti (dacoity) Department in the 1890s at a pay of Rs 4 a month. Allowed to live in official family quarters, they could be deputed to whichever police station their stories might take them—'liable to be transferred at Government expense . . . where their services may be required either temporarily or permanently', was how the rule book put it.

Paid approvers were curious creatures, nurtured in colonial India by a state determined to account for the Thugs in extra-legal ways. As these criminals were considered to belong to closed,

murderous fraternities, the department charged with their exter-
mination had devised the expedient of literally 'employing' a Thug
to catch other Thugs![19]

Approvers, whether Thug or peasant, were novel to India;
colonial historians even castigated the Mughal judicial procedure
as eccentric for not recognizing approvers.[20] The same colonial
implant was in evidence in the thirteen American possessions. In
Virginia, at least, if a 'person indicted for treason or any other
felony' confessed, made accusations against his accomplices and
had them successfully convicted, 'the "approver" received his pardon'. If his testimony failed to achieve the task for which it was
fabricated and the felon-accomplices were acquitted, the approver
took their place at the gallows.[21]

So, an eyewitness recall would not suffice. More was demanded. The approver had to confess to the crime as an *accomplice*: that was to be the guarantee of Shikari's testimony and
of his life. The committing magistrate had offered him a 'conditional pardon', a reprieve dependent on performance. Should he
perjure himself, or prove difficult in court, Mir Shikari could be
hanged for his admissions.[22]

Before he was recognized as approver, Shikari was just another
absconder. But this is to simplify matters somewhat. 'Shikari Sekh
is the leader of Dumari', we read in the list of volunteers compiled
at the police station in late January 1922.[23] A mālik of the Dumri
volunteers, Shikari was of special concern to the police from the
day after the riot. A quick raid on Chotki Dumri was aimed
specially at his capture. Unsuccessful, the police placed a reward
on his arrest.[24] In his absence Shikari's family was threatened with
loss of land. 'My relations sent a message to me, telling to come
and present myself or my houses and fields would be confiscated . . . and then what would they . . . live on?'[25] On 15 March
Shikari came out of hiding. 'I first went to Sardar Harcharan Singh
and through him presented myself to the Dy. Supt.'[26] (Harcharan

Singh was the manager of Chaura bazaar and a functionary of the Sikh estate, of which Chotki Dumri was a part.)

Shikari was, then, no ordinary accused. Nor was his first statement, a 'confession' duly recorded under the provisions of the Criminal Procedure Code, a rustic's rambling recall. Required by law, the magistrate had 'satisfied himself' that the prisoner was 'not under the tuition of anybody', that 'no police officer was present', and that he 'was making his statement voluntarily'. Shikari was allowed 'about half an hour' before the recording began 'so that he might think over what he had to say'.[27]

The confession was certainly well thought out. About Shikari's intelligence and character there appears to be little doubt: the judge commended him as 'active, quickwitted and intelligent', the Dumri people still recall his 'daring' and 'power'.[28] But the long confession of 16 March does not simply testify to the power of his phenomenal recall. The *pro forma* character of Shikari's utterances stands witness to an unwritten contract between the police and the potential approver. Here is Shikari confessing to the moment of the police–peasant encounter:

Then violent pelting of *kankars* [stones] began. I also threw kankars . . . As soon as they [the policemen] came out at the door, we, all those whose names I have mentioned to have been present at the gate of the thana, we killed them.[29]

Note how Shikari implicates himself as an accomplice: 'I also threw stones'; 'We: i.e. I and the others I have named—killed the policemen'. Note also the splitting up of the collective 'we', the way Shikari makes himself vulnerable in the eyes of the law so as to be allowed the freedom to legally frame everybody else. And notice the dangers inherent in Shikari offering himself and his stories to the prosecution, for this could elicit either punishment or reward. Even if 'nothing' is allegedly 'better known to the . . . shrewd' north-Indian 'villager . . . than that a confession of guilt *may lead* to the purchase of a pardon by his becoming an approver', how was Shikari to *know* that the prosecution would buy his story?[30]

Mir Shikari was not the only prisoner to have walked this tightrope. There were two others whose confessions were of special interest to the prosecution. Ramrup Barai, the *panwāri* (betel-leaf seller) from Mundera, was arrested on 5 March and confessed over two days. His duly recorded statement brims with pithy details. An idea of the inversion brought about by the power of local volunteer organizations is conveyed by the verbal abuse directed at the thanedar of Chaura. When Bhagwan Ahir, Ramrup Barai recalled, was admonished in Mundera bazaar on 1 February for being a disloyal government pensioner turned 'volunteer', Bhagwan Ahir replied with an abuse: '*Lund se*' (Fuck you)![31] This four-letter retort openly proffered to the local thanedar in the bazaar, was largely responsible for Bhagwan Ahir being beaten up by thanedar Gupteshar Singh—a significant link in the chain of events leading to the riot of 4 February 1922.

But the betel-leaf seller from Mundera bazaar was not just recalling a past altercation, inclusive of expletives; Ramrup had produced a 'confession' in the hope of a pardon. Self-implication in joint crimes and the slicing of the narrative into segments to better identify the accused are the tell-tale signs which his confession bears of an informal promise of approvership. Two such sequences, three days apart, in the run up to the riot give us some idea of what Ramrup had in mind when he dictated his confession to the Magistrate on 5–6 March 1922.

ACTION: Gathering at Mundera bazaar on 1 February 1922 to picket the bazaar.

IDENTIFICATION: 'Among the volunteers who were there *I recognized* Bengali Bhar of Bhartolia, Lal Mohd., Ramdas Kalwar, Bhagwan Ahir, residents of Chaura, Shikari and Nazar Ali, residents of Dumri. *I did not identify others.* The remaining others were of Raghuapur, Bale, Dumri and Chaura. *I do not know their names.*'

ACTION: Clash with the police.

IDENTIFICATION: 'Then all turned . . . towards the thana and began to throw kankar from the [railway] line: *I also* threw kankar from the line'; 'Then *myself*, Nazar Ali, Shikari and a Sain and many others pulled out the thana gate and broke it . . . '[32]

The police were clearly grooming Ramrup as a possible approver. He was kept in the city lock-up, far apart from his comrades clapped inside the district prison: the law required that potential approvers be kept separate from the accused.

This accused from Mundera bazaar was on the short list of potential approvers; he had only to wait in hopeful solitary confinement at the *kotwāli** for summons to appear in his new role in the makeshift court the magistrate had set up in the middle of the district jail compound. Ramrup's prolonged absence in the city lock-up led to a suspicion among the accused that he had been pardoned. Dwarka Gosain, when faced with an adverse mention in Ramrup's confession, replied: 'Ramrup Barai and I have no enmity. He names me as he has been given a pardon and had appeared as a witness.'[33]

Dwarka was proved wrong. Ramrup had been pipped at the post; the police officers had changed their mind; the mantle of approvership had fallen on Mir Shikari. For the prosecution it was a simple case of Ramrup's potential as approver being lower than Shikari's. The police officer in charge of the case was quite forthright. 'In every big case', he told the judge,

an approver is put up, therefore after the statements of Ramrup Barai, Bhagwan Ahir and Shikari had been taken, I and the DIG consulted as to who should be made approver out of the three; at last it was decided that Shikari should be made approver, and the Committing Magistrate was then approached.[34]

To Ramrup this decision appeared a betrayal. Having been tossed back to the wrong side of the law he pleaded pathetically against

* *Kotwāli*: city police station.

this deception: 'Daroga Lachhman Singh was standing there, when I saw him I salaamed and joined my hands and asked what fault I had committed that he had deceived me so. He said he had made me an approver but the Sahib had struck out my name and he was not at fault.'[35]

Now, facing his suddenly reversed circumstances, it was imperative for Ramrup to change tack. He made a desperate attempt to distance himself from his 'confession', repeatedly harping on the imagery of someone who was once freed and now returned to shackles. Ramrup retracted his confession in the sessions court; pathetically, he recounted his experience of police torture and the subsequent inducement of pardon and approvership. The High Court was unmoved by the plight of an actor who had been told, mid-play, that he had better act out another part. The judge took a narrowly legalistic view and ruled that he saw 'no reason to doubt that . . . [the confession] was voluntarily made'. The original death sentence stood confirmed.[36] Ramrup Barai was hanged on 2 July 1923.

And then there was Bhagwan Ahir.

A 'returned soldier' from the Mesopotamia theatre of the First World War, drill-master to the Dumri volunteers, proud owner of a military khaki uniform, Bhagwan had been beaten by the thanedar in Mundera on Wednesday, 1 February. A meeting of volunteers had been called for Saturday the 4th to discuss his case and demand an explanation from the station officer.

Arrested on 10 March in the northern jungles bordering Nepal, Bhagwan Ahir was also made to yield a 'confession'. In his *ikrārnāma*, Bhagwan named the persons who brought kerosene and burnt the thana, and a few others who killed a constable and the thanedar. But Bhagwan Ahir stopped short of implicating himself directly in the riot. He attempted instead to highlight his good deeds during the riot and underline the dangers of his shady position as a government pensioner/volunteer—one who fell outside the rigidly polarized theatre of violence at the Chaura thana.

His narrative is broken: this Bhagwan said he needed to go some distance to urinate, so that the riot happened behind his back! After this break, Bhagwan Ahir picks up the thread not in order to frame others by implicating himself, but to establish his role in the rescue of the thanedar's widow and her children—in other words, to stress his increasing distance from the rioters:

All the people were ready to kill the wife of the S.I.* Dudhai Bhar had a sword in his hand and proceeded to [try to] kill the S.I.'s child. I took up the child in my arms and requested Dudhai Bhar to spare the life of that child. Bhar [sic] then proceeded [towards] . . . the other child. I took up that child too in my arms . . . Then a large number of people whom I do not know fell upon her. I entreated these fellows also. Then I took the S.I.'s wife up to the field of Harpal . . . Then Inderjit Hajjam said, 'This man gets pension, beat him . . . The Sub-Inspector's wife will be witness for him'. Then Karia struck me two blows with a *patti*. Ramdas also beat me.[37]

Bhagwan was making a mistake. Being the alleged saviour of the dead daroga's pregnant wife was not good enough for the court: approvership was offered and pardon granted not for chivalrous heroism but for purposes with a clearer cut: helping the prosecution through self-implication in 'joint crimes'.

No indulgence was shown to Bhagwan Ahir: he too died on the gallows in July 1923.

Preparatory to the trial, proceedings began on 25 March in the Committing Magistrate's court with just Shikari as approver. On 18 April another accused, Thakur Ahir, came out of hiding and surrendered at Chaura. A milkman and carter from the small village of Bale just north of the police station, Thakur was an enrolled volunteer but had not been very active in the events leading up to the meeting at Dumri on the morning of 4 February. During his confession to the Deputy Superintendent of Police,

---

* S.I.: Sub-Inspector of Police, or daroga.

Thakur made 'important disclosures', particularly regarding the latter phase of the riot. Shikari by his own admission had run away while 'the riot and murder was still going on'. Thakur was of special interest to the police as he had provided detailed identification of the culprits who ransacked the thana and dismantled the telegraph wire and the railtrack, lest 'the sarkar getting information . . . thunder up' from the district headquarters.[38]

Thakur buttressed his story by giving the 'clue of 2 or 3 muskets . . . that Tirathraj had thrown . . . during the riot in the well near the thana'.[39] While his confession, made to a police officer, was invalid under section 25 of the Evidence Act (confessions to be admissible evidence had to be recorded by a competent magistrate), another section guaranteed the validity of the operative part 'by the discovery of facts in consequence of information given'.[40]

The police acted on this information the next day, and realizing the potential of Thakur as the second approver took steps to keep him under arrest in the dak bungalow, away from Shikari who was ensconced in the *kotwāli*. On 21 April a formal application was moved by the Public Prosecutor for the grant of pardon to Thakur Ahir, which ended with the request that 'if the Court considers it expedient and necessary for the case he [Thakur] may be tendered a conditional pardon, and examined as an approver. . . '.[41] The magistrate agreed. The quest for approvers had ended. Thakur was to supplement the testimony of Shikari. A complete case could now be built against the Chauri Chaura accused.

As required of an accomplice-approver, Thakur implicated himself in each of the culpable deeds of the rioters: 'I *also* beat the daroga'; 'many persons . . . went with Nazar Ali to cut the telegraph wire, *including myself*'.[42] This second approver therefore enabled the prosecution to identify the individual accused as part of a criminal collectivity which took shape at Dumri village on the morning of 4 February, which burnt and killed at the thana in the afternoon, and which wrecked rail and telegraph communications with Gorakhpur before the day was done.

Sahdeo, son of Jittu; I knew his name before; I saw him in the Dumri sabha; then I saw him at the thana gate, standing with a lathi and beating and knocking down anyone who came out of the thana; with him were many rioters. I saw him among the wire-cutters and among those who dismantled the railway.[43]

And so, in a similar vein, Thakur Ahir follows his instinct for self-preservation by doing duty for fifty-three others! Though he appeared 'dull, heavy-witted and stupid' to the sessions judge, Thakur was quite emphatic that he had seen the riot to its bitter end: 'I stayed in the riot until everybody left. Every one went off with me [when I did]'. Nervous and evasive when cross-examined by the counsels for defence—'I easily forget things'—Thakur seems to have managed his secondary role well.[44]

Both the prosecution and the judge, however, laid much more store by Shikari, whose fuller and prior testimony had set the stage for the competent performance of the second approver. More composed than Thakur, even Shikari was nonetheless afraid, in his own way, in court. It was no longer the dread of punishment which Shikari had felt while in hiding, nor the fear that 'persisted in my heart' (as he put it), 'until I was pardoned'. No, Shikari's pusillanimity had a more moral cause. 'I am in fear now', he said, answering a direct question from the judge, 'because I am afraid of mentioning someone who is innocent and leaving out someone who is guilty.'[45]

Towards the end of his gruelling week-long performance in the sessions court, Shikari appears to have become anxious about how he had fared as approver! Faced with the considerable task of successfully pressing charges against the 225 accused, the prosecution's main concern was to get hold of a connected narrative—a chain of events—leading up to and ending with the occurrence itself. No amount of rummaging by the police through confiscated Congress papers at Gorakhpur could do away with the need for 'hard' evidence about the background to the riot from Chaura, Chotki Dumri and tappa Keotali generally.[46] Shikari's anxiety is testimony of how crucial it was that he perform his narrative function; he spoke as if his life depended on it, which of course it did.

The approvers' narrative was not the only testimony to have been produced from the locality: agents of neighbouring landlords, peons and servants, constables and chaukidars who survived the massacre, also testified to the crime and to its pre-history.[47] But much of this evidence was fragmentary and did not cover the riot's entire course.

As for the accused, none came forward to make a programmatic statement. Even the ring leaders proffered only denials and alibis, ranging from Nazar Ali's plea of mistaken identity with his namesake, Shikari's uncle, to Lal Mohammad's claim that he was knocked unconscious by buckshot before the thana was stormed.[48] The accused attempted, by and large, to dissociate themselves from the evidence so as to escape punishment.

So we see here that the same fear of punishment which makes the accused economical of truth also yields us the figure of the approver, the 'criminal' turned Crown-Witness who, protected by the law and goaded by the prosecution speaks of the crime in an accusatory and systematic mode.

12

Shikari's Testimony

All witnesses in this country, but specially approvers, are fond of speaking with the vaguest generality . . . The moment he consents to be an approver, he stands in a different position from an ordinary prisoner making a confession. The latter is free to say as much or as little as he chooses . . . but [of an Approver] the greatest particularity of detail should be required.

—J.W. Mayne, *Hints on Confessions & Approvers for the Use of the Police* (Madras, 1906)

Shikari's was not only a particularly detailed narration: his testimony, much more than any other, was 'at the service of judgment'.[49]

Shikari had to testify so as to prove the factual basis of an assertion—the seven charges against the 225 Chauri Chaura accused.[50] The accusatory mode and its transactional character set Shikari's testimony apart from inquisitorial confessions wherein 'the accused himself took part in the ritual of producing penal truth'.[51] The difference, both stark and ironic, is that whereas in medieval Europe the more the accused confessed the greater became the justness of the punishment, in colonial India the more Shikari-as-Approver implicated himself in the crime of Chauri Chaura the better the chances became of his being pardoned.

The task before the approver was to narrate all the subsequences —'particularity of detail'—that were thought to be the basis of these culpable acts. He had to identify the accused at each step of their onward march towards crime. And he had to affirm that there were no legal or procedural limitations being put upon him to ensure his reliability in court. Shikari had moreover to testify as an accomplice-accuser. This dual character, operating from both sides of the law, marked his testimony out from everything else that was related in court. The prosecution, through its interventions, ensured that Shikari's testimony successfully performed these tasks for which it had been designed.[52] *'There were many others with me wherever I did anything. I recognized some of my associates in this riot.'*[53] Shikari as approver would have been useless to the prosecution without this constant switch between accusation and self-implication.

The Approver was not to limit himself to the crime but, as it were, to go behind it in order to help the prosecution fashion its pre-history. In this way the actions of the accused were imbued in court with a certain premeditation. In his testimony the narrative is broken up into sub-sequences leading to the crime, and at each juncture Shikari pauses and relates the names and the faces of his ex-comrades, whom he now 'recognizes' as the accused on trial.

If in this interpretation of Shikari's testimony actions were to relate to identification in such a way as accusation did to self-implication, the progression towards the crime would read as follows:[*]

ACTION 1:   Formation of the Dumri Mandal.

IDENTIFICATION: 'About 50 men of Mundera came to my door. And men of Chaura came. And a Brahmin whom I have identified here, a tallish man. Perhaps his name is Dwarka. And many men came with him. Abdullah of Rajdhani . . . and a Pandit of Rampurwa, whose name I know now to be Sham Sundar . . . Nazar Ali also came . . . Ganesh Bania of Mundera, Ramrup Barai of Mundera and Chedi Bhar of Chaura, etc . . . I do not know

---

[*] I have broken Shikari's testimony into short paragraphs to better illustrate the constructed nature of his evidence, where the recall of past events is obsessively peopled with the names and roles of those on trial.

who else was there, but all the men of my village were there. Some of the names—most of them—I learnt before the lower court. The rest I knew before.'

ACTION 2:   Recruitment of volunteers.

IDENTIFICATION: 'I and Nackched and Nazar Ali recruited eight or nine men. Nackched wrote the forms. Chingi Teli, Bihari Pasi, Phenku Pasi, Sukhdeo Pasi, Bindeshwari Sainthwar, Jangi Ahir, Dudhai Chamar, and two men of Bale whose names I do not remember. These were recruited. *Of them Phenku, Jangi are not among the accused.*'

ACTION 3:   Attempt at picketing Mundera bazaar in late January.

IDENTIFICATION: 'We went there with 30 or 32 volunteers; Nazar Ali, Bikram, Sukhdeo—I do not remember the other names . . . I started with 30 or 32 for Mundera but did not go there but to Bhupa.'

ACTION 4:   Meeting at Hata to counter a pro-government Sabha, 31 January.

IDENTIFICATION: 'Of the accused those who were in Hata assembly are Sukhdeo Pasi, Sadhu Sainthwar, Dudhai Chamar, Chingi Teli, etc. . . . I do not remember the others.'

ACTION 5:   Attempt at picketing Mundera bazaar on 1 February.

IDENTIFICATION: 'Of the people I have named today [see immediately above] Chingi Teli, Dudhai Chamar were not there, the rest were all there.'

ACTION 6:   Deliberations on the evening of 1 February at Shikari's house.

IDENTIFICATION: 'To that came Mahadeo of Chaura, Kheli Bhar, Bhagwan Ahir, Lal Muhammad Sain, Ramrup Barai, Nazar Ali. And others whose names I do not know. Kheli Bhar died in the riot. *The other five are among the accused.*'

ACTION 7:   Continuation of deliberations on the morning of 2 February.

IDENTIFICATION: 'The same people came to my house as had been there on the day before, and a boy named Nackched . . . That day five letters were written. By Nackched.'

ACTION 8:   Dumri sabha on the morning of 4 February.

IDENTIFICATION: 'I noticed carefully. Everyone was ready to go, no one drew back . . . *All the men of my village raised their hands. That is all the accused of my village who are present.* Also Ramrup Barai, Thakur Ahir (approver), Naipal Mallah, Ganesh Bania the Chaura accused whom I have identified; all these persons were among those who raised their hands. And Sham Sundar accused, and Meghu Tiwari accused, and Dwarka Pandey accused, and Abdullah alias Sukhi accused and Jaglal Kewat accused, and Kalu alias Lalu accused (Chamar), and Baran Bania accused; and many persons whom I do not remember. And I "recognized by face" several others.'[54]

An important juncture was a meeting of volunteers called on 31 January at the town of Hata, some twenty miles away, to which the Dumri contingent had been specially invited. Let us look at the making of this account more closely. In Shikari's confession of 16 March, the Hata sabha appears to have no real significance: it merely occupies a temporal space—the elapsed time between the January and early-February picketings of Mundera bazaar.[55]

During the committal proceedings, the prosecution elicited the following details from Shikari about the Hata sabha:

While the sabha was gathering I went to a relation of mine. When I returned the sabha was ending. A Panditji standing on a *chauki* was reciting, 'Mohd. Ali's mother says "son die for the Khilafat".'* I also heard some other things but I don't remember.

We were all affected by the speech, we became enthusiastic. Our heads swelled. We got up and shouted Gandhi's, Tilak's, Swaraj's, Bharat Mata's, Md. Ali and Shaukat Ali's jais. Then we formed into lines. We stood up opposite the tahsil and the thana and we put up a

---

* The reference is to a popular song, *'Bolin Amma Mohammad Ali ki jān beta Khilafat mein de do'.*

charkha [spinning wheel] and two or four flags in front, and we all went towards the bazaar by the tahsil. It was Hata Bazaar day.

In front of the tahsil we halted ten or twelve minutes and shouted all the jais mentioned above. The tahsildar, S.I., constables were there but no one arrested us.

We reached our office in Hata Bazaar. Nazar Ali then whistled . . . a whistle like this (exhibit 137) . . . We all knew the significance of the whistles from before as we had been instructed. This whistle was to stay and we stayed. The sun set. Then we left for Bharangua [and the next morning tried to picket Mundera Bazaar].[56]

Note that under questioning by the prosecution Shikari provides information about crowd discipline, response to prearranged signals, defiance of local functionaries of the state, etc. All these could easily feed into a different but related narrative which would present the proceedings after Hata almost as a prelude to 'Chauri Chaura'. In the court of the sessions judge Shikari repeats all this, but, crucially, he also *identifies* those of the accused who were present at Hata on that Tuesday afternoon. Shikari replies under cross-examination:

It was when I came into this [sessions] court that I first realized the importance of naming the persons whom I had seen at the Hata sabha. Before this I had not been questioned as to this: I mentioned it when the prosecution counsel asked me in the court.[57]

This was so because the Committing Magistrate in his 'order' had construed the Hata sabha as 'of direct consequence for the subsequent development of the story . . . '.[58] In the magistrate's master narrative, the importance of this sabha is established in sequential and symbolic terms. The holding of the meeting within earshot of the thana and the tahsil, and in opposition to a loyalist meeting convened by the *pargana hākim*,* is construed by Mahesh Dikshit, the Committing Magistrate, as an act charged with significance. For Dikshit it showed both 'independence of government control'

* *Pargana hākim*: a sub-divisional officer.

and of 'accredited leaders' of the Congress. The decision of Nazar Ali and others to picket Mundera bazaar flows from this victory over the 'authorities' at the tahsil headquarters; their reaction to the beating of Bhagwan Ahir the next day by the thanedar of Chaura is also overdetermined by the achievements of the Hata meeting. Having challenged the sub-divisional officer, they could not brook the assertion by a 'third-class' thanedar.*

The loss of power by the state at Hata leads to the loss of life at Chauri Chaura four days later. The 'tragedy of Chauri Chaura' was thus anticipated by the Non-Co-operation Movement generally and its particular manifestation at Hata tahsil on 31 January 1922: it could not 'be regarded as a stray act of rowdyism on the part of the non-co-operators and their sympathizers'.[59]

As the Committing Magistrate stated on the basis of the approver's testimony, the peasant-accused of Chauri Chaura had already taken the law into their hands at Hata three days before the occurrence.

As if to further rub in the lesson, and to show their independence not only of government control but also of their accredited leaders, they marched with the crowd to *both* the tahsil and the thana and rent the skies with their war cries.[†]

The police and the tahsil, however, ignored the challenge, and the crowd, flushed with victory, marched through Hata to the respective villages of their halt in the night, determined to picket the Mundera Bazaar next day . . .

The local village leaders took the matter up at once [of the beating of Bhagwan Ahir at Mundera Bazaar]. Their *amour propre* was hurt. An outlying sub-inspector had disgraced one of their members, while the tahsil and thana of Hata had quietly looked on at their antics. They wanted to take their revenge then and there . . . [60]

---

* The thana at Chauri Chaura was literally classified as 'third class', i.e. it contained a limited complement of police, as compared to bigger police stations.

† The use of the italicized *both* is a rhetorical device, as these were, and still are, in the same enclosure.

It is thus that the prosecution and the magistrate elicit episodic information which falls into a pattern which, for them and their purposes, makes the violence at Chauri Chaura intelligible in terms of a past. The episodic dimension gives rise to such questions as: and so? and then what? what was the outcome? But the activity of narrating does not consist simply in adding episodes to one another; it also constructs meaningful totalities by the grasping together of successive events.[61] Jurisprudence further involves identifying popular illegalities as culpable deeds, translating politics as crime, and building a case for the state against a crowd which, in different circumstances, might only merit individual punishment.[62]

13

The Approver and the Accused

The approver is so designated only because he produces a specialized testimony. It is his statement that makes him an approver. What is required of the prosecution is to establish that his testimony has been fashioned in terms of the procedures prescribed for the making of such statements by law. The prosecution wishes to restrict Shikari's testimony to the background and the minutiae of the crime. The question of Shikari's prior position and relationships in the village are immaterial for the prosecutor.

The counsel for the accused wants to destroy the self-sufficiency of Shikari's statement by contextualizing it, in the hope that this will expose its internal inconsistencies and prove its falsity. The defence attempts to socialize the event, implicate it—and hence the approver's testimony—into the reality of its milieu.

As opposed to the prosecution, which was content with half a sentence on the approver himself ('I pay Rs 34–7–0 rent a year'), the defence began by digging into Shikari and his family's past relationships with the persons named in his testimony. It emerged thus that Shikari's mother and sister had been *chalāned* for theft some years earlier by a chaukidar of the village who was now an accused; that some others named by Shikari had a history of disputes with the approver and his family, etc. When Shikari was offered to the defence, it attempted for three days to discredit his testimony by highlighting what it suggested were wilfully wrong statements motivated by prior feuds; by questioning the truth of the approver being an eyewitness to the events described by him, especially to the role of individuals accused in the riot; and by suggesting that procedural lapses may have been committed both in the manner of the taking down of his confession and during the identification parades. All this would invalidate the approver's testimony, making it inadmissible evidence and converting all or some of his statements into legal untruths. It is the task of the judge to adjudicate on such matters.[63]

What about the accused themselves? What do the court records tell us about their perception of the approver and his damning evidence? In reply to the question, 'Shikari identifies you as among the rioters. What do you say to this?', the accused could either think of no good reason why their ex-comrade should betray them so, or they dug into their common past to come up with explanations based on what, in most cases, the court described as 'frivolous and undocumented enmity'. The first type of response is typified by the comment of Gobardhan Pasi, a volunteer of Dumri: 'Shikari is of my village. I have no enmity with him. I cannot say why he entangles me [*humko kyon phansa raha hai*].'[64] Dudhai Chamar on the other hand had this to say in his defence:

We Chamars had bought a pig for sacrifice a year ago. It entered Ilahi Musalman's house and then Shikari's field. Shikari quarrelled with us at this. The Mukhia [headman] came and separated us. The Musalmans stopped our water. We dug our own well and take water from it.[65]

Dudhai inserted Shikari's behaviour in court within a history of communal differences within the village; Bikram Ahir, (Sita's uncle) an ex-chaukidar turned active volunteer,[66] pleaded personal enmity of a different sort:

Shikari is my enemy. When I was chaukidar, I chalāned his father over twenty years ago for theft; and about five years ago I chalāned his mother and sister for theft. All three were convicted. I identified the corpse of Shikari's wife when she was cut by the train. So he names me.[67]

And to complete the series, Kauleshwar Kurmi, a labourer from the nearby village of Jungle Mahadeva, thought up the time when 'Shikari wanted subscription' for the Tilak Swaraj and Khilafat funds from him, and he refused.[68]

Generally speaking, Shikari's testimony against the individuals accused was motivated not by past enmity but rather its opposite, fraternity in the days and weeks preceding 4 February 1922. On this count Shikari appears, even today in local memory, as a disembodied voice which names in an objective fashion, with malice towards none.

But neither legal fiction nor local recall can hide the instrumental nature of the betrayal which arraigns Shikari against his ex-comrades. This recognition is most poignantly brought out in the Memorandum of Examination of Abdullah of Rajdhani village. Abdullah accepted being a volunteer but denied everything else with which he was being charged: enrolling volunteers, attending the Dumri sabha and attacking the thana. Faced with the testimony of Shikari he comments ruefully: 'Shikari knows me from before. He has turned an approver and if he did not name a number of accused persons, how could he get off'.[69]

Here is a clear understanding of the transactional nature of Shikari's testimony. In a sense Abdullah also provides its contextualization, the context of the trial.

Of course the most significant question for the progress of the trial and the direction it takes is the way the judgment appropriates the approver's testimony. The court, though dependent on this testimony, makes it go through that crucible which alone can purge it of its originary impurities. Law books warn judges about this: 'accomplices are not like ordinary witnesses in respect of credibility, but their evidence is tainted and should be carefully scrutinized before being accepted . . .'.[70] The relationship between the approver's testimony and the judgment is however, carefully worked out within judicial discourse, and in the case of Chauri Chaura the overall context was provided by the politics of this trial.

14

Judicial Discourse

The task of the judge is to establish culpability. He seeks to fix responsibility by measuring out the legal and the illegal content of an action. Judgment is concerned with just and fair punishment, with evidence, and hence with 'truth'. Judicial discourse hopes to establish by certain well-defined procedures the *only true* narrative of past events. A product of Reason, it fixes a single, definitive, verifiable and proven meaning to the 'case', and this meaning must hold good. Judges validate this truth with reference to their records, a truth 'beyond reasonable doubt', a veracity evident to any 'reasonable person'.

Judgment is historiographical. The court places a premium on deliberation. Judges produce and present a harmonious narrative on the basis of a clash of accounts actuated by legal proceedings. Judgment is a representation of what 'really' happened. It produces a master narrative by shifting and shuffling through its own records as well as observations inscribed in the margin of the record of events. These observations are about the dress, demeanour, tone and expression of the witnesses. In this way judicial discourse presents itself as self-contained and internally consistent. This empowers the court to pronounce judgment on the culpability of the accused.

The final, true construction of events is effected fairly early in the course of the proceedings. At the highest level, the High Court, the question is not so much whether the narrative of the lower court is true or false, for the 'facts' of the case are no longer at issue; it is questions of inference, culpability and 'just' punishment which occupy the big-wigs of the judiciary.

But what is a true account of a riot like Chauri Chaura, where an estimated 6000 people were involved, 1000 suspects listed, and 225 put on trial? A judicial construction in a case such as this has to tackle two issues: (1) whether the accused arraigned *did* participate in the riot, and (2) re-present the pre-history of the occurrence in an intelligible fashion as *leading* the accused to riot on that particular day. But as 'Chauri Chaura' was an event which happened at a certain distance from the organized world of nationalist politics, the minimum requirements for both (1) and (2) had to be lowered.

The problems created by massive and anonymous participation in the riot open up for judgment the possibility of identifying participants by certain other indices. In this particular instance, the fact of being a volunteer—pledge forms; inclusion in the police-list of volunteers of thana Chauri Chaura; testimony of a landlord, his agent or a headman about volunteers in the village— were all adduced as further evidence of participation in the Dumri meeting and the subsequent riot at the thana.

Because it was practically impossible to fix motives for the storming of the police station for *each* and every accused, judgment takes recourse to generalizations. It settles down to providing a backdrop—economic hardship or a climate of political turbulence—which is raised to the level of a surrogate reason for the culpable actions of the individuals accused. In the present case judicial discourse could not get out of a political argument, even while it strove to deny that any political motivations went into the making of the criminal acts at the thana of Chauri Chaura.

There is yet another way in which the judge constructs the master narrative of the event. This is by accepting the prosecution's offer of Shikari's words as the *matériel* for his own story. A distance has, no doubt, to be created between the judge's prose and the tainted testimony of the approver: 'Perhaps the two most important witnesses for the prosecution are the informers, Shikari and Thakur', wrote Sessions Judge Holmes at the beginning of his long judgment; yet he never formally accepts the enormous degree to which his own account relies on Shikari's testimony.[71]

Within this broad category there were different orders of discourse, distinguished by their function in the judicial process, and indeed by their varying attitude towards the testimony of the approver. The case against the Chauri Chaura accused went through three distinct stages. Mahesh Bal Dikshit, the Committing Magistrate, conducted the preliminary hearings between 25 March and 18 June. It was he who, on the suggestion of the prosecution, created the two approvers, and after sifting through the evidence arraigned 225 persons to a sessions trial.

The case was then taken up by H.E. Holmes, the sessions judge of Gorakhpur. On 21 June Approver Shikari made his full-scale appearance as prosecution witness no. 1, followed by Thakur and a host of other witnesses. The recording of evidence and cross-examination for and against the accused continued till 30 October. Judge Holmes then sat down to prepare his judgment. He had to give an authoritative account of the 'general course of events, [and] to sift out and appraise the evidence as it affected each individual accused'.

In his judgment of 9 January 1923, Holmes acquitted 50 accused (3 had died during the course of the trial) and sentenced the remaining 172 to death. An appeal lay before the High Court at Allahabad against the death sentence. In their judgment on 30 April 1923, Judges Myers and Piggott of the High Court confirmed the sentence of the lower court in 19 cases, acquitted 38, and commuted the death penalty in 110 cases into lesser sentences of imprisonment. Beginning in the Gorakhpur jail, where the Committing Magistrate had set up his makeshift court to facilitate the production of such a large numbers of undertrials, the case reached its culmination thirteen months later in the final court of appeal, 200 miles south-east, in the important provincial town of Allahabad.[72]

It is significant that Mahesh Dikshit, the Committing Magistrate who tendered the pardon to the two approvers, is silent about them in his order of 18 June 1922. The only time that Dikshit mentions Shikari is as a rebel, never as an approver whose testimony had such a direct bearing on the committal proceedings. Why this omission, in sharp contrast to other judicial statements on 'Chauri Chaura'? The answer seems to be that Dikshit's was a committal order and not a judgment; it was nearer to an opening statement by the prosecution and therefore appropriated the speech of the approver to such an extent that it left no independent trace of it.

Judgment proper, on the other hand, has an equivocal attitude towards the approver. As we saw, judges are enjoined by law books to treat an approver's testimony with healthy suspicion.[73] At the same time legal pundits accept the obvious conclusion entailed in the juridical recognition of the accomplice as a 'competent witness':

It is not necessary that an accomplice should be corroborated in every material particular, because if such evidence be found it would be unnecessary to call the accomplice; but he must be confirmed in such and so many material points as to satisfy the Court or jury of the truth of his story.[74]

Although the Indian Evidence Act (section 133) expressly stated that 'a conviction is not illegal merely because it proceeds upon the uncorroborated testimony of an accomplice', a 'rule of prudence' (sec. 114, iii. b) was inserted which required corroboration of the approver's testimony. What could be construed as corroborative of the approver's statement was left undefined. This created two sets of discretionary possibilities. Judges could both rely upon and discredit different parts of the approver's testimony, without calling his entire evidence into question. Further, the High Court could, if it deemed fit, press for stricter criteria of corroboration than that accepted by a lower court. By being more legally prudent than the Gorakhpur judge, Justices Myers and Piggott were able to order a large number of acquittals without ever calling the 'facts' of the case into question. Not that Shikari's testimony was any the less important now—indeed it was crucial; it was just that the superior court was being stricter about corroborative evidence.

Judges, of necessity, broadly took Shikari at his word while casting doubt on his character. In fact this equivocation, though stemming specifically from what was perceived as the tainted nature of an approver's testimony, is rooted in the problematic relationship between punishment and justice, especially with regard to crimes committed during the course of anti-state mass action. In a trial such as Chauri Chaura the crux of the matter was to identify the criminals and mete out punishment, but this had simultaneously to be put across as the accomplishment of justice. The judge's equivocal attitude towards the approver, seen normally as part of a balancing act, arose in equal measure out of the requirement that judicial penalty hide its real nature from the outside world. There are numerous linguistic and other indications of this strewn through the various judicial statements on the riot, but the problem is perhaps most clearly stated by the High Court judge, Sir Theodore Piggott, in a book written in retirement and meant for the general reader:

I must warn the reader that for what took place between the afternoon of 1st February and the morning of 4th February *we have to rely, in part* on the statement of an approver who had turned King's Evidence in the *hope of saving his own neck,* and *in part* on the *reluctant* testimony of witnesses whom the High Court judgment describes as being 'as economic of truth as they dared'. *There is reason to believe that* the approver, a man named Shikari, was telling the truth when he described . . . [75]

The words italicized indicate an apologetic tone and an attempt, perhaps subconscious on the author's part, to overcome the judgment's complicity with Shikari's testimony: hence all the demonstrative reserve, displayed to convince a home audience about the sorts of problem faced while serving the Crown in India.

Despite their considered reliance on the approver's testimony, Justices Piggot and Myers recognized the problematic nature of Shikari's statement, and even briefly distinguished the person from the testimony. The judges of the High Court, following the lower court judge, characterized Shikari as 'an intelligent and even plausible witness'.[76] They then went on to cast doubt on his testimony in the following terms:

Shikari may have stretched a point against particular neighbours of his, for the sake of gratifying an antecedent grudge. Apart from this, the man was obviously under a considerable temptation to introduce into his story the names of any of his fellow villagers against whom he believed that the investigating police officers were entertaining serious suspicion. His failure to do so might, according to the mentality of a person [of this sort], create suspicion in the minds of the police that he was endeavouring to shield neighbours [of] whose doings he could not well profess ignorance.[77]

Here we have an attempt at contextualizing the approver's testimony, especially within Shikari's own village. In this instance the judges were expressing 'reasonable doubt' about Shikari's squealings against some of the Dumri men and felt that the sessions judge should have 'extended [this doubt] to a considerably larger number' of the accused.[78] But despite express reservations about the testimony of the approver, we get such sentences in the judgment of the High Court: 'The evidence of the approver against this man [Chingi] is therefore fully corroborated'; 'This accused is implicated in the evidence of both the approvers'.[79] Shikari was clearly the chief story-teller. Even where others came forward with their own tales, the judges paid greater attention to the approver; narratives other than Shikari's merely corroborated what he related.

Let us dwell a bit longer on the sabha at Dumri on the morning of 4 February, preparatory to the march on the thana. Justices Myers and Piggott had 'a very considerable body of evidence' on this sabha before them. They had 'the depositions of the two approvers', Shikari and Thakur. There were the confessions of Bhagwan Ahir and Ramrup Barai, among others accused. They also had 'more or less detailed accounts of the affair from three witnesses'. These were Bhawani Prasad Tiwari, a zamindar of the neighbouring village of Pokharbhinda; Jagat Narain Pandey of village Malaon, who was equally at home at nationalist meetings and at the Chaura thana; and Shankar Dayal Rae, a prosperous contractor from Mundera bazaar.

However, after discussing each of these three witnesses and the weight that could be placed on their testimony as well as their disposition towards the accused, the judges fell back upon the words of Shikari. 'The effect of [all] this evidence as a whole', they wrote, 'is to corroborate the account of the meeting at Dumri given by the approver Shikari, at least in its broad outline, sufficiently to enable us to feel certain of its straightforwardness and general accuracy.'[80]

15

The Alimentary Aspects of Picketing

While the judgment seeks corroboration of Shikari's testimony, it also grafts its own meanings on to the approver's episodic recall. The links within his testimony are picked out and strung together into quite a different chain, an ornament befitting the stately requirements of magisterial rule.

Let us turn, for the last time, to the High Court's understanding of the motivations behind the picketing of liquor and meat and fish shops, the immediate political cause that lay behind the clash outside the police station. The court 'traced with singular precision' how and why a movement intended by its organizers as a systematic picketing of liquor shops 'degenerated swiftly . . . almost . . . inevitably, into [an] appalling display of mass violence'. According to the court, the picketing of intoxicants at licensed shops suggested itself as a 'convenient object for activities of volunteer associations'. However, such activities could not have been restricted to intoxicants: something else was needed to 'appeal more directly' to the volunteers' 'personal sympathies'. Though the peasantry was suffering high grain prices, this could not by itself be the object of picketing as peasant producers were themselves 'anxious to sell in the highest market'. Therefore, 'the movement was against the sellers of meat and fish' who were required to bring down their prices or face closure and the looting of their shops. A 'great reduction in the prices of meat and fish' was in store for volunteers—a 'step towards the attainment of "Swaraj" which was to enhance their material prosperity . . . .'. This was possible only if they acted in concert, in 'overwhelming numbers'. This led to the clash with the police, first at the bazaar and then outside the thana.[81]

Note the economistic reading provided for the picketing of fish and meat shops by the volunteers of Chauri Chaura, negating with one bold stroke the complex process behind the widespread drive for abstinence and vegetarianism in the entire district of Gorakhpur.[82]

The people of Gorakhpur, and of the tract north of the river Ghaghra generally, were not known for their adherence to any strict dietary regimes. Well into the 1890s it was normal for all low-caste Hindus to eat meat. The only exceptions were the *bhagats* or *kanthīs* who had taken a vow 'to touch no flesh of any kind'. Normally a necklace (*kanthi*) of basil, sandal, or *neem* beads was worn as an outward sign of vegetarianism and a pious life among these low-caste bhagats.[83] The injunction against eating fish seems to have been rather lax—slaughter and purchase were not required, and the catch, especially during the monsoon months, was ample and ready at hand. The amount of fish consumed in Gorakhpur was immense, according to an official source. 'Hindus and Muhammadans of all castes and class[es] eat it', stated the 1881 *Gazetteer* of the district. In neighbouring Tirhut, even a kanthi was reportedly 'glad of a fish dinner when he can get it'. A well-informed traveller from the Hindu heartland of Banaras commented in 1880 on 'the strange Brahmins' of Gorakhpur who 'ate meat, fish, everything!'[84]

It was a sign of changed times that four decades later low- and middle-caste *panchāyats** were imposing novel dietary taboos in the very tract where the 'strange meat-eating Brahmins' had been spotted in the previous century. On 27 January 1921 the sweepers, washermen and barbers of Naugarh, in neighbouring Basti, meeting in panchāyats of their various brotherhoods,

---

* *Panchāyat*: a caste assembly with the authority to punish dietary, sexual and social transgressions.

decided that 'anyone who partakes of meat, fish and liquor would have to pay a fine' of Rs 51 towards the upkeep of vagrant cows! Patrons of washermen and barbers persisting with unreformed dietary ways were to be boycotted.[85] For the low castes and the untouchables to give up meat, and to shame their social superiors into following suit to boot, was not simply a gesture of ritual self-purification. Such acts on the part of the impure amounted to a reversal of the signs of subordination; dietary taboos were very often matched by a refusal to let womenfolk work as housemaids, and the withholding of forced labour from the sarkar and the landlord.[*]

Gandhi, during his visit of 8 February 1922, did not press his Gorakhpur audience to forsake fish and meat: he only wished the nationalist public to abstain from intoxicants, both liquor and *gānja*. All the same, his speech at the district town and the perorations at all the railway stations, including Chauri Chaura, generated considerable discussion on the virtues of nationalist vegetarianism.

The back issues of a local newspaper allow us to eavesdrop on reported dietary conversations. In the spring of 1921 the sons of a betel-leaf seller near Bhatni station slaughtered and ate a goat. 'Some persons tried to dissuade them, but they paid no heed'. The consequences were phenomenal. 'All of them started vomiting and got very worried', reported a local correspondent to the Gorakhpur nationalist weekly. But there was a way out of their discomfort: vegetarianism. They could in fact have spared themselves the pain if only they had heeded the ascendant nationalist opinion: 'In the end when they *vowed* in the name of Mahatmaji

---

[*] The presence of a low-caste woman inside an upper-caste house always made her available for the lust of males. An upper-caste male could refrain from exercising this aspect of caste power, but the 'morals' of these working women were invariably related in high-caste imagination with how far inside the house they worked. Women who came as far as the kitchen to sharpen the grindstone are regarded even today as of particularly loose character.

[Gandhi] never to eat meat again, their condition returned to normal.' From neighbouring Basti came the story of a Brahmin who had refused, despite repeated admonitions, 'to give up his habit of eating fish'. 'I shall eat fish, let's see what Mahatmaji can do', defiantly shouted the Pande of Rampur to his interlocutors. When he sat down to eat the fish, 'it was crawling with worms'![86]

Suggesting verbal tussles for and against abstinence, these stories, significantly, invoke Gandhi's name as a part of their argument. A calamity which befalls a non-conformist, its subsequent social impact, and finally the victim's repentance, are then connected in the popular imagination with the undesirability of going against locally imposed dietary decisions. Would it be farfetched to see in this emphasis an extension of the Gandhian idea of self-purification (abstinence from intoxicants) to a context where prohibition was enlarged to include meat and fish—this indicating, in turn, 'religiosity' and lower-caste assertion at the same time?

When Shikari, Nazar Ali and other volunteers of Dumri elected in January 1922 to picket liquor, meat and fish shops they were making a significant move. Apparently, these nationalists regarded an alimentary change more important than the switch over to Gandhian handspun cloth![87] Why else would they have allowed retailers of imported cloth to ply their trade in Mundera and Chauri Chaura?

I am not claiming that Shikari and others became vegetarians in 1922. It could well have been that meat-eating volunteers were enforcing a boycott of butchers and fishmongers in the name of Mahatma Gandhi. A certain ambiguity usually characterizes popular actions of this sort. What we know for sure is that just three miles away from Shikari's village an orgy of meat-eating took place for a fortnight every year. Held in the first half of May to honour the goddess Durga, the site of the Tarkulha fair marked the public hanging of the local landed rebel and hero, Bandhu Singh, by the British in 1858. A wrestler and devotee of Durga, Bandhu Singh was naturally protected by the goddess in his hour of need. Many a time, local memory has it, the noose round Bandhu Singh's neck would come unstuck. It was only when the rebel disavowed his protector by mouthing a profanity against her that Durga let the English successfully hang him.

Bandhu Singh's death and the confiscation of his estate led to a redrawing of the landed map of the area. The Majithias, loyalist Sikhs from the Punjab, were rewarded with the grant of his Dumri estate; another portion, a jungle tract across the road from Shikari's village, was farmed out to a prominent banker family from the neighbouring district of Azamgarh.

Daily attendance at the fair in the early 1920s was around 1000; the gathering yielded an income of Rs 1300, the bulk of which came from a 4-anna levy on every goat slaughtered in honour of Durga and the local *ghadar* hero, cooked and eaten in earthenware, and with lots of spices, as happens even to this day.[88]

To successfully prevent the sale of fish in villages adjoining the site of the fair, as the volunteer-leader Dwarka Pandey did in Rampur Raqba (a collection of five villages belonging to the banker family), or to press the butchers of Mundera not to ply their trade, as Shikari and Nazar Ali tried unsuccessfully (with historic consequences), were acts charged with symbolic meaning, and with a degree of ambiguity.[89]

The ambiguity is clear in two slightly different statements made by Shikari in the courtroom. During his cross-examination Shikari stated that 'the stopping of sales of flesh [*sic*], fish, toddy and spirit in the Mundera Bazar was in accordance with the teachings and orders of Hakeemji', i.e. Hakeem Arif of the District Congress Committee, who formally established the Dumri unit of volunteers in early 1922. During his testimony for the prosecution Shikari made a moral economy argument about enforcing a 'just' and lower price for meat through picketing.

We were stopping the sale of meat and fish because they were dear. We wanted meat and fish sold at 2 annas a seer and fish at 4 or 6 pice. Meat was then being sold at 8 or 10 annas and fish at 5 or 6. We wanted to make the sellers consent to sell cheap or to compel them to do so. We told them that if they would not sell [cheap] we would throw it away.[90]

It was by a selective reliance on Shikari's words that the judges arrived at a rational, or in other words a narrowly economic, explanation of the activities of the Dumri activists. Picketing was aimed, in the judges words, at a 'great reduction in the prices of meat and fish'; it was 'a step towards the attainment of "Swaraj"' which was to 'enhance [the] material prosperity' of the volunteers.

There was other evidence on record which the judges chose to disregard in 'tracing with singular precision' the motivations behind the picketing of meat and fish shops in Mundera bazaar. The assembly at Hata, attended by Nazar Ali and Shikari, had been exhorted: 'Picketing, liquor, *tāri*, foreign cloth, fish and meat *have been entrusted to volunteers*. They should do it, because these things are against religion. Go out and accomplish this task'.[91] It was on their way back from this meeting that the Dumri contingent sought to picket liquor, meat and fish shops at Mundera bazaar. At the same sabha one Shakur Ali Dafali had declaimed: 'Nobody should eat meat, because mutton, beef and human flesh are just the same.' There was no question here of a concerted effort to get meat at rock-bottom prices; the message of the Hata assembly was clearly one in which religiosity and politics were brought together to forge a united Hindu–Muslim front on abstinence and vegetarianism. This evidence was also on record, but by relying solely on the words of Mir Shikari the judges brushed it aside in favour of an even more economistic reading of picketing than was strictly warranted.

So, it would not be unfair to assert that this judicial reasoning tells us less about the motivations of Shikari, the activist, and more about the politics of the judgment itself.

16

The Politics of the Trial

In early 1923 the 172 sentenced to death for rioting appealed against the decision of the sessions judge of Gorakhpur. In its final verdict the High Court upheld the view that the deliberations at the Dumri sabha on the morning of 4 February 1922 'amounted to criminal conspiracy'. An 'intention to assault the police in certain eventualities', the judges said, 'was therefore a part of the common object of the whole assembly of volunteers from the time they left Dumri'. After the police shot the first 'effective volley' into the crowd, which, in response to the earlier firing in the air had swung back to stone the thana, its 'object was . . . *to do simply what they did*, namely to take life in revenge for life'. Procedural and substantive objections raised by the defence counsels against the joint-trial of 225 accused, as well as arguments for a separation between the actions at the Dumri meeting and the rioting at the thana a few hours later (so as to necessitate two separate trials) were dismissed by the High Court. The crowd that marched out from Dumri village and clashed with the police three hours and two miles further down the road *was* a single collective agent. Every accused person who was 'proved by evidence to have continued to be an active participant in the riot after the moment when *kankar* [clods and stones] began to be thrown' at the police was guilty under section 302/149 of the Indian Penal Code. This charge, when proved, carried the death penalty.[92]

But was the death sentence to be confirmed on each of the 172 persons accepted by the sessions judge to have constituted this murderous crowd? Concerned to avoid the charge of being vindictive, the High Court judges began to whittle down the exceedingly large number of death sentences. They did this first by trimming the figure of persons proven to have been in the crowd. And here the issue of corroboration of Shikari's evidence surfaced once again. Second, where applicable, the judges decided to commute the death sentence to various lengths of rigorous imprisonment.

The fate of a large number of accused hung on a final evaluation of Shikari's testimony. Judges Myers and Piggott agreed that Shikari had 'proved himself an intelligent and even plausible witness'. They were 'satisfied that the witness had made up his mind to earn his pardon honestly by making a clean breast of the facts so far as known to him'. But Shikari *was* an approver, and for that very reason, though reliable, a man of dubious moral character. Firm corroboration was needed, for Shikari, *according to the mentality of a person of his class*', may have simply added the names of several individuals so as not to 'endanger his own pardon'. He 'may have stretched a point against particular neighbours of his' because of past enmity; he may have wrongly identified individuals against 'whom he believed that the investigating . . . officers were entertaining serious suspicion'.[93] The approver may, in other words, have played his part to a fault.

The sessions judge had 'convicted no one on the murder charge who was not directly implicated in the evidence given by one or both the approvers'. In Judge Holmes' judgment, the individuals who were seen as constituting the Chauri Chaura crowd were largely those recalled by Shikari and Thakur. For Judge Holmes, the fact that 'a particular accused was an enrolled volunteer'—as proved by the discovery of his pledge form—'was, under the circumstances of the case, sufficient corroboration, as against him, of the accomplice's evidence'. The High Court refused to accept this inference.[94] The rule of prudence, which required corroboration of an approver's testimony, had, in their view, been interpreted loosely by the sessions judge. The great majority of the thirty-eight acquittals ordered by the High Court 'turned on . . . [this] question of principle'. This was a legal position which underscored how crucial Shikari's testimony had been in the final determination of punishment.[95]

With these acquittals, the number constituting the crowd of culpable murderers came down from 172 to 129. In its judicious juggling with the life of these 129 peasants, the High Court confirmed the death penalty on 19 'ring leaders', commuted the sentence of death to life imprisonment for the remaining 110, and tempered this further by recommending shorter prison terms for a great majority of such individuals.[96] Awarding the maximum (death) penalty, the Gorakhpur judge had expostulated that: 'for anyone proved to have taken part in a fiendish outrage as the Chauri riot, hardly any punishment can be too severe.'[97]

And so the High Court arrived at a less harsh view of the culpability of the Chauri Chaura accused. There were grounds, it argued, for limiting the death penalty only to select individuals. All 'proven' members of that violent crowd now no longer needed to die for their joint crimes. This argument, proffered on behalf of the accused, deserves scrutiny, for while it saved over a hundred lives, it also brings us face to face with the limits of a sober judicial understanding of the riot.

The High Court judges were prepared at most to grant a political *backdrop* to the crimes: any political *foregrounding* of the event would have cast them, so the judges thought, into 'apologists for the lawlessness of the crowd'.[98] At the highest level of the provincial judiciary, 'Chauri Chaura' remained a series of criminal acts rather than a violent instance of mass peasant politics. If a plausible case could be made for the reduction of death sentences (from 172 to a lower figure) it could only be by characterizing the accused as 'in the main ignorant peasants', the 'great majority' of whom were drawn into the business by misrepresentation of fact and preposterous promises concerning the millennium of 'Swaraj', the arrival of which was to be forwarded by courage and resolution on their part. Some indeed were apparently influenced by the belief that Mr Gandhi was a worker of miracles.[99]

Deluded peasants . . . objects of manipulation . . . goaded into committing criminal acts by pangs of hunger . . . , in short, criminals who had some *attenuating* circumstances in their favour— these were the grounds on which the High Court agreed to tone down the extreme penalty prescribed by law.

For their part the nationalists inside and outside the court did not attempt to contextualize the riot within any kind of political activity. On the contrary, they sought to delimit 'true' Congress politics by distancing the organization at Gorakhpur from the acts of their Chauri Chaura volunteers weeks before they turned into so-called criminals. It may have been the context of the trial, forcing the District Congress to either own or disown Nazar Ali, Lal Mohammad and Bhagwan Ahir as their godchildren, that forced Dasrath Dwivedi, editor of *Swadesh* and Secretary, Congress Committee, into launching this diatribe against the Dumri volunteers:

I refused the request [to send a drill master to Dumri], as I considered that the volunteers were undisciplined, that they had signed the pledge forms without considering the undertakings; that each worker was pulling his own way; that volunteers had been formed in an unauthorized way; that they had begun crowding round about the courts, and that they had started acting as watch and ward in an unauthorized way . . . The majority of the volunteers were illiterate and of a low class . . . [100]

The Committing Magistrate gratefully borrowed this vocabulary to condemn the peasants who assembled at Dumri on the morning of 4 February as a 'mob of enraged *untouchable* volunteers'.

An *ordinary crowd* would have good-humouredly laughed at being thus moved and would have run off. Even angry crowds have been charged by the police with batons and dispersed all over the world. They do not usually burn and kill the police for this reason.[101]

The nationalist newspaper *Aaj* was not being very different either
when it characterized the volunteers of Chauri Chaura as a bunch
of rascals (*dusht*), in awkward opposition to other political creatures whom it chose to call *samajhdār* (sensible).[102]

In his book of reminiscences Piggott, the retired High Court
judge, explained the reasons for putting a criminal rather than
political construction on the riot.

From one point of view, undoubtedly, the peasants who stormed Chaura
police station were simply rebels against the established Government.
They set out on their march with cries of 'Victory to Mahatmaji Gandhi';
they hailed their victory with acclamations, triumphantly proclaiming
that they had established his 'kingdom'. Mahatma Gandhi they unquestionably regarded as the embodiment of opposition to the Government
under which they lived.[103]

If 'Chauri Chaura' had happened in the West, the government
would have punished its leaders and granted 'the widest possible
amnesty . . . to their deluded followers'. Situated in colonial India
and carried out by 'wretched peasants', this 'uprising against the
established Government', such as it was,

came to an abrupt end after a single . . . overwhelming victory for the
'rebels' . . . Before the next morning's sun rose the wretched peasants
knew that no new 'kingdom' had been set up; *each man felt himself
marked out for the vengeance of the irresistible power which, in a moment
of madness, he had challenged.*[104]

Further, there was no 'rival authority to which they could appeal
for countenance or support'. For all these reasons

it was futile to treat this mob of deluded peasants as 'rebels' and impolitic
to *dignify their riot* by forming indictments for such high-sounding
offences as 'waging war against the King' . . . The only alternative was
to deal with the *offenders as ordinary criminals*, and to employ against
them the cumbrous machinery of the ordinary law. They had committed
offences enough against sections of the Indian Penal Code quite other
than those dealing with crimes against the state.[105]

In these arguments, penned by this retired puisne judge who had helped reduce the death sentences in the Chauri Chaura case, we still find the articulation of thoughts in the idiom of punishment. Implied in Piggott's case for a criminal reading of 'Chauri Chaura' are a series of oppositions: movement/event; successful resistance/quick failure; attack on the state/fear of its power. Not all of these are of equal weight. The duration of an episode of resistance cannot by itself mark the significant difference between 'crime' and 'politics'. It is the extraneous criteria of political/criminal, buttressed by the rule of colonial difference[106]—India was another country—that appears crucial in fixing the event and the accused. The retired judge, writing in his cottage, was speaking of colonial order and not law alone. For all his professional concern for the other point of view, Piggott's reminiscences fed into the discourse of colonial power.

The point was not just, to paraphrase Piggott, that the next day did not bring about the dawn of Swaraj, howsoever the peasants understood it or read the signs of its impending arrival. The significant issue, missed by the judge, was that the accused were unwilling to talk about motivations and expectations in court because any true recollection there would have stuck them even more deeply within the mire of criminality prepared by the prosecution. The judicial discourse on Chauri Chaura—'This Tale of Murder'—had put its definitive stamp on the accused. To relate the event outside the story of crime is a task that historiography must strive towards. That the Chauri Chaura accused were 'ordinary criminals' is a piece of legal fiction that sits uneasily in the colonial archive. The notoriety of the crime of Chauri Chaura lay not solely in its brutality; it was the expression of that violence as an aspect of peasant politics that unnerved the judge and saddened the Mahatma.

Judge Piggott, who in his reminiscences denied the peasants the epithet 'rebels', had earlier made a clever connection between the crime and the rest of subject India, for which 'the tax payers' had to pay. Justifying the disbursement of a rather high Rs 5314 as defence counsels' fees for the 172 poor-accused, Piggott had noted in April 1923:

When all is said and done, it is no bad thing that the public in general should realize that *outbursts of revolutionary enthusiasm* such as that which materialized at Chauri Chaura on 4/2/22 *are expensive things for the tax payers.*[107]

Wry humour aside, the discourse of criminality lived on. When a legal occasion—the revision of his eight-year sentence—brought Kamla Kewat of Kusmhi, incarcerated in Bareilly Central Prison, to the attention of a District Superintendent of Police, he scribbled on Kamla's Revision of Sentence sheet:

He used to earn his living by labour and construction. The recent disclosures made by some accused persons show that the Police circle Chaura in which the man resides [*sic*] abounds in criminals and he is very likely to join them on his release. He was a volunteer in the Non-co-operation army, the aim of which was to subvert the Government and in furtherance of this they burnt the Chaura thana and killed all police officers and chaukidars etc., they could find in the thana and committed other acts of unparalleled barbarism on them. The Government has already reduced his sentence, hence his release before the expiry of his term is strongly opposed.[108]

The stigma of crime was very much there on the person of Kamla, but even the police could not brand him as a dangerous criminal without reference to his career as a volunteer. The area under the Chaura thana was no den of criminals, nor was Kamla Kewat a plain murderer. In fact after the sun rose the next morning (*pace* Piggott) Kamla openly proclaimed the dawn of a new order to the *patwari** of his village: 'Leave your Government employment or else as the Chaura thana had yesterday been burnt and all the police had all been killed by us we in the same way will kill you.'[109]

So strong was this tendency towards a criminal reading of the

---

* *Patwari*: a village account, locally powerful as an official functionary.

114   EVENT, METAPHOR, MEMORY: CHAURI CHAURA 1922–1992

history of Chauri Chaura that in the summary of evidence against
the accused, the above 'fact' relating to Kamla was translated as:
'confessed—exultingly—to having burnt thana . . . '.[110] An open
proclamation appeared then as a confession to the clerk of the
court: a 'form of apology which involves the individual separating
himself into two parts: the part that is technically guilty of an
offence and the part that disowns itself from guilt and swears
allegiance to the norms which have been violated'.[111] Kamla Kewat
was of course doing no such thing on the morning of 5 February
1922 in his village on the outskirts of the Kusmhi jungle.

A suitably ironic indicator of the longevity of judicial discourse is a letter from the Officer on Special Duty, Political
Pensions, to the District Magistrate, Gorakhpur, written thirty-
five years after the event, a letter which now forms the opening
document to the judicial dossier on Chauri Chaura:

I am directed to say that a large number of applications for pensions or
monetary help from persons associated with the well-known Chauri
Chaura case are under the consideration of the Government. It has not
been possible so far to take a decision in the matter as there are no
records at this end to show that the said case was *purely of a political
nature* . . . It may . . . be kindly intimated whether records available at
your end show that the Chauri Chaura case was purely of a political
nature.[112]

Ten years after independence, the Office of Political Pensions
was unable to find the evidence to judge adequately the 'well-
known Chauri Chaura case'. Was it purely political? How could
one be sure? The 'ex-rioters' were already making demands on the
state. Substantive records had to be furnished; but these were
about a complex of crimes—'unlawful assembly', 'mischief by
fire', 'rioting'—all of which together constituted the case called
Chauri Chaura. To appeal to the records of the case—literally an
'instance of a thing's occurring', or a 'statement of facts in cause
sub judice'—was to circumscribe that occurrence as a fact, shorn
of everything other than the mere legality that it was *sub judice*.[113]

Part Five

'Except in the strict pages of history, memorable events stand in no need of memorable phrases'.

— J. Borges, 'The Other', in *The Book of Sands*

17

Historian's Dilemma

Almost in story-book fashion, my account of Chauri Chaura has kept coming up against successive hurdles. Contemporary nationalist tracts have no time for a history of the event, only for its lessons. Authorized post-colonial retellings proffer stereotypical descriptions of colonial violence and nationalist resolve. They fail to account for the actors, men such as Nazar Ali, Abdullah, Dwarka Gosain and Shikari. In the court the accused decline to speak about their 'criminal' past. They address a judge, not History. This economy of rebel speech leads me to the enforced utterances of Approver Shikari. In this Mir Shikari, the approver of the records, the historian finally has access to the actual words of a leading actor. But the presence of the first person singular is, in this case, inadequate guarantee of the speaker's nearness to his own speech.[1]

Disappointed in one archive, it is the business of the historian to turn to another. During my visits to Chauri Chaura I attempted to grasp the event in the moment of its recall. The riot had already been nationalized, and a memorial, the last nail in the coffin as it were, was now being put in place. In February 1989 I had hastened from Delhi to garner the local people's reactions to this official celebration, choreographed by a local politician who had been elevated to a ministership in Rajiv Gandhi's cabinet. In August 1991 another state minister had unveiled a stone tablet purporting to be the 'Golden History of the Martyrs of Chauri Chaura'.

While interrogating several local narratives of the riot, this part of the book concentrates on family accounts from Chotki Dumri. The recollections of Naujadi, the wife of a rioter, and of

Sita Ahir, the son of a chaukidar, are deployed to construct the world of the peasant nationalists. These *otiyars*, to use Naujadi's remarkable Bhojpuri creolization of the familiar 'volunteer', were Gandhi's men all right; everything connected with popular nationalism of that time possessed a generic Gandhian quality. But Naujadi's otiyars were Gandhian in curiously unrecognizable ways.

I seek to chart the distance that separates the volunteers of Gandhi's *Collected Works* from the otiyars of Naujadi's recollection. I also try to explore the possibility, with the help of Sita and Naujadi, of generating an independent narrative, a story which does not have crime for its title. My attempt is not quite successful. This is not because the basic facts of the riot are incontrovertible: the same characters can, after all, be made to play several different parts. The difficulty of my effort to generate an entirely alternative narrative of the event, I might even say its failure, illustrates, rather, the hegemonic power of judicial and nationalist discourse. The subalterns make their own memories, but they do not make them just as they please. The gallows and the prison ensure that, decades later, judicial pronouncements live to be heard even in the familial recall of an event. And so it is with Chauri Chaura. Peasant narratives that I collected were inescapably tainted or vitiated or coloured in varying degrees by the hegemonic master narratives.

The experience of historical fieldwork was not without its ironies. On my very first visit to Chotki Dumri I was taken to meet the *grām pradhān*, a sort of elected village headman who represents the village to the outside world. Sharfuddin, my host, was Mir Shikari's son! He chipped in to 'translate' slightly garbled sentences from an older informant's mouth. Ever so often, as befitted his rank and intelligence, Sharfuddin would, while translating the words of our old companion, underline the dominant nationalist spirit 'of those times'. But he proffered no insights into his father, Shikari, nor did I feel the urge to press him.

Sita Ahir, the leading male narrator, turned out, as his story unfolded, to be the son of a village policeman killed in the riot. He was also the nephew of one hanged for the killing and burning at the police station.

From their story-telling it was apparent that the politicization of the case had altered the state's perception of the rioters: now, documents pertaining to an individual's proven crimes bore the impress of their reverse—a heroic nationalist significance.

18

Dumri Records

The typical document available in Dumri is a certified copy of the punishment meted out to the convicted rioter for his 'participation in the non-co-operation movement of 1922 (Chauri Chaura outrage)'.[2] The equation of the kānd (outrage) of 1922 with the freedom movement of that year, as well as the use of the verb 'participate' and the third person honorific (*bhāg liye the*) are grammatical evidence of the relocation of the riot in the narrative of nationalism.[3] By 1972, that is in the twenty-fifth year of Indian independence, this well known case had been accorded a 'purely political character'. This late admission was not based on a radical rendering of the event: Gandhi's condemnation of what he called the crime of Gorakhpur had ruled out that possibility. Instead, the power of the nation-state to reorder its pre-history was used simply to transform the record of death and imprisonment into one of reward and recognition: punishments were translated into pensions. When Naujadi, the wife of Rameshar Pasi, refers to things 'written on my paper' (*hamār kagda par likhal ba*), her paper is the same recent copy certifying that Rameshar had undergone eight years' rigorous imprisonment. Family records, favoured by an entire generation of historians, turn out in Chauri Chaura to be fragments of a judicial sentence.

Could it be that very few records were generated in Chauri Chaura in the winter of 1921–2? Oral transmission was no doubt important,[4] but so were missives, composed in the unsteady hand of a schoolboy or a semi-literate peasant. We have on judicial record three letters written in January 1922 by a volunteer-leader of Chauri Chaura. In these successive letters, Lal Mohammad 'Sain' offers his services to the Gorakhpur Khilafat Committee, reports on the success of his recruitment drive, and lodges a complaint against the local thanedar.[5] The crowd of 4 February, it requires repeating, had assembled in response to an express written communication.

Writing and recording were integral to the constitution of the volunteer movement. Completing the pledge form, securing thumb impressions, maintaining registers, and corresponding with district headquarters were important tasks of the functionaries of volunteer units.[6] One of them, Lal Mohammad, was his own correspondent; Nazar Ali and Shikari, for their part, went around with a literate Dumri boy in tow. A lad of ten who attended school at Chaura, Nackched Kahar would write letters on behalf of low-caste fathers to migrant sons in Rangoon; in early 1922 he functioned as a writer to the Dumri volunteer unit. 'I and Nackched and Nazar Ali recruited nine men. Nackched wrote the forms', Shikari stated in the court of Judge H.E. Holmes.[7]

The district headquarters was full of nationalist paper. When the city police raided the Khilafat and Congress offices on 5 February, they carried away scores of registers, receipt books, maps, files, budget proposals, pledge forms, and abstracts of correspondence, including Lal Mohammad's letters. Most of these were put on record.[8] A similar raid on the mandal office of Burha Dih, a

few miles north of Dumri, again yielded a rich haul.[9] Burha Dih
had a developed sense of non-co-operation. In December 1921,
the nationalist village panchāyat was mediating in property disputes, and the mandal secretary had with ceremonial hauteur
furnished a complete list of the illegal volunteer corps for 'necessary action' to the thana.[10]

Why is there nothing on record from Chotki Dumri, especially as the village was raided the day after the riot? The Dumri
papers may not have been as wide-ranging as the Burha Dih
collection, but nationalist paper there must have been at Dumri.
It appears that the same police force that went about impounding
each and every scrap of paper, including waste and blank paper,[11]
deliberately destroyed the Dumri records in the early hours of
5 February 1922. Sita Ahir, the young son of Surajbali chaukidar,
who was mourning the death of his father, recalled: 'When the
thana was burnt, then everyone ran away. Not a soul, not even
a little bird was left; only I remained.' (*Ek chirai ke put nāhīn
hamār gauwān mein rahal.*)

Nobody was willing to take charge of Chauri Chaura thana. (*Kehu
Daroga bīra na kha rāte ke Chauri Chaura ke.*) Then Lachman Singh,
captain of Deoria thana—a very tough man he was—he came down at
midnight to take charge of the Chauri Chaura thana. It was the month
of Māgh . . . Then at the crack of dawn—I of course was crying by the
feeding-trough—and my mother, she was crying as well—Lachman
Singh emerged from the Chamar quarters, walking up the railway track
. . . Then two of his *sipāhīs* hit me with their rifle butts. I forgot all
about my [dead] father; I now thought only about myself. Oh yes! My
body became stiff as wood [laughs].

Sita, now recognized as the village chaukidar's son, was ordered
to lead the way to the houses of the Dumri leaders. '*Najar Ali-
Sikari ka ghar batāo*', he quotes Lachman Singh in imitation
Hindustani. 'And so I took them along' (*te liya ke chalalīn*), he
recounts in local Bhojpuri. In Sita's recall 5 February 1922 is
punctuated by a series of forceful exhortations. All that happened

in the village that morning echoes Lachman Singh's command: 'Najar Ali-Sikari ka ghar batāo!'[12]

The raiding party wreaked its vengeance on just about everything. Doors of houses were busted, earthen ghee-pots were smashed, and ghee gobbled up by the mouthful. Onwards to Shikari's house the police party went. This is described thus in the local tongue:

Khapra ke ghar rahe—paith gailan sab. Jaune dehri mein māren kul, taune mein se bhak-dena dhanwe nikre. Te kaha tāna kul, 'dhān bāndho!' Kahlīn, nāhīn hajoor, hammen dhān-aun nāhīn laukat-ta, hamme apne dāda ke chāhat-tāni, ta inhān se lautalān kul.

At Shikari's house—a substantial tiled structure—several large jars of rice were smashed, and the son of the dead chaukidar asked to take the loot home. There is a noteworthy parallel here between the wreaking and extravagant eating that Ranajit Guha finds in peasant insurgencies and the symbolic and material damage done to peasant property by Lachman Singh and party.[13] To translate Sita's recall of the scene at Nazar Ali's house:

And so [Lachman Singh] said, 'show us the house of Nazar Ali.' And so I brought him there. . . . Nazar Ali's house was a thatched [hut]. One could see the *kolhu* etc.* Then this bugger Lachman Singh [Lachman Singhwa]—one box-full of volunteer-paper was in the house—Lachman Singh brought it outside . . . He brought the box out and started tearing and throwing away the papers. And he said, 'Sister-fucker!' lives in a thatched hut and goes out and commits such a big case—(*Ehé bahanchod! phoos ek mutha nahin hai aur etna bara 'khes' kar diya!*)

At the thana the volunteers had torn the police turbans to tatters; in 1942, during the course of the Quit India Movement, when crowds battled with the police in numerous places in eastern India, public burning of the red *pagrīs* was punished by collective fines of Rs 20 per headdress burnt;[14] in Dumri in the early hours of

---

* *Kolhu*: a sugarcane press.

5 February 1922, a police officer, fresh from the smouldering Chaura thana, had wreaked his vengeance on the pledge forms. No wonder only one such pledge from the village could be produced in court.[15] In Chotki Dumri the police had destroyed the record—with a vengeance.

In view of this I had to ask: What then are the narratives that can be tapped around Chauri Chaura? I discovered four: stories told by local youths; accounts from Mundera bazaar; the narratives of distant localities; and the remembrance of lost times among surviving family members of those who participated in the riot.

19

The Youthful Account

The narratives of the slim Dumri youth are thin on sequence but supplement the actions of a grandfather or a grand-uncle with physical prowess and cunning insight. Volunteers here appear as *pahelwāns*, trained in the *akhāra* of Nazar Ali, the leading wrestler of the village.* Native of another village, Nazar Ali like many others from the region, had migrated to Rangoon and returned in December 1920 to set up a tailoring shop in Mundera and a wrestling school in Chotki Dumri. A noted pahelwān, with the tell-tale sign of a cauliflower ear, Nazar Ali was a powerful presence and a leader of men.[16]

Wrestling or pahelwāni was the distinguishing mark of an outstanding male personality among peasants. Wrestlers had their

* *Akhāra*: lit. a place of wrestling created by digging up the earth and moistening it with water; by extension an arena, a band, a 'school'. *Pahelwān*: a wrestler.

patron saints, but the truly great wrestlers were those who had been gripped by the female Shakti form, incarnated in the goddess Durga. A Musalman, Nazar Ali's powerful body was not the abode of any divine power. But Bikram Ahir's son Neur, one of the promising lads of the Dumri akhāra, was 'in the grip' of Durga, and so, despite his small stature, a real champion.[17] Bandhu Singh, the local landed rebel of 1857 who was strung up from a tree by the British, was also a wrestler and a devotee of Durga.

In a culture where docile postures and genuflexion were the palpable signs of subordination, pahelwāni amounted to a literal and metaphorical flexing of peasant muscles.[18] So ingrained was this notion of bodily subjection among peasants that the herdsmen's freedom and access to fortifying milk products was commonly regarded as the reason for the large number of wrestlers among the cowherd Ahir/Yadav community.

The pahelwān leader was a memorable figure in peasant lore because resistance to authority was invariably met by the attempted or actual thrashing of the ring leader. Strong rustic bodies normally served as auxiliaries to a superior force—as in-house wrestlers or as clubmen in the army of a local landlord. To run an akhāra independent of a superior's patronage, as Nazar Ali did at Dumri, was to make an exhibition of peasant prowess.[19]

Nazar Ali's akhāra was renowned far and wide; here, local lads like Neur and the master himself would train and pin down challengers on home turf. For the grandson of Bikram Ahir (Neur's father: hanged, 1923), it is *bal* and *chhal* (power and cunning) rather than *tyāg* and *tap* (prayer and sacrifice) that constitute the plot of his story of Chauri Chaura:

Gandhiji had come, but he did not stop over; he just met people with folded hands and went away. The thana was attacked twice. The first time it 'failed'. The second time bullets turned into water by the blessings of Gandhiji.

Nazar Ali, Bikram Yadav and Neur used to wrestle at the akhāra. It was Nazar Ali's akhāra: he had 2–3 *bighas* of land. They did not farm everyday—nobody does—they would set off with their lāthīs and roam around [the jungle].

One day Bikram Yadav was grazing buffaloes [in the jungle]; he came across a rifle. He deposited the rifle at the thana, thinking that this way he would earn goodwill [*khair-khāi*]. Bikram Yadav [consequently] became a chaukidar. This way [they] were able to infiltrate (*ghus-paith*) the thana. The first thing they burnt were the [thana] records.

It could well be that the burning and the killings at the thana have in themselves led to an overemphasis on the strength of the tough Dumri volunteers. Nazar Ali reportedly 'seized' a fleeing daroga 'and threw him down' with a wrestler's hold before others beat him to death.[20] In local retellings, the brutality of this violence is naturalized by ascribing it to acts of individual prowess: 'Getting hold of one leg they tossed them into the fire'* is the phrase most commonly employed in Dumri; in its local inflection it suggests more a one-sided wrestling bout than death in a riot.

It is peasant-wrestlers and daredevil herdsmen which people Shardanand Yadav's account, cited above. The power of the Dumri volunteers resides in tough masculine bodies, it does not emanate from an androgynous Gandhian sense of sacrifice.[21] Quite the contrary; the focus on bal or strength creates the space for the fictive presence of a dreaded wrestler-dacoit of the 1920s.

* '*Tangri pakari ke phenk delān āgi mein.*'

20

Komal-Dacoit

In conversation, Shardanand briefly mentioned the name Komal Yadav, the common caste marker 'Yadav' obscuring the fact that Komal was no ordinary Yadav but the notorious 'Komal and his gang' of the police records. Shardanand was unable to knit Komal into his sketchy account, but he reminded Sita Ahir, the eyewitness, not to leave the tough guy out of his story of 'Chauri Chaura'. Sita did not ascribe any leadership role to the dacoit, but he admitted that it was Komal who had the guts (*karēja*, lit. 'liver') to torch the police station.[*]

An interjection, 'Komal always carried a spear', completed the picture. The irony of Komal's fictive presence emerges when counterpoised with the police version of the story. 'Expenditure of energy' in apprehending and prosecuting the Chauri Chaura rioters had 'prevented the police from devoting their full energy to organized crime'.[22] 'Surveillance was poor' in 1922 and 1923, 'and, to a large extent over the wrong men'. The district, noted the commissioner, 'was harassed by bands of dacoits', notably, 'Komal and his gang'. With the 'capture and conviction of Komal . . . things improved' in 1924.[23]

'Very few people in the . . . district would be unaware of Komal Ahir' (i.e. Komal Yadav), began the nationalist weekly *Swadesh* in the first of its four-part story on this 'fantastic wrestler-dacoit'. Noted for his exploits in central Gorakhpur, Komal was apprehended, after much effort, in the summer of 1922, the time

---

[*] *'Leader' te nāhin rahlān, Komal. 'Leader' te Najar Ali aur Abdulla rahlān, baki phuk-le Komal-e-ke karēja rahal.'*

when the Chauri Chaura accused were kept shackled together in
the district jail. Komal wanted Neur, the young wrestler-accused
to escape with him. According to his cousin, Neur's courage failed
him on the appointed day.[24] Komal scaled the jail walls along with
another inmate on 18 July 1922. He was not rearrested for another
eighteen months, then was convicted and hanged in the summer
of 1924.[25]

Sita: Komal was really a very tough Ahir. He cut his chains bit by
         bit. It took a full month. When just a little bit of the shackle
         remained, then [they] threw a rope from the outside. There
         was real strength in his strides; and his eyes!, they were this-big!
         He held the small bit of the *beri* [shackles] by the hand. His
         strides, they were powerful—like a Punjabi. He was from
         Sahuakot, and had been to the jail many times. He got involved
         in this thana-affair as well. He was a pahelwān.

Naujadi: I have yet to see a stronger fellow than he. I saw him at the
         Gorakhpur jail.

Sita: He was tough-and-cruel (*jābir*), like a Punjabi.

Komal was no ordinary pahelwān. About this Naujadi and Sita
leave you in little doubt. The real significance of the character
Komal lies in the fact that 'he got involved in the thana affair as
well'. Police files offer an altogether different trajectory to the
dacoit's career; from the Chauri Chaura court records Komal is
simply absent. Nevertheless, in local memory Komal remains a
powerful presence, one that evokes the magnitude of the violence
at Chauri Chaura. It is the physical prowess of this wrestler-outlaw
that places him alongside Nazar Ali and his associates on that
extraordinary day—a reminder of the idea of the tough otiyars in
the minds of the Dumri folk, young and old alike.

21

The Babu-saheb of Mundera

The tough otiyars of Dumri appear in the bazaar account as 'rustics, ruffians and rogues', in that order.[26] In Mundera the riot is remembered as an episode from the history of the bazaar itself. Its hero is the legendary *zor-talab* zamindar, Sant Baksh Singh, ably supported by his clever functionary, *kārinda* Awadhu Tiwari.*

After the riot the rival Chaura bazaar lay in ruins; Mundera, the *phulwaria* (lit. garden) of Babu saheb (Sant Baksh Singh), rode the storm. Chandi Tiwari, the kārinda's grandson, draws on his memory of the event as follows:

Satyagraha had started at the behest of Gandhiji . . . [Volunteers] were insisting that the sale of meat, fish and liquor be stopped. Grandfather requested the thanedar to beat the fellows down; it would be the end of the bazaar, he said, if these fuckers were allowed to carry on with their riotous ways (*dhīnga-karna*). So Gupteshar Singh came. He had his sipāhīs bring these fellows in, and they were slapped and threatened (*do-char thappar māra gaya, darwāya gaya*).

The italicized phrase implies that the thrashing of the volunteers was as much the work of the kārinda as of the thanedar. In fact the construction—*māra gaya, darwāya gaya*—can be taken to mean the narrator as well as his grandfather. Chandi Tiwari's tone suggests that Awadhu thought of the volunteers as mere peasants. The fellows no doubt meant mischief, but police kicks and curses were considered adequate to rid them of their pretensions. The Dumri activists took the beating more seriously than expected, a surprise which is echoed in Chandi's recall:

* *Zor-talab*: forceful, oppressive in the present context; *kārinda*: a functionary.

After the volunteers had been beaten back [on Wednesday], these fellows
sent out letters saying that we should all go to the bazaar [on Saturday].
And return they did in strength. And a whole lot of *goondas, badmashes*
and *dākus* [i.e. rogues and ruffians] were there with the set purpose of
looting Mundera Bazaar. And that's what [nearly?] happened.

But Awadhu Tiwari, the kārinda, stood up for the bazaar. He
picked out Ramrup Barai, a leader of volunteers from Mundera
(hanged 1923), and taunted the *panwāri**. (*Ka ho Ramrup!
Hamariye kapāre pe ee chura chali?*) 'This crowd is beyond my
powers to control', replied Ramrup. Awadhu ordered him to
'divert the crowd towards the thana'. In this Ramrup was apparently successful: the bazaar was spared; the thana got burnt.

It is hard to miss the element of filial exaggeration in Chandi's
recall. Awadhu Tiwari, by his own account 'remained the whole
night on guard in the bazaar',[27] but the volunteers knew their
geography; the procession did not require an astute diversion to
find itself outside the thana.

In the bazaar narrative it is not so much the riot as the babu-
saheb's ability to stand up to its consequences that is the object
of copious remembrance. Chandi recalls the pillage (*loot-mār*) that
accompanied police investigations. 'A "force", hundreds-strong,
including cavalrymen [sowārs] raided the villages . . . Whole ham-
lets were deserted; only the old and the infirm remained' to face
the wrath of the state.[28] 'After 1922, Chauri Chaura bazaar . . .
was ruined because of the raids; Babu-saheb on the other hand
kept the police out of Mundera.' This was a prodigious feat, and
it is remembered so:

In 1922 when the thana was burnt . . . the Collector came. Sant Baksh
Singh [Chandi recalls] went out to meet him at the station. They talked.
The Collector said, 'Babu saheb! You got your bazaar saved and had my
thana burnt!' Sant Baksh Singh gave a [stunning] reply. He said, 'Why

* Barai is the caste name of betel-sellers and betel growers, hence Ramrup
Barai. The former class, who usually operate from a kiosk which has stacks of
bricks for support, are also called *panwāri*, from *pān*, i.e. betel leaf.

shouldn't your thana be burnt, you who make a fetish of your laws'
[*Kyon na āp ka thāna jala diya jāe, jab āp kanoon se bor-ke roti khāne
wāle hain*]. 'You people are hamstrung by rules and procedures: First
fire blanks, then fire in the air, then below the knees. Me! I would have
fired to kill.' The Collector shook his head and asked for help: provisions
[*rasad*], some labourers, and cloth for the shrouds of the dead policemen. Babu saheb had all this supplied from Mundera without difficulty;
but he did not let a single policeman enter the bazaar.

The dialogue between the babu-saheb and the collector was
a powerful and imaginary one. Sant Baksh Singh was certainly in
attendance at the railway station on 5 February—a clutch of public
men had also arrived by then from Gorakhpur—but it was
Chandi's grandfather who was 'ordered' by the Collector 'to help
with coolies and supply 2 *thāns* (bolts) of cloth and 8 bullock
carts'. Mundera traders were told to supply food gratis to the
troops at the thana.[29] Awadhu Tiwari was of course acting on
behalf of his mālik, and it is his master who figures as a hero, both
in Mundera bazaar and in Tiwari's own family. A ruthless zamindar and a toady of the British, Sant Baksh Singh is remembered
even today with a mixture of awe and adulation.[30] Local memory
credits him with protecting his subjects from the ravages of the
law.

Mewa Lal Jaiswal, a trader-intellectual who frequents Ram
Awadh's bookshop in the commercial wing of the local Arya Samaj
mandir, offers a bazaar view of the activities of the babu-saheb.

[After the thana was burnt] people pulled down their shutters and just
scooted. Then Sant Baksh Singh rode into the bazaar on elephant-back.
[He lived five miles away in Gaunar.] *Purāna rupaya* [i.e. old, regionally
minted coins, collected as bazaar dues], ghee and *bhandāri* [i.e. provi-
sions], he offered as gifts [*dāli*] to the English collector. It was then that
the *angrez* calmed down somewhat. Sant Baksh Singh said, 'My phulwāri
Mundera Bazaar will be ruined'.

1. Rubber stamp impression of Mahatma Gandhi on the Register of Volunteers, Gorakhpur Congress Committee. A similar 'image' (*murti*), with customized name and address, was marketed in 1921 for a rather high Rs 3.50.

2. A 'Swadeshi Commodity' of the time of the Khilafat-Non-Co-operation movement. The names of Shaukat and Muhammad Ali are engraved alongside Mahatma Gandhi.

3. Receipt for a one-rupee contribution to the Tilak Swaraj
Fund, 1921.

4. A more elaborate receipt for contribution to the Khilafat
Fund, 1920.

5. Cartoon in *Amrita Bazar Patrika*, Calcutta, 15 August 1947.

SOME photographs of the ruined thana were taken by private persons after the massacre at Chauri Chaura in the Gorakhpur district of the United Provinces. These have been printed for private circulation among responsible persons. It is thought that the sight of these horrible pictures may make the public realise what are the dangers of exciting the latent ferocity of mobs of ignorant villagers who in this instance battered to death with lathis twenty-one policemen of different ranks and all of their own blood and race.

J. E. GOUDGE,
Publicity Commissioner.

6. Prefatory Note to the pictorial catalogue of the violence compiled by the Provincial Government.

7. The aftermath of the violence, from the official album on Chauri Chaura.

8. Lal Mohammad 'Sain' and Qazi outside the courtroom
on 22 September 1922.

9. Sita Ahir, Chotki Dumri,
February 1989.

10. Naujadi Pasin, Chotki Dumri,
February 1989.

11. A group photograph of the accused on trial.

Stanley Mayers, the Gorakhpur police chief, was raiding the neighbouring villages non-stop. It was this massive police hunt that made Sant Baksh Singh plead for 'his people'; otherwise, babu-saheb had a reputation for keeping the police at bay.[31] 'Even the postman had to enter the bazaar wearing civilian dress!' For Mewa Lal, who made this observation, the divesting of state authority was enforced after the riot as well. The police, 'when they came into the bazaar', did so 'in plain dress'. Sita and Naujadi describe a sea of red turbans (*lalri-e-lalri*), lashing out against the neighbouring villages. The local chaukidar, however, 'never saw any daroga or constable coming [in] to Mundera' during the entire course of police investigations.[32]

The man in charge of investigations was 'won over'. 'My men will go with you, and my peons will get the culprits you want', the inspector was told. Mutton etc. was 'supplied' for the police to feast on,[33] he adds in parenthesis: *'Hamāre qasbe mein koi sipāhi nahin āyega (Bakri-shakri sab thane mein 'supply' kar di). Jo 'list' chahiye de-dijiye, ham pakrawa denge.'*[34] Mewa Lal Jaiswal maintained that this enabled Sant Baksh Singh to 'shield the real ones'. 'Babu-saheb got all the rogues and ruffians [*lafange, chor-chikār*] arrested. In this way 'these [low caste] people [who were actually hanged and imprisoned] became [political] sufferers: *asli log back mein chale gaye* [i.e. the real people went into the background]'.[35] In Mewa Lal's account the success of Sant Baksh Singh has paradoxically enabled the descendants of those rogues and ruffians to draw political pensions for what can only be termed wrongful confinement. There is nothing but convoluted high-caste pique to Mewa Lal's words. The Dumri crowd, we know, was composed of low- and middle-caste men—'a mob of enraged untouchable volunteers' is how they appeared to the Brahmin magistrate; the social composition of those convicted was no different.[36]

22

The Madanpur Narrative

The real agents (*asli log*) involved in the riot are, again, other people altogether in the narrative from Madanpur, a Pathan-trader dominated market village twenty miles south-east of Chauri Chaura. Located at the junction of Majhna and Rapti rivers, Madanpur is an old settlement consisting of a residential site and a separate *gola* or marketplace. Boats containing iron, grain, cloth, molasses, tobacco and spices regularly docked here till the 1880s, connecting Madanpur through the river Ghaghra to the markets down the Gangetic plains, all the way to Calcutta.[37] Madanpur was soon to lose some of its carrying trade to the railways, but its Pathan trader-cartmen were still active in the 1920s, bringing in the produce of northern Gorakhpur for distribution in the southern part of the district.

The Madanpur account places the riot in the context of a stylized understanding of the nationalist movement, and it ascribes agency to the trader-cartmen who happened to be around on the afternoon of 4 February. '*Namak āndolan chal rahā thā* [i.e. It was the time of the salt satyagraha]', begins Mohram Sheikh of Madanpur, pushing the event eight years forward into the nationalist future. 'The volunteers were trying to encircle the thana, but were being beaten back by the police.' The peasants told the cartmen (*gāriwāns*) their plight; the gāriwāns replied: 'Let us tether our bullocks, and then we shall see what can be done.'[38]

In this account it is the Madanpur cartmen who suggest that stones lying by the railway track be used as missiles; it is they who supply the kerosene which sets the thana afire. Having caused the riot, the traders drove their carts, laden with rice and raw sugar,

back to Madanpur, threatening another thana en route.[39] A massive police raid (a cannon is mentioned) on Madanpur finds a
village united and ready to defend its 'criminals'. Village elders
parley with police officers. The English superintendent cries 'real
tears', saying '*hamāri insult ho gayi hai* [i.e. we have lost face], our
thana has been burnt down'. Guns looted from the police station
are hidden in the village well; these lie undetected, but the police
manage to arrest forty suspects. Appeals are made in the name of
the nation: '*pahchanon mat! Āzadi kā sawāl hai! Yeh sab ke liye
kiya gaya hai*'. To give evidence against these men would be 'to
betray the nation'.[40]

The Madanpur narrative is an account of nationalist success.
Transporter-traders from a distant market village make their contribution (*yogdān*) while going about their business; exhorted on
behalf of an ongoing struggle, and aided by the powers of a
Muslim worthy, these men enable the village to rescue its violent
heroes from the clutches of judicial penalty.[41] The ubiquity of
nationalist discourse takes on a particularly interesting colour in
this fanciful fabrication of a pleasing local victory.

23

Malaviya Saves Chotki Dumri

Village solidarity is important within the successful denouement of the Madanpur narrative. In Dumri, the story is
altogether different. Here it is said that the village was
deserted (*ek chirai ke put nāhin rahal*) and Shikari had turned
approver. There is no question of police officers parleying with
village elders: Dumri felt the full impact of police raids.

From the court records we know the following sequence. Shikari makes a confession on 16 March; Chotki Dumri is again raided early next morning; eighteen people are arrested and packed off to the district jail.[42] Sita Ahir recalls the raid (*chāpa*) of 17 March as follows:

A month after the riot, when people had started coming back to the village, there was a big raid. They surrounded the village from all sides. Whoever ventured out—in the middle of the night, or at dawn, even to shit—was nabbed by the police.

According to Sita, cannons had been brought over to blow Dumri up, but a legal luminary made an ingenious plea which saved the village from utter destruction.

They had brought cannons with them. Madan Mohan Malaviya sahab then argued [*bahas karlan*]: 'Sir', he said, 'four-legged animals have not burnt the thana, cows-and-buffaloes have not burnt the thana, birds have not burnt the thana. It is the two-legged creatures, men [*du-gora: manhi*] who have burnt the thana. Catch *them*! . . . If you fire the *tōp* [cannon] then all life—*chirai-chirau, goru-bachru*—will be destroyed.' With this the English agreed; the cannons were not fired.

How are we to read this amazing account of Dumri's success in surviving the wrath of the avenging colonial force? There was no way in which Malaviya, a veteran nationalist, could have pleaded with the police: *bahas* (argument) is reserved for the court-room, and the Allahabad pleader did not set foot in Gorakhpur till July 1922. But Malaviya *had* been in touch with the events of Chauri Chaura almost immediately after 4 February. His son toured Chauri Chaura as a member of a fact-finding team, and K.N. Malaviya was Counsel for the Defence in the sessions court.

The convicted rioters were defended in the High Court by a team of five lawyers, paid for by the state: the peasants convicted, as we saw, were too poor to afford their fees.[43] Madan Mohan Malaviya was an additional counsel and argued on a substantial point of law. His plea was that no offence of a criminal conspiracy had been committed at the Dumri meeting on the morning of 4 February 1922, and that whatever offence was committed at the police station in the afternoon could not fairly be regarded as 'committed in the same transaction'. There had therefore been a misjoinder and conflation of charges 'sufficient to invalidate the entire trial' in the lower court.[44] The High Court judges refused to accept this plea, and, when they reduced the sentences, did so on grounds of attenuating circumstances. This led them to look favourably at most of the accused, apart from the ring leaders.

For Sita, though, it was Malaviya sahab who had been instrumental in saving Dumri village from ruin by getting the Angrez (the English) to restrict punishment to select, culpable individuals. Not that Sita does not know the final judgment: he even claims to have had a copy of it. However, in his recall the discretion exercised by the superior judges on behalf of the Dumri accused is of no consequence; nor are the five Indian lawyers who defended the accused. His memory of the police party swooping down in rage, and of the vulnerability to it of every individual in Dumri, is so overbearing that it leads him to visualize the aftermath of the riot as comprising imminent and summary collective punishment. The figure of the enraged police force, and of the judge before whom Malaviya pleaded, are fused into one. The people of Dumri were not saved by the Allahabad High Court. The village as a whole, represented in Sita's voice by its living organisms, young and old, bird and beast (*chirai-chirau, goru-bachru*), was saved by a famous nationalist lawyer who Sita knew had argued with the English judges on behalf of the Dumri accused.[45]

24

The Great Betrayal

If, as the last chapter shows, this is how the shadow lines of punishment and justice are etched in Sita Ahir's memory, there is no ambiguity about the fact that the case had to await the discovery of an approver. Without this mnemonic spur, it is clear, as Sita puts it, '*Mukadma chale ke jōg nāhin rahe* [i.e. There was very little chance of the case getting off the ground].' However, Shikari's betrayal was not an individual act. He was made to renege by a historic renegade—the Sikh zamindar of the Dumri estate whose father the English had rewarded for his services during 1857 by the grant of a confiscated estate.

Sita picks up the thread of his narrative of how the village was saved, and now the story takes on a different turn.

And then, Sardar saheb, he is a toady of the English (*Angrez ke khair-khāh hauwwen. Inheen ke pakral gail*). It was him the English got hold of. Then he [the sardar] went out in search of his own men, his own tenants, and turned them into approvers. (*Uhe mukhbir bayān dihlan.*) It was these approvers who testified in court; It was then that the trial could commence, don't you see!

The grateful Sikh owners of the Dumri estate remain true to their renegade selves; they betray the peasants in 1922, as they had the landed rebel Bandhu Singh in 1857. With their thirty-four villages already confiscated for rebellion, 'Bandhoo Singh and others' were, in early 1859, 'still lurk[ing] in the . . . jungles', committing 'dacoities and murders', as the commissioner put it, and causing the main road from Gorakhpur to north Bihar to be 'frequently . . . closed'. Officials desired this estate to be conferred on 'some loyal Seikh [Sikh] or Afghan' who 'would probably purchase quiet by giving up to the former proprietors a proportion of the profits'. No local 'Rajah or Zemindar . . . could hold his own against the influence of the . . . [Dumri Babus] . . . with whom the tenantry sympathized.'

The colonial search stopped with Sardar Surat Singh and his heirs, 'on condition of continued loyalty and good service to the British government'. The title Bahadur, a formal deed, and Bandhu Singh's villages, were all conferred on these Sikh Punjabi outsiders. These Dumri sardars did not accommodate the ex-proprietors.[46] However, another branch of the same Sirnet Rajput clan as Bandhu Singh was allowed by the British to retain its share of the remaining thirty-four villages, including Mundera bazaar. Sant Baksh Singh, the Babu Sahab of Mundera, was a second generation kin of Bandhu Singh. Umrao Singh, the owner of Chotki Dumri and Chaura, was in contrast the son of the loyalist grantee Sardar Surat Singh Majithia.

The memory of the Great Betrayal of 1857, which made the Sardars of Majitha village in Punjab the leading landholders of Gorakhpur, still rankles with the people of Chauri Chaura. Nau-jadi referred deprecatingly to the Majithias, who owned Dumri and much else besides, as *Sardarwa*; even their lowers, the estate functionaries, were accorded the higher title Maharaj in the 1920s, revealing just how deep the acrimony against them had settled. Mewa Lal Jaiswal was still more severe: 'The Majithias', he said, 'will always remain renegades (*ghaddārs*) in this area, howsoever they may prosper (*chāhe jitna uth jaen*).'

The contrast between the loyalist-collaborator Sardar saheb of Dumri who offered his tenants as approvers, and the Babu saheb of Mundera, who as usual held the police at bay, is a characteristic trope in most local retellings of Chauri Chaura. In the local mind it is not the destruction of state apparatus—the police station—that evokes the tumult of 1857. Rather, it is the renegade help given by the Sardars for the re-establishment of colonial authority that both marks these Sardars out as objects of scorn as well as brings to mind their turncoat colour during the Great Mutiny.

25

A Powerful 'Mukhbir'

'Shikari was also in the *kānd* [riot], but became a *mukhbir* [approver]. It was Sardar Harcharan Singh who made him a mukhbir.'[47] So says Sita Ahir, whose brief account of the making of the approver has an interesting tie-up with the Dumri Sardars. Harcharan Singh, an old-time official of the estate, had brought Shikari's father, says Sita, from Punjab. This man, Mir Qurban, was given 'a pension' by the estate. Of his son, Mir Shikari, Sita says:

Shikari ke majgar ghar rahe . . . Shikari ke khēti bahut rahal, 12 bigha—akele rahen, khēti karen . . . Chamra-o bechen, obha-chobhi, jaise ki kauno bajār jāwen, kauno na jāwen . . . Kheti ke tāo aa ja te khēti-e karen.[48]

When translated, this reads:

Shikari was a man of substance: with a large holding and additional income from leather trading, he lived alone;[49] he had no need to slave over his 4 acres of land. He would sell skins and hides every now and then, or turn to agriculture, if it took his fancy.

This biographical information, which casts Shikari as a carefree, well-to-do individual, was not offered in order to explain Shikari's betrayal. There is nothing in Sita's account that suggests a valid reason for Shikari, of all people, turning approver. Sita, and especially Naujadi, remember Mir Qurban's son with a certain resignation quite free of pique. In their recollections Shikari appears as a forceful person, a leader of men whose power was not diminished by his stellar performance in court. This is backed up by another account, where the lead taken by Shikari in court figures as an aspect of his leadership qualities in general: Ramji Chamar, son of a convicted rioter, employs the term mukhbir (approver) in a complimentary way. He recalls Shikari as the mediator in the affairs of the state, be it the thana or the court, and as the self-assured man who took the lead for the greater good. All this he says in his own idiom:

Te jaise das admi mein ek admi jarūr mukhbir rahe la, har cheej mein, te ee [Shikari] thāna-adālat mein uho jamāna mein rahen: kisi se daren nāhin, jāke bāt-chīt karen . . . bhalāi tabbe karen, ta! . . . Aosan khandān mein ab kehu ba nāhin. Nāhīn, kehu ke nāhīn ba.[50]

'He was powerful, he was fearless', says Ramji, in sum. Clearly, Shikari's betrayal in court has not tarnished his powerful image in Dumri even today. Nor of his family: 'there is no one like him in that family anymore'. People in the village were still in awe of Shikari after his return from the trial. Nobody, affirms Sita, castigated him for his part in the proceedings, everyone was afraid of his prowess: *'Hai ke kahe? Dar ke māre, ee kehu kahe!—darāe sab'*. And why were they afraid rather than just plain angry? Obviously—'Because he might [very well] implicate them in some other case.'

Shikari's return was then a successful one, almost the return of a prodigal to the fold. Approvership imbued this leader of Dumri's men with an altogether different sort of power. That Shikari's son was elected village headman (*grām pradhān*) in the late 1980s suggests that no stigma attaches to the approver and his family. The recounting of the event for the visiting historian also took place at Shikari's old house. For me, there really has been no getting away from Mir Shikari.

This is especially true with the eighty-year-old Naujadi, wife of Rameshar Pasi, incarcerated eight years for his part in the riot. Naujadi, a low-caste woman, is roughly the godmother of Shikari's grandson. The little boy was sold for his weight in grain to the old Pasin as his siblings had all died in their infancy.[51] Naujadi, who regards herself as a 'member of the [Shikari] household, then [in 1922] as now [1988]', remembers the powerful approver with hardly a trace of regret. For her Shikari was first and foremost a leader of men: *'Ek mutthi mein kihle rahlān. Unke mutle chirāg barat rahal.'* She believes it was Shikari who kept everyone united. He possessed real power: 'one could light a lamp with his piss', says Naujadi, wonderfully adapting a local epigram to her own ends.[52] After the riot, she says, her own husband tried saving his skin by running away to his sister's village; but all this was in vain, for Shikari had spoken. *Pahichān* (identification) by the approver got men the gallows or the jail, but she believes there was no vindictiveness in what he said.

For Naujadi there was a certain inevitability about the punishment. Having challenged the might of the state via a frontal assault on the thana, what could one hope for except a temporary reprieve? There is no room in her recall for the ones that got away. It was immediate kin who persuaded absconders to come out of hiding:

Jab paulīn hāl ki [Rameshar] chutihen te nāhīn, aa pa jaihen [pulis] te mār ke bekām kar deihen—te ānkhi se sab dekhat rahlīn. Te kahlīn, kahlīn, ki chutihen te nahīn, te kāhe ke dēh radd karāwal ja—le āwa, unke bharti kar jāwal ja, te . . . bula ke le-ailīn.

Naujadi knew well the treatment that awaited her husband Rameshar; she had little hope that he would successfully evade the police for long. *Bharti**—surrender—was better than 'having one's bones broken'. She went to her sister-in-law's house in a distant village and brought Rameshar back.

* Lit. 'to deposit'.

Sita's uncle, Bikram (hanged 1923), was similarly forced out of hiding by the prospect of the raiding party arresting his wife in his stead.[53] The effect of police raids and Shikari's testimony was overpowering.

Te māre gārad se, māre ghora se, 'kham-kham-kham-kham',[54] ailen san, eh Babu! Kehu dehri mein dharāil, kehu rahta [rasta] mein dharāil. Aa, eh Babu! hum jhūt nāhīn kahīn, hamre Sikari-Babu ke dehe ke biyān, nāhīn bhail na? Jahār [jānch] karlān, kahlān-sunlān, kehu ke bekār nāhīn karlān, haan! Bekār nāhīn karlān. Humman-o-lōgan ke pahichān karlān; bekār nāhīn karlān.

Using evocative imagery Naujadi is here saying that though people tried to run away from the horses' hooves when the mounted police (*māre gārad se, māre ghōra se*) came looking for culprits, it was in vain. No matter where they tried hiding, inside houses or outside the village, the police caught up with them. Puranmasi Chamar was dragged out from a pumpkin bush.[55] With 'Shikari-babu implicating his ex-comrades almost to a fault', she says, 'he also showed us up, but not without reason.' For Naujadi it was both really and justifiably the end of the road for Rameshar and Nageshar, Lal Mohammad and Nazar Ali.

But do I really wish to suggest that Shikari was *never* regarded as a betrayer in the village? Could not the resignation towards the inevitability of his squealing-dealing that I discovered in Dumri in 1989 have been a result of the passage of time? An alternative explanation for the apparent lack of hostility towards Shikari can be advanced, which, in the absence of evidence, can only remain a hypothesis. This is that Shikari would have been regarded as the betrayer of a cause, and of persons connected to it, only if the event had been considered a political act in the village in the *aftermath* of the riot. But nationalist condemnation and judicial punishment had foreclosed this possibility. Disavowed by Gandhi and the nationalists locally, the Dumri people may well have come to accept their men as the notorious criminals of Chauri Chaura— more than a hundred of whom were lucky to have escaped with their lives—and therefore Shikari's enforced condemnation of them may have come to seem as worthy of exoneration among the locals.

Gandhi, it needs recalling, had advised the 'guilty and the repentant to hand themselves voluntarily to the Government for punishment and make a clean confession.' The functionaries of the District Congress in Gorakhpur had been urged to deliver 'the evil doers . . . into custody'. And indeed a few were so delivered. The relatives of the rioters and the convicted in jail would then have had to maintain a firm sense of national belonging, and this while being shunned all the while by self-respecting nationalists as criminals who had shamed and stigmatized the nation. Not every convicted rioter was a Dwarka Gosain, who, after fifteen years in jail harangued the Congress chief minister of UP in 1937 for forgetting that 'whoever fought against Imperialism and for swaraj, be he right or wrong, violent or non-violent [was in the right, for] the goal is the same.'

Paradoxical as it may sound, Shikari was able to come back to the village not only because his court performance had imbued him with still greater power in the eyes of the Dumri people; one could go further and suggest that, within the context of the Gandhian understanding of Chauri Chaura as crime, the need for repentance and confession, the failure of the accused to follow this advice, and given the established ways of the courts in such matters, Shikari had indeed helped bring the guilty to justice.

Nonetheless, even as the approver performed in court, his 'accomplices' gasped with dismay at the impersonal and transactional nature of his testimony. The tie-up between torture and speech was not hidden from the accused. Scores had been made to 'confess'; of these at least two other than Shikari had been short-listed as potential approvers, only to fall short and be hanged for their crimes. Faced with the Dumri leader's damning testimony,

Abdullah of Rajdhani responded with the straightforward hatred of one who discerns the hangman: 'Shikari knows me from before. He has turned approver and if he did not name a number of persons, how could he get off?'[56] Abdullah (hanged 2 July 1923) spoke thus because he never came back to confront Shikari outside the court.

But Rameshar, Naujadi's husband, did return after eight years in prison. What did he think of Shikari? We don't have access to Rameshar Pasi's memory. All we know is that Naujadi, for perhaps a complex web of reasons, still remembers Shikari-babu with a respect untainted by rancour.

26

The One-Seven-Two of Chauri Chaura

If Shikari's role is etched out as a matter of fact in Naujadi's mind, the judgment makes a shadowy but deadly appearance in her recall. Every time the old woman refers to an assembly connected with the event, she uses the figure *ek-sau-bahattar*, i.e. 172, to give it its proper numerical form. 'Ek-sau-bahattar people gathered on the morning of 4 February'; 'there are 172 persons mentioned on my paper'.[57]

Now, 172 was the number of rioters sentenced to death by the sessions judge, Gorakhpur; the High Court reduced the death sentences to 19. One-seven-two has remained, however, the real number for Naujadi. The reasons for this lie in the system of colonial justice. Under the Indian Penal Code death was the 'ordinarily right and appropriate' sentence to pass on each and every member of an assembly proven to have committed an offence under section 302/149. Section 302 was a murder charge; under section 149 every member of a crowd which committed a grave offence 'was liable to punishment for that offence as if he had committed it himself.' Judge Holmes had then quite rightly considered the crowd as one legal person, and, given 'the adequacy of the evidence in each case, the conviction of these hundred and seventy-two men on the charge of murder was right, and indeed inevitable'.[58] The Gorakhpur judge could have been more lenient, but he would then have had to explain why he was not doing his duty by awarding the maximum punishment. The natural inclination of district judges was to recommend the hangman's noose, secure in the knowledge that 'no capital sentence can be carried out until it has been confirmed by the High Court'. This of course 'tend[ed] to weaken the sense of responsibility in the trial courts',[59] but it also enabled the harsh face of death penalty to serve as a local warning to a colonial population.

The contrast with eighteenth-century England is instructive. Douglas Hay has noted that while a large number of persons were sentenced to death for relatively minor crimes against property, 'pardons were very common'. Though vested in the sovereign, 'the prerogative of mercy ran throughout the administration of the criminal law, from the lowest to the highest level'. Magistrates and assize judges on circuit employed a certain discretion and 'used the pardon when necessary to meet the requests of the local gentry or to propitiate popular feelings of justice'. Indeed, in the localities, 'within the immediate experience of the poor', pardons were very much a part of 'the tissue of paternalism'. Petitions for mercy were routinely drafted by gentlemen on behalf of labourers. 'It was an important self-justification of the ruling class', argues Hay, 'that once the poor had been chastised sufficiently to protect property, it was the duty of a gentleman to protect "his" people'.

Discretion—of JPs, magistrates and the gentry—one might say was the better part of eighteenth-century English justice.[60]

In colonial India the situation was quite the reverse. In cases such as Chauri Chaura, punishment was to be handed down in the districts; it was then up to the convicted to appeal against the 'ordinarily right and appropriate . . . death sentence'.[61] Till justice could be won at the High Court, all of Naujadi's ek-sau-bahattar were as good as dead. The dissonance between local punishment and provincial justice can be heard in familial recall of the event. For Naujadi, who made weekly trips to the Gorakhpur jail—a portion of which functioned in this case as a court—it was the initial 172 that represented the crowd as well as the convicted.

The idiosyncrasy in Naujadi's recall becomes intelligible in terms of the working of the judicial process.[62] Sita's comment, 'Yes Abdullah was in it; he was the first to be hanged' is equally revealing.[63] Abdullah topped the list of those sentenced to death by the High Court; it was in this alphabetical sense that 'his was the first hanging'. It would be a naive historiography which would expect to find subaltern recollections untouched by the prose and procedures of punishment: judgment was, quite literally, a matter of life and death for Abdullah and 171 others. It is remembered as such.[64]

27

The Policemen Dead

When Sita asserts that 'nineteen died at the thana; nineteen were hanged', he creates a flawed equation but one which establishes a symmetry between the extent of the crime and the degree of punishment. It is true the High Court finally sentenced these many to death, but the toll within the police force was twenty-three. Transposing the number of 'rioters' hanged on to the figure of policemen killed suggests a displacement far deeper than a simple arithmetical error of four. It points to the silencing of the police in most local retellings of the riot.

In Dumri the policemen who died do not count. They triggered the riot, with their ineffective firing in the air, no doubt, and the gathering in the village that morning was in response to the police inspector's beating of volunteers. Yet, for all this, they lack agency in current accounts. It is Nazar Ali and his men who activate the stories. In Sita's account, there is a far greater recognition of the tie-up between the thana and the district. He recalls that armed guards had been despatched from Gorakhpur, and that orders had not been received from the Collector to open fire. But he has little to say about the local police force. Or at least Sita's considerable knowledge of the regular and auxiliary police force is not fully deployed by him in his narrative of the riot.

The force that confronted the Dumri marchers, we know from court records, consisted of armed guards, constables and a motley collection of 'rural policemen'—chaukidars and goraits resident in their villages, and normally indistinguishable from peasants in appearance and attire. Of the two, the goraits were of inferior status, usually of the untouchable Chamar, Pasi and Dusadh castes. Required to subsist on a small rent-free allotment, the gorait was very much a 'servant of the zamindar', 'employed to fetch, carry and perform menial services', including ploughing the master's fields free of charge. Attached to lowly untouchables, the term gorait had 'become one of reproach' and was 'by itself . . . a great obstacle to men of good caste taking up the post'.[65]

Chaukidars, by comparison, were paid servants of the state,*

---

* They received Rs 3 per month in 1860; and Rs 3 in 1914 as well!

had a dignified ancestry (from *chauki*, i.e. outpost), and came from middling social groups. Mostly Ahirs or middle-ranking Musalmans, a few like Chedi and Tribeni Pande of Sant Baksh Singh's estate even belonged to the upper crust of Brahmins.[66] Sita Ahir's grandfather, when he elected to leave the paternal home in the overpopulated southern tract by the river Rapti and follow his wife to her natal village Dumri, also made the transition from being a road-runner (*harkāra*) to a chaukidar. The chaukidari of Satrohanpur village had some freshly reclaimed land across the road from Dumri, in the newly carved jungle estate of a powerful merchant-banker family, which then devolved in Sita's family. From the grandfather it went to an elder uncle, then to his father Surajbali, who was killed in the riot. Sita's mother received Rs 100 for her husband's death in the line of duty. Her thumb impression survives on a receipt marked no. 447(13) in the court records. Harpal Chamar of Dumri, an erstwhile gorait whose lowly office had been merged with that of chaukidar by a special dispensation of 1919, survived the riot.[67]

After his father's death, Sita recalls being offered a post in the provincial constabulary. He passed the physical examination; his eyesight was normal: '*Inspittar āil rahal; ānkhi rumāl-umāl bāndh ke ehi tarah ginaulas, te laukat rahe, sab gin gailīn.*'* But Sita wanted to stay back and desired the chaukidari of a neighbouring village: he had a widowed mother and three sisters to look after. The request was turned down at the highest level: '*kul Lāt-Governor, Jarnail-pharnail jawāb deh dehlen*'. Uma Chamar, whom Sita calls 'Umva' by inflecting a low-caste name with the requisite disdain—had a prior claim. The chaukidari of neighbouring Bharatpur–Satrohanpur villages lapsed in Sita's family with the death of his father on 4 February 1922.

---

* Optical examination for the police and army service consisted in illiterate recruits counting dots, twelve in number, at a distance with each eye. See Maulvi S.N.A Jafri, *Jangi Novel, ya ek Sipāhi ki sarguzasht ka saccha photo* (Sitapur, 1917).

Chaukidars like Sita's father were auxiliaries to the regular police stationed at the thana. Chauri Chaura was a 'third-class' police station, which meant that it had no more than eight constables and just one daroga or sub-inspector of police.[68] But the thana covered over a hundred villages, and had about that number of chaukidars attached to it. Though not under direct everyday control, these chaukidars fell under the jurisdiction of the local thana.

These rural policemen were expected to report serious infractions of the law as well as register the incidence of births and deaths in the village to the thana every week.[69] They also had to walk up to the police station to receive their monthly pay. Saturday, 4 February, was a pay-day. A large number of chaukidars were present at the thana, dressed in their officious red turbans. On such occasions they would be ordered around, pressed to labour gratis for the daroga or his establishment—perhaps repair the tiles on the thana roof, weed the garden-patch of the thanedar, and even run an errand to the nearby bazaar despite the orders in force since 1887 which prohibited excessive use of chaukidars as coolies at the thana.

Subordinate to the regular police force, chaukidars were also made to appear a bit different. Not for them the starched khaki of the police, roughly textured to allow it to breathe during the hot and humid months. (Polyester first adorned the bodies of motorcycle cops only after the 1970s.) Formalized in the 1870s, the dress of chaukidars consisted of a *mirzai* (padded jacket) 'of blue drill', a four-yard long red pagri (turban), and 'the usual dhoti', or long loincloth.[70] From the waist down it was the dhoti which kept the rustic chaukidar from rising above the ordinary peasant. The billowing khaki shorts and khaki leggings were not for these chaukidars.

It was the blue coat that distinguished village policemen from peasants. It was this official blue which got Dukhi Kewat (two year's rigorous imprisonment) into trouble with unfamiliar comrades on the evening of 4 February 1922. Dukhi attempted to make away with a dead policeman's rifle which had survived an attempt by some rioters to break it in half. He was set upon and beaten by a section of the crowd. Dukhi's black mirzai, subsequently displayed in court, was mistaken for a chaukidar's blue! 'They considered that as he had on a black mirzai he was a chaukidar', explained the watchman of Dukhi's village to the judge.[71]

It was not just chaukidars but the entire police force that had blue as their official badge till some thirty years before the 1922 riot.[72] A high-level investigation of a dacoity in the central UP district of Unao in 1889 resulted in the regular police switching over from blue to the distinctive khaki—a colour, which because of its connection with the colonial constabulary, has since come to stand for formal organization, discipline and the exercise of paramilitary force. (The numerous Civil Defence Corps which sprang up after the Sino-India War of 1962 had khaki for their uniform; the cadres of the authoritarian Hindu organization, the RSS, also don khaki shorts.)

The reasons for the change to khaki in 1890 are not without interest. The indigo dye used for the blue uniform emitted unwholesome vapours during the sultry monsoon months. Medical officers in charge of the police frequently reported on the fumes 'with which . . . constable lines' were 'filled in the rains'. But the switch to another colour had to await the arrival of synthetic dyes; only then could the cheap indigo produced by the British planters of north India be substituted in the official department. By 1890 German dyes were in the market.

More importantly—and this brings us back to the armed robbery of 1889—'a dark dye obtainable in every village easily passed for blue at night'. In many instances dacoits taking advantage had 'pass[ed] themselves off as police and obtain[ed] entry without difficulty into the houses of [shopkeepers] and others'.[73]

In the summer of 1890 the governor, after inspecting some

men in the new uniform, approved the change from blue to khaki. As a distinctive mark, armed guards were permitted to retain 'only the fringe on the top of the red pagris . . . blue'.[74] Once khaki was chosen as the livery of these myrmidons of state,* strict control began to be exercised over its distribution and wear and wash. In 1902 an order was promulgated, deprecating the 'growing tendency in several departments to dress subordinates in uniforms closely resembling that prescribed for the police'. His Honour was 'pleased to direct that *employés* of other Departments must not be allowed to wear khaki clothes, together with red *sāfās*—a uniform which must be confined to members of the police force.'[75]

So the lowly chaukidars had only one thing in common with policemen proper—the red turban. Everything else about their attire was different.† Blue *vs* khaki; dhoti *vs* shorts; leggings and boots *vs* unshod feet. It was the turban and its distinctive red colour that proclaimed the two as a composite coercive corps of the state.

Great weight is attached to the pagri as headgear in most parts of rural India. With some communities it is the headman alone who may wear the headdress; in Gujarat it was a privilege violently guarded by the dominant caste of Patidars.[76] It was a significant gesture, then, to have conferred the pagri on the lowly chaukidar along with the policeman proper. It was this pagri that the chauki-dars flaunted most; it was this four-yard strip of red cloth that peasants attacked even after its owner was dead. 'The red turban was particularly offensive to the non-co-operation lamb', wrote the Committing Magistrate in anger. 'Minute strips of these turbans,

---

* Gramsci writes somewhere that peasants mostly encounter the state in the guise of policemen.

† True, both wore belts with buckles, but again with a difference. The buckles of the policemen had a personal identification number on them, those of the chaukidar gave only the name of the thana. Thirty-two chaukidar brass-buckles, and thirteen from police constables, were recovered from the burnt thana. CCR, I, p. 484.

two or three inches long and a quarter inch broad, were lying all over' the thana on the morning of 5 February 1922.[77]

When Ram Lal Chamar, chaukidar of Lachmanpur, came for his pay on 4 February, he was sporting his headgear. 'I had not had my uniform renewed for a long time and it had got torn. I had not brought my belt or lathi. I had only come for my pay with my turban on.'[78] Confronted with the crowd yelling 'death to the red-turbaned bastards', Ram Lal threw down his pagri at the thana door and ran into a wheatfield. Others, more fully attired, had to divest themselves of all their accoutrements. Manohar thrust his 'uniform, safa, belt and mirzai', into a corner of the burning thana 'and with an *angocha* [kerchief] of coarse cloth tied round [his] loins . . . ran out by the east door . . . and joined the crowd. They could not identify me; they were so many.' Siddiq, the sole surviving constable (many more chaukidars managed to escape), who was standing near a mango tree away from the thana, saw the crowd bolt the door on the policemen seeking refuge in the station.

I then knew that my uniform will kill me. I took off my uniform and ran off in my shirt. Running . . . I heard a woman saying, 'Here is a policeman going this way', pointing towards me. No one followed me. When I had gone a mile or half a mile, I seized a kerchief from a lad's head and ran on and then tied it round my loins.

Siddiq ran for another six miles to the next police station and filed the first report on the riot. Badri scurried out half-clad and picked up a fistful of stones to appear like your average rioter. Jeodhan threw off his uniform and turban 'and went out with *kankar* in both hands pretending to be one of the rioters and calling out "Hit him, hit him" '. Bhagelu of Sonbarsa, a late arrival, was spotted at some distance by his brass-capped lathi and a suspicious looking bundle. He was accosted by five men carrying an injured comrade back to their village. 'They put down the injured man and two men seized' Bhagelu. 'One man wanted to open my bundle and said they would kill me if a turban should be found in it.'[79]

There is no room in the Dumri stories for Bhagelu and his comrades. When Sita mentions the escape of a policeman (Siddiq), it is to identify the person who lodged the first report at the next police station. The violence of Chauri Chaura, gruesome as it was, is recalled in Dumri as a matter of fact. It is narrated from the point of view of those hanged in 1923, not of the policemen killed at the thana. The death of policemen fails to register as a fact independent of the burning down of that precinct. The son of a chaukidar, the wife of a rioter, the grandson of a bazaar functionary, all relate the event as the 'setting afire of the thana'. 'The day the thana was burnt' is how the event is phrased to mark out a momentous and historic occasion. This is true as much of Sita's recollections in 1989 as it is of the more immediate recall of several witnesses in the court in 1922.

'Running away from the hail of stones they locked themselves inside the thana. The building was set on fire; whoever came out was thrown back into the flames', says Sita. All local accounts of the police–peasant encounter build up to the destruction by fire, paying particular attention to where the kerosene was got from. 'They got the oil from a storage tank next to the railway gate' ('okre bād tel gail tanki tūr ke'); it came 'from the Madanpur traders who had carts loaded with kerosene'; it came 'from Mundera Bazaar'—'a canister of oil was there [at the thana], and there were matches as well'.*

The last of these statements, by Naujadi, wife of Rameshar Pasi, allows the incendiary agent to appear on its own! In Naujadi's

---

* Recalling 'the *day* the thana was *burnt*' rather than the death of policemen could well be a way by which members within a face-to-face society escape remembering the actual killing of local watchmen who were familiar figures in the villages. (I am grateful to Natalie Davis for this suggestion.) Conversely, enumerating the *number* of policemen killed appears to be central to all other accounts of the riot: in this case it is the killings that underscore the extent of violence.

eyewitness account—'we are only labourers, sir, I am re-telling what I have seen with my own eyes'—the blaze is all-consuming; it accounts for at least two young lives which we know were not lost at all that day.

Singing and shouting they [the volunteers] left for Chauri Chaura . . . The roof of the thāna was tiled—this I shall never forget . . . Then daroga saheb fired. They were hit.
     Then Babu! They turned around, turn back they did, and started throwing clods and stones. (*Hammani ke bar-majdoori karat tāni, Sarkār!, dekhle ānkhi-ke kahat tāni. Babu-ho!*) They turned back and started pelting [the police] with stones.
     A canister full of oil was kept there, and so were matches . . . They started setting fire to the thana. The darogāin was standing there . . . They set fire to [the daroga's] house, burnt him alive, his children too! There the kids were—the two of them—back from school, standing with their satchels—they threw them into the fire as well.

The daroga's two daughters who, along with their mother, narrowly escaped death, here get thrown into the inferno. Naujadi does not relate how the trapped policemen were attacked and killed, their bodies charred by fire. That day the thana, and everybody and everything connected with it, was simply set ablaze.

Within a month of the occurrence a pictorial catalogue of the violence was compiled by the publicity department of the provincial government in Lucknow. Based on photographs taken the day after the riot, when the charred and battered bodies were arranged for identification, six 'horrible pictures' were printed 'for private circulation among responsible persons'. The object was to 'make the public realize . . . the dangers of exciting the latent ferocity of mobs of ignorant villagers.'[80] One of these photographs is reproduced here, along with the prefatory note that accompanied the album. A senior police officer had desired 'an enlargement of the head' of the dead constable in one such photograph, 'with the object of showing . . . clearly' the way in which it had been 'battered about', but the photographer was unable to produce the desired effect.[81]

These documentary indices of the riot were considered too explosive—and perhaps gratuitous in view of the nationalist condemnation of the violence—to be published in Indian newspapers; the provincial government however forwarded fifty copies to the India Office for suitable use. The mandarins in London sat tight on the packet, noting that were American newspapers to get hold of them 'they would probably be published . . . as photographs of Indians massacred by British troops'. A copy of the album was withheld even from the House of Commons' library. Consigned to the files in London and Lucknow, a photographic version of the dead policemen's story was hidden from public view.[82]

The crowd outside the thana was not looking for particular policemen; nor were its actions animated by routine past enmities. The Dumri leaders were agitated about the recent prevention of picketing by the daroga; theirs was an attempt to marginalize the police and short-circuit its authority by a massive show of numbers. Harpal, the village chaukidar, kept popping in and out of the Dumri meeting, reporting on its progress to the daroga. Unmindful of the local watchman, the volunteers deliberated the course of their collective action.[83] The gathering then marched out to the thana to demand an explanation for the forceful prevention of two earlier attempts to picket Mundera bazaar. The daroga would be given a chance to explain his conduct, perhaps made to apologize. Guns and muskets, meant to terrorize them, would be braved. The bazaar *would* be picketed. The *paulic* (public) would see that the police were powerless. According to Sita, 'This is what they [had] decided. They would "pay their respects" to the daroga and then picket Mundera bazaar. That's all. [*Ihe sab sarmat (sah-mati) kailān ki thanedār ke salaam kar-ke chalal jāi rokal jāi.*]'

The riot of that day was a contingent event; it followed the wilful acts of local activists. It comprised three thousand peasants, with the activists within it distinctly attired, all marching in unison to bow their heads before the thanedar in mock subjection before picketing the bazaar *as volunteers*. That was the scenario, imagined, within local recall, in Dumri that day more than seventy years ago.

There must certainly have been tension between the village and the thana. Two weeks before the clash the thanedar had listed all the activists, village by village, paying special attention to the leaders and how they could be shown to have broken the bounds of the law. Nos 227 to 240 in this list were from Dumri village. Nazar Ali's name was at the top, followed by Shikari, with Nageshar Pasi (Naujadi's brother-in-law) in fourth position. A marginal comment in the daroga's hand reads: 'Shikari Sekh is the leader. Evidence can be had under sec. 107 of the Criminal Procedure Code.'[84] Police constables had been attacked in the district; popular animosity lived in the proverb that God punishes darogas by seldom blessing them with sons![85] In local memory the event, 'this burning of the thana', does not *result* from identifiable *causes*; it is part of a story, a sequence activated by local volunteers. It follows a clutch of events, not all of which are traceable to an originary animus against the police.

It is worth reminding ourselves that Sita Ahir, a major eyewitness narrator (died 27 August 1991), was the son of a village chaukidar killed in the riot. His father's death obviously figures prominently in Sita's recall. The police officer searching furiously for Dumri leaders the morning after the riot saves a disconsolate Sita from hard-hitting rifle-butts of his sepoys and escorts him to the thana where 'nineteen [*sic*] corpses were laid out side by side'. The son is asked to identify the dead father, and is unsuccessful. Surajbali chaukidar's body was unrecognizable: it was 'charred like charcoal [*jhaunsal . . . kāth ho gail rahe dehiye*].'

Despite these details, Sita's account is really about the deeds of the Dumri activists. The police appear after the event as the avenging *forus* (force) wreaking Dumri, rather than as kinsmen killed during the riot. Sita, the dead chaukidar's son, speaks *for* the village. Till his death in August 1991 old Sita was regarded as the most authoritative reteller of the kānd (event/outrage). Would Sita have always told his story in this way? I am not sure. The discourse of pensions may be at work here, aided by the fact that Sita's uncle, himself an ex-chaukidar, was hanged as a rioter.[86] Young Sita had visited his uncle, Bikram Ahir, several times in Gorakhpur jail, and had also made the long journey to Meerut prison to be present at his hanging.

Bikram Ahir had a chequered career. A chaukidar for over fifteen years, he had joined the regular police in the late 1910s, handing over the chaukidari to his brother, Sita's father.[87]

Chaukidāri hamre dāda ke de-ke apne 'Line' mein bhailān. Par kawāid nāhīn pār lāge—bara kawāid tab hokhe. Gor-or toot gail—pār nāhīn lāge. Itāpha [Istīfa] de-ke ghar baith gailān.

To paraphrase this in straight English, the 'parade and drill [*kawāid*]' at the police lines were very tough in those days; Bikram Ahir just couldn't take it. He resigned and came back to Dumri. On his return from the 'Line', the shenanigans of his wrestler-son got him a six-month jail sentence. Neur Ahir—a tough young lad of the local akhāra—who was to be subsequently employed as an informer by the police to get the Dumri leaders arrested and was then arraigned in court and finally released—had in 1920 stolen some timber from the nearby Tarkulha jungle.[88] The lumber having been traced to Bikram's house, the father offered himself to the police in his stead. A stint in jail meant that Bikram could not come back to his chaukidari post. And anyway, Sita's father had already succeeded to that family position.[89]

In late 1921 Bikram of Dumri was a recognized volunteer. A fat, officious-looking Register of Volunteers of Gorakhpur which

had a rubber-stamp image of Mahatma Gandhi for effect, lists
Bikram as a volunteer.[90] In court, the village policeman presented
this composite picture of chaukidar–volunteer Bikram Ahir.

This accused is Bikram of my village Dumri . . . I saw him in a previous
sabha in Dumri, in which he was wearing a Gandhi cap and, as chaukidars move people on at fairs etc., he was in that sabha making the people
sit down and acting as leader. He is a volunteer.[91]

Bikram produced an alibi: he was, he claimed, fifty miles away on
the day of the riot, buying a pair of bullocks in Gonda district. A
receipt testifying to the purchase was produced in court, as were
countercharges of his participation in the riot. Eyewitnesses apart,
'a prima facie strong point against him [was] that he did not
accompany his brother's widow when she went to the police
station to get compensation for her husband's death.'[92]

   Sita's uncle and Neur's father got the death sentence. Young
Sita visited his uncle several times in Gorakhpur jail, and finally
made the long trip with Neur to Meerut, where Bikram was to
be hanged.

In Meerut [jail] the hanging kept getting postponed. It was to be on
one day, but then it would get fixed for another. In this way we stayed
on in Meerut for one full month. I would see *chāchā* [uncle] every
Sunday.
   After a month chāchā said, 'You fellows go home and look after
your work. Don't stick around here! Go back home.' We came back to
Dumri, and a wire arrived to say that the hanging has been fixed for
tomorrow!

It was not just a rioter uncle who displaced a policeman father.
In Sita's and several other local retellings, the widow of the station
officer assumes a role which is as significant as it is ubiquitous.

28

The Darogāin

S
ita has an intriguing reference to the darogāin, the widow of the daroga killed at the thana.

When night fell, the darogāin was unhurt. Two or three men saved the darogāin—they surrounded her saying, 'Don't kill her.' The *olantiyars* wanted to throw her into the fire as well, but for these men. Meghu Tiwari of Menhian took her to his house. She was pregnant. They did not listen to her entreaties and dishonoured her (*beijjat karlān*); he [Meghu] did not listen to her. With tears she wrote down her plight on her *ānchal* . . . And when the trial began . . . Meghu Tiwari got the gallows for his 'valour' [*bahaduri*].

The darogāin figures in other local accounts as well. 'She was pregnant. Meghu Tiwari took her [*Darogaji ki istri garbhwati thīn. Meghu Tiwari usko lekar ghar chale gaye*], was how the episode was described in chaste Hindi by the Vaidji (naturopath) of Mundera.[93] For the Chauri Chaura judges the dishonour done to the darogāin consisted in a *pardānashīn*[*] woman being confined in another man's house.[94] The woman herself, Rajmani Kaur, describes her escape as follows:

The rioters took possession of all my jewellery, clothing, utensils, cash and in fact everything. . . .

The house was burning and my two girls were carried out and my servant was turned out and I followed . . . As I got out of the house there were 2000 or 3000 men round it who were shouting . . . Out of the mob *one or two men said that we should not be beaten as I was pregnant* and we were women. The mob fell in with this view and I walked aimlessly with my daughters.

* *Pardānashīn*: one who keeps purdah, and so remains inside the house.

I was met by two or three men who commanded me to follow them. I obeyed, as they said they would kill us. We followed them into a courtyard [*osāra*] where we were seated. We remained there all night and we were neither offered refreshments nor shown any hospitality nor given bedding. No womenfolk came near us.[95]

This passage was paraphrased in the judgment; even the Committing Magistrate, otherwise so full of abuse and anger, did not hint that any misdemeanour or beijjati was done to the darogāin. 'She was given no food nor was she treated well', was all Mahesh Bal Dikshit had to say.[96]

But in Sita's and Naujadi's account, and in local memory more generally, the confinement of the darogāin by Meghu Tiwari amounted to a sexual assault on her person. So strong is this idea that the daroga's wife is the subject of obscene, sexist jokes at the Chauri Chaura petrol station, a meeting place for all the landed-lumpens of the area.

The figure of the darogāin is etched out in greater detail by Naujadi. The old woman could not recollect Meghu Tiwari's name, but for her this Bābhan (Brahmin) of Menhian appears as the culprit who, instead of protecting a pregnant (*sānpat*) woman, went out of his way to dishonour her: 'It was to that Brahmin's house they took her so that her honour [*ijjat-pānī*] would be safe: she was pregnant, you know. But that fellow not only looted her but dishonoured her as well.'

Hann! Ohi Babu! Ahir hauwwe ki Bābhan? . . . (Bābhan), Ohi ke gharwa le gailān ki ijjat-pāni bachi rahi . . . sānpat na rahi! Okre ghar le gailān. (Uu) lehu lena (dhan) aur beijjat-o-karlān; Bedharam-o-karlān aur dhan-o le lihlān.

This is how Meghu Tiwari disgraced the wife of thanedar Gupteshar Singh. But the darogāin, who remained in her house till 'stones and kankar were thrown' at the thana,[97] is also made to play a crucial role both before and after the riot. Let us go back to Naujadi's account of the police–peasant encounter. It is late afternoon of 4 February, and the Dumri gathering has just left for Chauri Chaura.

Singing and shouting [*gāwat-bajāwat*] they went at four in the evening; they went to Chauri Chaura through the thāna. The thāna was a tiled structure, this I cannot forget. *And the darogāin was standing. And these people* [*Nazar Ali, Shikari, etc.*] *were on their march, singing and shouting. And the daroga was seated. When they passed the thana the daroga fired . . . And the darogāin was pregnant*; she was standing and reasoning with the daroga to let the crowd go, but he did not pay heed, and fired. [*Darogāin sānpat rahal, minha karat tāri: 'chale jāe do, kāhe ko gōli chalāega, chale jāe do'. Te ee na manlān, na manlān, chala delān.*]

In Naujadi's account the darogāin is the voice of moderation and of justice. The riot occurs *because* the daroga pays no heed to his wife. No doubt she was looted and dishonoured by some of the crowd, but she had given her husband sane advice.

The sequence in Naujadi's story of the darogāin is confusing: In this version the darogāin is both confined for the night in Chauri Chaura and also arrives from Gorakhpur the next morning to speak up for the public [*paulic*]. But there is no doubting the importance of her testimony:

Uhe darogāin! jab unhān-se inhān ailas—char-ke motor-pe gail— 'tekāsi' [taxi]-pe—uhe darogain asal-asal bolali. 'Sarkār! Koi-ka dos(h) nahīn hai, paulic kuch nahīn dos(h) hai; hamāra goli chalāega, hamāra mārega.'

To translate this passage adequately is to prune it of its ambiguity. Naujadi's attempt to mimic the speech of the high-caste darogāin results in grammatical slides, such that the possessive pronoun *hamāra* (mine), in the absence of a qualifier (husband), becomes the subject which causes the riot! 'It was no fault of the public', she is saying to her interlocutors when apprehended. In Naujadi's version the darogāin, witness to a tragic truth, lessens the enormity of a public occurrence by blaming her husband, albeit obliquely.[98] Further, it is the darogāin's critical presence, and intervention, that saves Dumri from ruin: 'But for the darogāin, Dumri would have been totally destroyed.' [*Te darogāin je na rahe te kund par jāe Dumri-Mundera*]. 'Without her there would have been apocalypse [*sarvnāsh*]', is how one person translated this emphatic statement.

We are back here to the theme of the crucial intervention that saves entire localities from utter ruin after the riot. Surviving the aftermath is an important motif in all local remembrances of the event, with varying degrees of extraordinariness attached to it. In the Madanpur narrative, it might be recalled, the saviour is village solidarity *and* a Muslim worthy (*buzurg*);[99] in Mundera it is a patriarch-landlord; in Sita's account it is Madan Mohan Malaviya. With Naujadi, a sympathizing woman, it is the widowed darogāin herself who helps avert the *sarvnāsh* or utter destruction. This last seems a poignant slip of memory in the direction of solidarity with a woman who had suffered much.

29

The Presence of Gandhi

In Dumri the end of the event is remembered for its immediate result, not for its national consequences. Repression, punishment, survival—these are the themes with which Naujadi, Sita and others close their accounts of Chauri Chaura. They do not locate its significance in the grief the riot caused the Mahatma and the brake it put on the fight against the British. None of the relatives of the rioters framed their stories in terms of what 'Chauri Chaura' meant to an ongoing freedom struggle, or to Mahatma Gandhi for that matter. Not that they have no recollection of Gandhi Maharaj. Gandhi's presence in Dumri is in fact so dominant that it has the effect of displacing every other nationalist actor, apart from the local volunteers, from recollections of the event.

Strands of the tie-up with the district headquarters lie scattered throughout the records. The Dumri unit was formally established by Hakeem Arif, a district functionary; Nazar Ali had gone to Gorakhpur with a request for a drill-instructor; Lal Mohammad sent up a written complaint about the beating of volunteers in Mundera bazaar. The Allahabad judges 'strongly suspect[ed]' that the Dumri leaders had in fact acted upon instructions sent out from the district headquarters.[100] Lal Mohammad Sain, who initially arranged Hakeem Arif's visit to Dumri in January, had sent a letter to Gorakhpur after the beating of the volunteers in Mundera bazaar. In this 'report', the Sain from Chaura made the standard gestures of political deference:

We therefore report this matter to you, Sirs, so that you could come over and ascertain for yourself. And it is because of you, Sirs, that we have not taken any offensive action, for we would act only after seeking the advice of [you] our officers [afsars].[101]

Much was made of this letter in the court. The judges suggested that since the confiscated Congress records contained no evidence of a written reply, 'an oral answer was returned [to Chaura] . . . of such a character that those responsible for it could not commit it to writing.'[102] Gorakhpur, in other words, was instrumental in causing the riot at Chauri Chaura.

Important as these events are for historical reconstruction, they seem to have slipped out of local recall. An erasure caused by time, perhaps? Or could it be that those who recounted 'Chauri Chaura' to me were not privy to all that transpired between Dumri and the district? It is significant that in our long conversations, not a single district nationalist's name ever cropped up. It was Gandhi and the volunteers who peopled the Dumri stories. What we have here are mnemonic traces, perhaps, of a desire to construct a world larger than the local, a world of volunteers from which the Gorakhpur superiors are necessarily absent.

There is in fact hardly any place for the District Congress in local accounts of the event. It is Nazar Ali's letter—*tār* (wire) in Sita's words—summoning an urgent meeting at Dumri which is most strongly remembered. No one seems to recall Lal Mohammad's 'report', which is lodged as an exhibit in the court records.[103] Hakeem Arif, the Gorakhpur nationalist, who for the judge 'definitely formed . . . the local . . . Dumri circle . . . of the non-co-operation movement . . . in January 1922',[104] is similarly displaced by the activities of local volunteers. For Naujadi it is an existing band of volunteers, called into being by Gandhi, who confabulate and organize, unaided by people from Gorakhpur (*apne mein log 'kumeti' kail*). The district headquarters is referred to by Naujadi once as the site of the jail, never as the seat of the non-co-operation movement.

In Dumri the district does not count. The volunteers owed their existence directly to Gandhi's personal appearance at the Chauri Chaura railway station on 8 February 1921,[105] eleven months before Nazar Ali, Shikari and others turned full-time volunteers.

In Naujadi's recollection that extraordinary visit is heralded by celestial apparitions—a snake-like figure and two commoner objects appeared over the Mundera-Dumri sky. In response to my question about Gandhi's arrival, Naujadi launches into an intriguing tale of the women lentil-splitters of Mundera being roused from their grindstones by strange stirrings in the sky. These heavenly signs were invariably recognized by their form, but their ominousness was open to debate. The old woman is at some pains to dispel the disbelief that her story might arouse among her listeners. Naujadi begins by eliciting an agreement on some basic propositions first:

Oh regarding Gandhiji! You see sir! Now you are sitting on this cot towards the south, right! And *sirkar* we are labourers, right! . . .

You see! It was the month of Māgh. Everybody is splitting dāl [in special chakkīs in Mundera Bazaar]. It was a bazaar day, Wednesday, or Saturday perhaps. Har-har-har-har [the chakkīs go round and round], everyone is grinding and splitting dāl. And then Babu! From *this* very corner—I am not lying, I tell you—from this very side *it* arose, and then went round and round and round, and formed a complete circle. Then it subsided . . . Like ash, like smoke in the sky it was.

People said it's a python, a python has descended from the hills. There was great commotion. Merchants and brokers, labourers and dāl-grinders, all went to see this *tamāsha*, this sight, from rooftops. Next day a broom [*barhani*] appeared in the southern sky, then a ploughing plank [*henga*]. And then a long twig broom [*kharhara*].*

God save us now! With this kharhara people and their houses will be swept away. No one, nothing will remain, people said.

Unable to understand, all of this, I asked Naujadi to elaborate. 'Everyone will die. All will be lost. It is the end of time [*ant kāl*],' she stressed, raising her voice to effect communication. Sharfuddin, the village headman, tried to link all this to the future catastrophe—the riot, the repression, the deaths and imprisonment—which were to destroy the locality a year later. But for Naujadi the omens, though unsettling, were part of a set of strange happenings. She had heard that shrubs would shoot up into big trees, that and other such happenings would augur Gandhi's arrival in February 1921.†

Sita Ahir, then a twelve-year-old son of a village chaukidar who was at the station with 10,000 others that day, has a more dignified and evocative recollection of Gandhi-Baba: 'Fair, tall and of slight build, he gave a lecture [*bhāshan*].' A few words uttered by Gandhi from the door of a rail carriage here fill up to

---

* *Barhani*: broom used by women when sweeping out the house; *henga*: flat plank dragged along the ground after ploughing, while a man stands on it to give it weight; *kharhara*: broom made of twigs, used for sweeping out leaves and stray rubbish.

† Gandhi's day-long stay in the district on 8 February 1921 was to give rise to fantastic rumours about his 'message', as understood locally. For an analysis, see my 'Gandhi as Mahatma', *Subaltern Studies III*, ed. Ranajit Guha, pp. 1–60.

an entire 'speech', and a brief stopover extends into a day's stay. [*Gandhi-Baba ke dekhle rahlīn. Gora, patra-ke rahlān, lamba. Bhāshan karlān. Bahut bheer! . . . din-bhar ruklān.*]

He had come by train. He stopped over. People from all over had gathered at the station that day. What a crowd! He was surrounded by his servants and attendants [*chākar*]. At the godown-siding west of the station, money and coins [*kaccha paisa, dabbal*] were being thrown from every direction.* He—he was least bothered! Wearing a dhoti as I do, hands folded *like this,* he went round greeting the people. (*Hamre laikhan dhoti karke . . . hāth jore, panchan ke hāth joren.*)

Gandhiji was slightly better built than I. [*Hamse taniye karēr rahlān Gandhiji.*][106]

It was a stupendous welcome, by any account. The train carrying the Mahatma stopped at each and every station on the sixty-mile rail stretch that traversed the district from east to west. A leader of the Gorakhpur Congress reception party would first explain Gandhi's message to these wayside crowds. 'After the din and the excitement had subsided Mahatmaji would appear at the door of his carriage and give his message.' Gandhi refused donations en route; people were advised to deposit their gifts with the District Congress Committee. However, at Chauri Chaura 'a trader managed to hand something over. Then there was no stopping the people', goes the authoritative account of Gandhi's train journey through Gorakhpur. 'A sheet was spread out and currency notes and coins started raining down. It was a sight.'[107]

There is a close correspondence between the authoritative and remembered accounts: donations figure prominently in both. But Sita, significantly, makes Gandhi's train stop at the godown (*mālgodām*), well to the west of the railway station proper. (*Mālgodamiya par, tīsan ke pacchum!*) In a subsequent retelling Sita suggests that Gandhi's carriage was uncoupled at Chauri

* *Kaccha paisa*: the regionally minted copper coin, used locally for small purchases and the payment of bazaar dues in Mundera. 5 kaccha paisa = 1 anna. *Dabbal* ('double'?): the two paisa, or the half-anna, coin. 16 annas = 1 rupee.

Chaura for a few hours. Did the bogie carrying the Mahatma get shunted out to the warehouse, awaiting the next train connection, while the populace milled around it at leisure? There is no evidence of this on record, though on occasion Gandhi's 'compartment was detached [and] . . . drawn up in front of a reserved platform', as happened at Madras Central in September 1920.[108] Should we discount Sita's precise location—'at the warehouse, to the west of the station'—as the site where Gandhi appeared before the people of Chauri Chaura, only because it is a fact omitted from the published account? The unwritten rules of historical evidence would suggest we do. Unsure of the right answer I would push the question a bit further. Why should Sita confuse the māl-godām and the platform, especially when he makes it a point to distinguish between the two?

Sleepy stations like Chauri Chaura were dominated by their godowns.[109] They were built to facilitate links between local production and consumption with the national and world markets. The warehouse precincts could have accommodated the 10,000 who had gathered to greet Gandhi that day. When Sita makes Gandhi's train stop at the warehouse, he enables us to better appreciate the significance of railside bazaars like Chauri Chaura.

The essence of Gandhi's train tours, which he conducted to personally propagate the message of non-co-operation, lay in the stops he invariably made at numerous stations. This afforded 'an expectant and believing people' to 'come from all quarters within walking reach to meet me'—as Gandhi himself put it in October 1920.[110] 'People groaning under misery and insult' flocked to the meetings he addressed at the bigger towns, and so did many more to meet him from 'within walking reach' of railside marts like Chauri Chaura or Gauri Bazaar (to name just two of the seven stops that Gandhi made that day in Gorakhpur district). Sita Ahir, for instance, had to walk just one mile to the mālgodām to be in the presence of Gandhi-Baba. Small stations dominated by ware-houses allowed the nationalist public a far better view of the Mahatma than was accorded by monster meetings like the one Gandhi addressed at Gorakhpur on the afternoon of 8 February 1921.[111]

Gandhi was apparently pleased with the crowd and the money collected at Chauri Chaura, as he was with the reception at the next station, Kusmhi,[112] eight miles up the track in the middle of a jungle that, thirty years earlier, had skirted Chotki Dumri itself. But railway stations were also the sites where the *darshan*-seeking public appeared as mobs to the Mahatma.* These 'insistent and assertive crowds' were bent on viewing and touching Gandhi even when he was asleep, and ended up in a 'tug of war' with his companions. They pulled up the shutters of his carriage, lit up torches to quell the darkness, and demanded that Gandhi show himself. Sometimes they even engaged in a slanging match with the Mahatma—as happened on the journey back from Gorakh-pur. It was these mobs that Gandhi wanted disciplined by trained volunteers.

When large crowds demanded darshan in the middle of the night, after the Gorakhpur train took a turn at Bhatni junction for Banaras, Gandhi lost his temper: 'I got up and peeped through the window . . . It was quite cold but, in my temper, I didn't feel it. I pleaded with the people in a raised voice. Their shouting of slogans grew louder.' To Gandhi's angry question—'How could you expect darshan at night?', the crowd responded with even louder cries: 'Victory to the Mahatma!' 'What was I to do?', Gandhi wrote twelve days later. 'Should I jump from the window? Should I cry? Should I beat any of them? Should I stay back at the station?' Gandhi hit his forehead twice in anger, but with no apparent effect on the unruly people who had gathered at Salem-pur station. Gandhi hit himself for the third time. It was then

---

* *Darshan* : paying homage to a holy object or a saintly person by presenting oneself in the vicinity of the personage.

that 'the people got frightened. They asked me to forgive them, became quiet and requested me to go to sleep.' Gandhi's secretary, who 'could not contain . . . [his] anger . . . had the cheek to tell a lie in the very presence of Gandhiji.'

Many of these devotees do not even know how their 'Mahatma Gandhi' looks. A few of them thrust themselves into our compartment, and began to bawl out, 'Who is Mahatma Gandhiji? Who is Mahatma Gandhiji?' I got desperate and said 'I'. They were satisfied, bowed down to me and left the compartment.[113]

Gandhi had formulated elaborate rules for the shepherding of such unruly demonstrators. Large crowds were not to be allowed inside railway stations, and people were to be let in just before 'the notified time of arrival' of Gandhi's train. 'Demonstrators' were to keep 'motionless and silent', and move only under a 'pre-arranged signal from an authorized volunteer.' Shouts of 'Victory to Gandhi' (and to the Nation) were not to be raised till after the arrival of the train.[114] The reception recounted by Sita Ahir and the midnight madness at Salempur suggest that people at railway stations were quite literally seeing their Mahatma in their own ways, unmindful of the disciplinary cordon that Gandhi had advocated at such sites! To see the unruly platform people only through the bleary eyes of Gandhi is to miss out the Mahatma that got fabricated at and on the way to smaller stations.

'When Mahatma Gandhi was going back on the night of 8 February from Gorakhpur . . . there was a huge gathering at Salempur station to have his darshan', reported a local correspond-ent in the nationalist weekly *Swadesh*. There was a Barai lad in that gathering. 'It is said that he had asked the wife of a high-caste Brahmin for a [cloth] wrapper to come to the station. She reprimanded him and refused to give him the blanket. The poor soul came shivering to the station, had darshan of the Mahatma and went back.' But the suffering of that young boy—'it was quite cold' that night, though Gandhi in his anger at the darshan-demanding crowd 'didn't feel it'—had become a part of a story. Next morning the village was agog with the rumour that shit was raining all over the house of that mean, anti-Gandhian woman who had denied the boy a blanket. This demeaning punishment was not the end of the story: 'In the end, only when she kept a fast and did ritual praying to the Mahatma did peace finally return to her.'[115]

In Gandhi's own account of the encounter with the Salempur mob, the hero is a local gentleman-nationalist who 'at every station . . . would plead with the people, restrain their eagerness for darshan and persuade them to remain quiet'.[116] In the south-eastern corner of the district, it is this young low-caste lad who goes out into the cold to the nearby station where Gandhi would stop, and, by his personal suffering, humbles a foul-mouthed sceptic—it is the son of the Barai who is the hero for having sought the Mahatma out.

The things that occurred at the station—i.e. Gandhi lost his temper, he beat his forehead thrice in anger and thus frightened people into leaving him alone—seem to have been immaterial to the way the Mahatma's presence was felt in the nearby villages. Gandhi's story of his encounter with the Gorakhpuri mobs is enshrined in his *Collected Works*: it forms a part of the discourse of discipline. The stories of the *individuals* who sought Gandhi leaked out that night into an eddy of rumours about the Great One, adding to an imaginative crafting of the figure of Mahatma Gandhi.

'Gandhiji was only slightly better-built than I', [*Hamse taniye karēr rahlān Gandhiji*] recalled the eighty-year-old Sita, establishing a physical connection between the people of Dumri and the author of non-co-operation. Naujadi for her part makes another link between Gandhi and his otiyars. Her account commences: 'To begin with, all were otiyars in Chauri Chaura; when Gandhi Maharaj's raj came, there were otiyars.' [*Chauri Chaura mein pahile sab otiyar rahlān; Gandhi-Mahatma ke jab rāj āil— otiyar rahlān.*]

The phrase about the Mahatma is significant, for it makes the otiyars contemporaneous with Gandhi-raj. This is a novel perspective on the Rule of Gandhi. Gandhi's raj is then not an impending event which had to be divined by a reading of its signs, nor is it an object attainable by militant means.[117] For Ramesharvolunteer's wife the time of the otiyars *was* the time of Gandhi-raj. The proximity created by Gandhi at the Chauri Chaura station on 8 February 1921, 'wearing a dhoti as I do' (Sita), paradoxically left no room for the District Congress Committee.

The presence of Gandhi in Gorakhpur seems to have left no separate space for Shaukat Ali and Mohammad Ali, the two charismatic leaders of the Khilafat movement, aligned to his non-co-operation campaign in India. We know from records of individuals, 'reading out Gandhiji's books and displaying Shaukat Ali's picture along with Gandhi's at Bhopa', the makeshift leather trading bazaar where a large contingent of Muslim peasants and traders and Chamar tanners congregated every Saturday. Mohammad Ali had also made that train journey to Gorakhpur along with Gandhi on 8 February 1921 and addressed the massive meeting at the district headquarters. In the countryside, however, the enthusiasm generated for the Khilafat cause and its high profile leaders was not separate from the popular regard for Mahatma Gandhi. At the Dumri meeting on the morning of the riot, a man 'wearing green glasses', whom Shikari could not identify but 'who from his words appeared to be a Musalman' came forward and 'began to read from a slip of paper', singing a song exhorting the gathering to embrace imprisonment, like Mohammad and Shaukat Ali, for two years' each. The man slipped away after the song, but the crowd which had been bound together by oath by

Nazar Ali started its march to the thana to the cry of 'Victory to Mahatma Gandhi'. The pan-Islamic cause of Khilafat and the Indian fascination with the Mahatma were compounded in Dumri that day.[118]

Just as Gandhi was associated in Gorakhpur with a variety of miraculous occurrences—'We have not seen the miracles of the Mahatma; we have only heard of them', testified Sukhari, an accused of Amahiya village, in court[119]—so did his name lend itself as a label for all sorts of public meetings, pamphlets, and of course for that polysemic word 'Swaraj'. Lal Mohammad of Chaura sold two sets of 'announcements in Urdu', most probably exhortations to oppose the British published by the Khilafat Committee of Gorakhpur, 'which he said were Gandhiji's paper'. Shikari who bought one such appeal in November 1921, priced at a low 2 and 4 pice each, was told 'to take the paper and return it when *Gandhiji asked for it*'.[120] The receipt for the more substantial donations to the Khilafat fund, which bore a superficial resemblance to a one-rupee bank note, though much larger in size, was referred to as a 'Gandhi note' by the peasants of Gorakhpur. Villagers, pro-government sources alleged, interpreted its non-acceptance (as legal tender?) as an act of opposition to the Mahatma.[121] Whether peasants genuinely failed to recognize the difference (as officials in some Awadh districts implied),[122] or whether this was just a conscious manipulation of an ambiguous printed paper to force non-believers into acceptance, we do not know for certain. What is clear, however, is that we have in the 'Gandhi note' an index of the popular tendency to look upon the Mahatma as an alternative source of authority.

However, as local-level volunteer activity entered a more militant phase in late 1921, the coming of Swaraj was perceived— contrary to everything the Congress stood for at that time—in terms of the direct supplanting of the authority of the police.[123] Thus Sarju Kahar, the personal servant of the thanedar of Chaura, testified that 'two or four days before the affair [he] had heard that Gandhi Mahatma's Swaraj had been established, that the Chaura thana would be abolished, and that the volunteers would set up their own thana.'[124]

As the High Court judges observed, the local peasantry 'perceived of it [Swaraj] as a millennium in which taxation would be limited to the collection of small cash contributions or dues in kind from fields and threshing floors, and [in] which the cultivators would hold their lands at little more than nominal rents.'[125] While recruiting volunteers to the newly formed Dumri mandal in January 1922, Nazar Ali and Shikari appear to have held out such promises. 'Shikari and Nazar Ali told me to become a volunteer', testified Sampat Chamar, a labourer from Chaura. 'Shikari told me I would get 2 or 3 bighas of land [at low rent] if I got myself enrolled . . . So I became a volunteer.'[126] Thakur Ahir, the second approver, was promised a substantial reduction in his rent, and also a volunteer's salary just below the current daily wage rate:

Nazar Ali and Shikari and a small boy [Nackched Kahar, the school boy who filled the forms] made me a volunteer . . . I became a volunteer because I was told that the Maharaj's [Gandhi] Swaraj would come and I should [only] have to pay 4 annas a bigha, and would get Rs 8 pay a month.[127]

Surveying the background to the Chauri Chaura riot, the judges of the High Court found it 'remarkable . . . how this name of "Swaraj" was linked, in the minds of the peasantry of Gorakhpur, with the name of Mr Gandhi. Everywhere in the evidence and in the statements made . . . by various accused persons', they found that 'it was "Gandhiji's Swaraj", or the "Mahatmaji's Swaraj" for which they [i.e. the peasants] were looking.'[128] We have it on local testimony that peasant volunteers proceeding to a sabha at Dumri on the morning of 4 February 1922 (hours before the clash with police was to occur at the Chaura thana, a couple of miles away), claimed that they were 'going to hold a Gandhi Mahatma Sabha' which would bring about 'Gandhi Swaraj'.[129]

What is significant is that the phrase 'Gandhiji's swaraj has come' was used as an exhortation for each and every reversal that the Dumri volunteers brought about that day. When the daroga tried to save the day by apologizing to the crowd and letting it move towards Mundera bazaar, 'then the gathering clapped their hands', jeered that the daroga was 'shit scared', and said 'Gandhiji's swaraj had come to pass'. Once the police had sought to recover the lost ground by firing and the crowd had begun brickbatting and clubbing the policemen, leaders like Lal Moham-mad and Meghu Tiwari were reported to have shouted: 'Kill the sister-fucker-policemen, Swaraj has come. Burn the thana.' 'Until the thana has been burnt and the police have been killed, there will not be Gandhiji's swaraj', another man rushing in to join the riot was reported shouting.[130]

According to Harbans Kurmi of Mangapatti, Narayan, Bal-eshar and Chamru of his village said on their return from the riot that 'they had burnt and thrown away and Swaraj had come'.[131] Or, as Phenku Chamar told the sessions judge in August 1922:

Bipat Kahar, Sarup Bhar and Mahadeo Bhuj were coming along calling out 'Gandhi Maharaj, Gandhi Maharaj' from the north, the direction of Chaura, to [the] south, the direction of Barhampur. I asked why they were calling out 'Gandhi Maharaj' and they said the thana of Chaura had been burnt and razed to the ground [by them] and the Maharaj's swaraj had come.[132]

Of course, all this evidence was produced in the court so as to prove a connection between public proclamations made by in-dividual accused and the crimes for which they were jointly on trial. But this is not reason enough to disregard these paradoxical and cruel cries in the name of Gandhi. First, several analyses of contemporary volunteer activity in other parts of north India suggest that peasant-nationalists were invoking the Mahatma to rough up opponents, punish waverers, and attack bazaars and police stations.[133] Second, the foregoing discussion of the presence of Gandhi suggests that the issue of violence apart, the Mahatma of the peasants was not as he really was but as they had thought him up. This is the case in the villages around Chauri Chaura even today.

Ramji, an untouchable and therefore living in the segregated Chamar quarters on the outskirts of the village, remembers Gandhi's arrival and his message with a profanity that ends up implicating the Mahatma with the riotous actions of the Dumri volunteers!

This son of Puranmasi Chamar (convicted for eight years), Ramji came to know 'Gandhi Maharaj' only after seeing him. He did not know about him earlier. And Gandhi Maharaj,

did he leave a single village untouched? Oh no! And what did he tell everybody? Just this much: 'Fucking-hell! take back your raj; turn out these mother-fuckers; kick out the Englishman!' In every village this is what people talked, thought and agreed on. You know, this business about the thana—the burning etc.,—all this leads back to him, to Gandhi Maharaj! [*Are hamman unke, Gandhi Maharāj ke ta bād mein jiyānal gailīn: magar pahilwān hamman nāhin jāni, magar Gandhi Maharāj ekko gāwn chorēn! Khāli ehe kahen, ekar bahin-chodo ee raj āpan le la, aa eke sāle ke khed da . . . angrej ke kheda! Ehe te hokhe gāwn-gāwn sarmatiya, uho gaur karen. Hai thanwa-onwa ākhir unhi ke jari se jaral.*]

At least in this account, everything, including the violence, seems to derive from Gandhi!

It may be argued that it is because of the riot that Ramji Chamar remembers Mahatma Gandhi in such an obscenely violent way. However, there is other evidence to suggest that the Dumri volunteers, in their attempts to do 'Gandhi Mahatma's work',[134] were equipping themselves in a markedly different fashion. Months before the clash with the police, the ways of Nazar Ali and his associates were already at variance with, and often in actual opposition to, the dictates of the Mahatma and the requirements of the District Congress Committee of Gorakhpur.

We therefore turn to the image of the volunteer in Dumri village to chart the career of Nazar Ali, Shikari and others before the picketing of fish, meat and liquor shops began; before Bhagwan Ahir, returned soldier turned volunteer, was beaten by the police inspector; before Nazar Ali sent letters to other volunteers inviting them to a meeting at Dumri on the morning of 4 February to 'stop the Mundera bazaar after paying our respects to the daroga'.

30

Otiyars

An otiyar (volunteer) was one who begged for his food and who wore *gerua* (safflower-coloured) clothes.

That is how Naujadi began her account on 18 August 1988. It was raining appropriately in patches, for the lunar asterism [*nakshatra*] was Maggha, and all of us—a small inquisitive set—were sitting in the tiled verandah [*osāra*] of Shikari's old house. Sharfuddin, Shikari's son and the elected village chief had asked Sita and Naujadi, the two surviving witnesses to Chauri Chaura, to come over to his house. Besides Sharfuddin and myself, there was Shikari's four-year-old grandson, Shikari's daughter Jaibul, Sita Ahir, Naujadi, and a couple of young men from the village. The interview with Sita had concluded for the day; it was Naujadi's turn to speak. She said:

'In the beginning there were otiyars in Chauri Chaura. When Gandhi Mahatma's raj came there were otiyars. They asked for alms'. Shikari Babu, 'this gentleman's father', Naujadi points to Sharfuddin, 'was there; Nazar Ali was there, Salamat-father-in-law [*bhasur*] was there; Nageshar, my *devar* [husband's younger brother] was there; Rameshar was there.' Naujadi, taken in by this roll call uncharacteristically identifies her husband by his first name and not by the euphemism *hamār parāni* (lit. 'my life'). 'And Awdhi was there. I am telling you the story of *that* time.' With this temporal emphasis, Naujadi comes round to identifying the otiyars by their attributes. First they got organized, they got together and discussed things (lit. 'did some "committeeing"') among themselves (*apne mein log Kumeti kail*). And like beggars asking for alms (*bhīk*), they asked for a pinch of grain [*chutki*]. 'They had flags, pink, no gerua long shirts (*kurta*), caps, flags.' She now turns to the otiyar's uniform.

Chauri Chaura mein pahile sab otiyar rahlān. Gandhi-Mahatma ke jab rāj āil—otiyar rahlān. Bhīk māngat rahlān. Babu-ke dāda rahlān.[135] *Ohmen Shikari-babu rahlān, Najar Ali rahlān, Salamat-bhasur rahlān . . . Sahadat rahlān, Nagesar, hamre devar rahlān, Ramesar rahlān, Awadhi rahlān . . . Sun tāni! Oh-samay ke bāt ba!*

Okre bād mein inhān-se Sarkār jab apne-mein log 'kumeti' kail, aa chutki māngat rahal, te ohi-mein khāt-o rahlān aa dharāt-o rahal . . . Mane khāt-o apne-mein rahlān, aur dhara-jāt rahal jo besi ho.

Khariyāni nāhīn lēt rahlān.[136] *Jaise bhikmanga chutki māngele na? Mānge-lān bhīk!!—Ohi-tarah log bhīk māngat rahlān.*

Jhanda rahal, gulābi-kurta rahal—gerua-rang; dhoti rahal, topi rahal, aa jhanda rahal.

In Naujadi's mind chutki, bhīk and gerua clothes together distinguished the otiyars of Chauri Chaura.

31

Chutki, or the Gift of Grain

'They would come abegging and ask for a pinch of grain', says Naujadi, wife of Rameshar Pasi of Chotki Dumri. Demanding chutki was regarded as evidence of a volunteering past in the court as well. However, chutki was here so closely associated with *chanda* (subscription) as to have become synonymous with it. 'We were all told to collect subscriptions [*chanda* and *chutki*]' is how Shikari's implicit distinction between these two was blurred in the official record of the trial.[137] In the judicial probe, chutki was one fact among many by which the accused were identified as volunteers: donning a Gandhi cap, patrolling the village at night, 'behaving as a policeman' at a fair or a gathering, signing the pledge form—all these formed the set of incriminating evidence.[138]

With Naujadi it was chutki that mattered most. It was what distinguished a real otiyar from a nominal one: her brother-in-law from her husband, for example:

Otiyar khāli uhe, chotka [Nageshar-devar] rahal. [As for Rameshar, her husband?]: Are likhaule rahlān, mane māngat nāhīn rahlān. Uu [Nagesar] māngat rahal—gerua . . . sab pahir le-lena, lugga-kapra. [Ramesar] khāli likhaule-bhar rahlān.

Translated, this is roughly what she says: 'It was only he—Nageshar—the younger one, who was the otiyar. As for Rameshar, well, he had himself enrolled but never asked for chutki. Nageshar, he would ask for it, he had gerua clothes, the works.'

It was chutki-begging and not enrolment that made a volunteer. And the volunteers asked for chutki, *like beggars*, Naujadi stresses, her voice rising in exasperation at my inability immediately to grasp the meaning of the term. 'Send out a pinch of flour, mother! [*Bhejyo māi, chutki*]' was in fact a mendicant's cry in north India.[139] The housewife, before cooking the day's food, would set aside some lentils, rice or flour as her share for volunteers. It was not so much the reason as the reasonableness of the demand —'they did not come for it everyday, did they? [*rōj nāhīn-na kahēn? . . . dusre-tisre din diyāt rahal*]—that Naujadi remembers. Out of the chutki so collected, every third day or so the volunteers would cook their own food; the surplus chutki they would stock up.

This short paraphrase of Naujadi's long statement on chutki provides a housewife's view of the Chauri Chaura volunteers.[140] Nationalism in the guise of the alms-seeking volunteer appeared literally outside Naujadi's door: '*Aa hamār duāre-pe aa-ke khara hoilān bhikmanga! Hamre jo-kuch jutal: chāur-dāl jutal, pisān jutal, diyāi.*' Whatever could be managed, she says—rice, lentils, flour— I gave. Since the peasant household parted with a portion of its food, it fell to the housewife to make arrangements for the upkeep of these full-time peripatetic volunteers.[141] They were not given the leftovers, as was 'the stated rule' with *sanyāsīs*;[142] otiyars claimed a fraction of the food at the point at which it was to be cooked by the housewife [*grihasthin*].*

Chutki lay in the domain of the domestic. This pinch of grain was what the peasant family volunteered from its own consumption. And unlike *khalihāni* or harvest dues collected periodically at the threshing floor, chutki-giving tied recipients and donors in a continual, quotidian relationship. In local parlance chutki was not a *hak* (a right) but *bhīk* (alms); its recipient was a beggar-like person, not a superordinate claimant.

Chutki-giving for non-ascetic or political purposes was not novel in the region: the militant kine protection leagues that had emerged in the 1890s to safeguard the Hindu community's holy

---

* *Grihasthini* in its proper Sanskritic rendition.

cows from being slaughtered by butchers and at Muslim religious ceremonies had laid down elaborate chutki-gathering rules.* 'Each household was directed to set apart at each meal one chutki (equal in weight or value to one paisa) of foodstuff for each member of the family.' And in keeping with the cow-centred discipline of the sabhas, 'the eating of food without setting apart the chutki' was tantamount to eating beef! *Sabhāsads* (agents) were deputed to garner these contributions. They were to convert chutki-grain into hard cash and remit the money to regional treasurers.[143]

An analogous network of converting chutki to cash and its onward transmission to headquarters was proposed by the Gorakhpur Congress Committee in 1921. In a front-page notice, *Swadesh*, the nationalist weekly, exhorted 'each and every village . . . claiming faith in Mahatma Gandhi' to 'take out *chutki . . .* and *khalihāni*'.[144] Raghupati Sahai, who became the famous poet Firaq Gorakhpuri in later years, was initially in-charge of these collections. Maulvi Subhanullah, the District Congress President, replaced him in May 1921. In a public notice Firaq enjoined 'one or two persons in every village to take responsibility for the collection of *muthia* and *khalihāni*'. Responsible individuals were to sell the chutki-grain 'in the village or a nearby bazaar' and forward the cash by money order to the District Congress Committee in Gorakhpur. The preferred mode was for collectors to come over to the headquarters and deposit the cash personally.[145] Chutki Registers were in existence in villages like Burha Dih near Pipraich, and in Padrauna tahsil.[146] Small wonder then that the 1921–2 budget of the District Congress had estimated an income of Rs 5 lakhs from chutki-muthia collections. A realization rate of ½ *chatānks* chutki daily per house of 10 persons, with a 33 per cent 'discount for unrealized houses', when sold at an average rate of 12 seers to the rupee, yielded an annual value of Rs 5,09,352

---

* Such chutki or *muthia* (*mutthi*: fist) collections could, for instance, support full-time Sanskrit students at an informal *pathshāla*. For an example from north Bihar, see Rahul Sankrityayan, *Meri Jeevan Yatra*, i (Kalkutta, 1951), p. 21.

for the entire district.[147] The rate of conversion was arrived at keeping in mind the different foodstuffs—*pisān, chaur, dāl* in Naujadi's composite phrase—that were offered as chutki. As the secretary, Gorakhpur Town Congress Committee, told the court, 'various corns [*sic*] were collected in the handfuls [*muthia*], so it was considered that they will sell for 12 standard seers to the rupee.'[148]

For the Congress Committee chutki was a subscription; it was another name for chanda. It had to be collected, forwarded and accounted for. Lists of authorized chutki and chanda collectors were often published in nationalist newspapers;[149] district accounts ledgers have such entries as 'direct muthia from a Salempur village, Rs 7–12'.[150] Chutki or muthia collections were certainly not meant for the upkeep of local volunteers—there was no provision for this in the budget for 1921–2.[151] When Hakeem Arif came to Dumri on 13 January, 'he told Lal Mohammad and Nazar Ali and (Shikari) to make over to Bhagwati Bania the subscriptions . . . (*chanda* and *chutki*) collected by us.'[152] This order, Shikari testified in court, was not obeyed. 'Collections . . . made by Lal Mohammad and Nazar Ali' were 'apparently embezzled', said the judge, basing himself on the approver's testimony.[153]

32

The Feast of 4 February 1922

A ll this is a far cry from Naujadi's idea of chutki. Chutki for Naujadi was what sustained full-time volunteers. It was not a contribution meant for ultimate deposit in the District Congress treasury.[154] Naujadi's otiyars in fact straddled the distance that separated chutki, a public levy, from chanda, a nationalist subscription. The surplus chutki was laid aside (*dharāt rahal*) in the village for a suitable public use.[155] According to Naujadi, the big Dumri gathering of 4 February feasted on the chutki collected by the volunteers of Chauri Chaura. Shikari in his statement did not mention the storage and the feast. He alluded, however, to the *gur* or raw sugar that had been collected for the meeting.[156] Naujadi maintained that it was a regular feast (and not 'modest provisions', as the judge noted) that took place on the day of the clash with the police:

I mean sweets were there, vegetables were there, rice and dāl, this-and-that was there. All this was cooked, they ate, they drank, and only then did they move. [*Aré mītha āil rahal, mane mītha, tarkāri āil rahal, dāl-chāur āil rahal, dūsar-tīsar āil rahal . . . banal, khailān-piyalān, tab uthlān.*]

It is difficult to miss the hyperbole in this statement. But it is precisely such excess of description that enables Naujadi to underscore the public and festive nature of that gathering. Here, issues were debated, food consumed, oaths administered and the march to the thana commenced amidst fanfare.

Are you listening! In the month of Māgh there was a gathering here. [*Suni! te Māgh-ke mahinna mein inhān bator bhail.*] It is the same month now! There was a gathering; everybody came. All the chutki that had been kept—all that chutki—was sent to the *kāli-māi-ke-thān**. It was at that place that the feast took place [*Ohi-ja banal bhandāra*]. They ate and drank; thick, real thick garlands were prepared; and then the drums [*dholaks*] started their song.

It was from such a meeting that the otiyars marched, singing and shouting, on to the thana.[157] Note the effervescent nature of the Dumri sabha; and note specially the feast that Naujadi repeatedly emphasizes. Brought up on a diet of Indian anthropology, I wanted to know whether the grain was cooked or offered un-cooked, *sattu*-like.[158] At this Naujadi lost her patience:

Now, whether they cooked it or consumed it uncooked [*kaccha*], this I did not see with my own eyes. I didn't see who ate and who didn't, did I? It was in his house—in Mir Shikari's house . . . and in Salamat's house [Shikari's daughter's in-laws'] that all the stuff was kept . . .

Everybody, young and old [*larka, parāni, manahi*], everybody carted the stuff away. Whether people cooked it and ate it, or they didn't eat it—the stuff left [Shikari's] house.

'I am telling you, all the grain was sent for the feast [*Ajji! sajji jinisiya gail khāe-piye ke; Bhandāra mein chal gail!*].' The construction of this passage is significant: it is not as if the grain was kept in a storehouse (*bhandār*); in fact, on the morning of 4 February it was sent out to the *bhandāra*.† Now, bhandāra means both a 'storehouse' and a 'feast' (of jogis, sanyasis, etc.). '*Bāba-ka bhandāra bhar-pūr rahe*' was a benediction of plenitude that alms-seeking mendicants showered on householders. The beggar's second cry, '*Mhāre bhandāre mein sājha kar-ke māi, mhāre bhandāre mein*' was an invitation to the alms-giving housewife to share in the mendicant's feast/storehouse in the next world.[159] In Nau-jadi's recall chutki and bhandāra unite the individual volunteer to

---

* The village threshing floor (*khalihān*) was also known as Kali-mai-ka-thān, after the small Kali temple, laying adjacent to it.

† A sister word, *bhandāri*, is still used in Mundera for Sant Baksh Singh's provisioning of the police raiding parties after the riot.

other volunteers and to the 'paulic' (public) at large. The bhīk given to the otiyars remained in the village, but it made a substantial contribution to the success of a major political meeting.

Do the terms bhīk, chutki and bhandāra suggest that Naujadi's otiyars should be thought of as sadhus and sanyāsīs, renouncers and religious mendicants? I do not think so, for several reasons. First, during her long exposition on chutki Naujadi nowhere employed these familiar terms. She repeatedly used the descriptive *bhikmanga* (beggar), not Baba, which is the generic term for a religious mendicant. '*Baba duāre mānge dāl-o-pisān ho!*' is how a Bhojpuri poet was to describe the usual chutki-seeking ascetics of eastern UP.[160] Naujadi, however, refrained from characterizing Nazar Ali, Shikari or Nageshar, her brother-in-law, as Babas in nationalist garb. Even when someone glossed over her comment on gerua clothes with the stock phrase, '*vairāgya mein aa gaye*' [they appeared as ascetics], she did not nod her head in assent. For Naujadi the chutki-seekers of 1922 were political activists from the village: all householders whom she knew, and whose physical strength and organizational skill she admired. They begged bhikmanga-like for chutki,[161] but that did not make them sanyāsīs or ascetics.

Volunteer—a new idea—comes into the village. This term is neither translated into the standard Hindi, *swayam sevak*, nor absorbed into the more common baba or sanyāsī. The word is peasantized. It would not help to translate this peasantization, namely otiyar, any further. The cultural significance of this term would in fact be denied if we failed to accept that peasants play with, transfer and transform alien concepts into idioms which fit with their daily lives. We don't gain anything by translating one native term into another. So, it would help to stay with Naujadi's otiyars for a little bit longer.

33

The Colour Gerua and Proper
Nationalist Attire

The chutki-seekers of Naujadi wore *gulābi* (pink) or gerua clothes. In our second meeting in February 1989, Naujadi elaborated on the coloured clothes of the volunteers:

When Gandhi-Baba came—what did he give [us]? He took out [*karhlān*] otiyars. Otiyars he took out. He first sent word that people should become otiyars. Red, black—no, not black—red—geru . . . everything geru. Then the cap was got dyed, this, whatsitsname, dhoti, was got dyed. And this big flag and lāthi . . . And the flag was used for gathering chutki.

Now the dyeing of dhotis was not the norm in eastern UP and Bihar. Markīn, i.e. machine-made cloth with the distinguishing mark of a Lancashire or Bombay mill, was the cloth most used for dhotis, and it was usually white.[162] Shikari's uncle recalled seeing 'a large number of men' going towards the thana, 'some with yellow and *some with ordinary cloth*'.[163] Where white was the norm, the dyeing of cloth had a special significance attached to it. Dhotis are still dyed primarily for marriages and other ceremonies, and they are dyed by the *rangrez*, the professional dyer commonly pronounced angrez! Buchanan-Hamilton, that trusted companion of medieval and modern historians, comes in handy here. 'The dyers in most parts of the district', he wrote in his notice on Bhagalpur,

are chiefly employed to dye the clothes of those who attend marriage parties . . . and during the three months that the ceremonies last, the

dyers make very high wages; but at other times they have little employment.

    [Those in the town of Munger] dye chiefly with safflower, with
which they give two colours, kusami [*kusumbi*: cloth dyed with safflower, *s.v.* Fallon], a bright pomegranate red, and Golabi a fine red like
rose; and each colour is of two different shades . . . The safflower,
Carthamus tinctorious or kusum is most in demand.[164]

Gulābi, lāl and geru were used interchangeably by Naujadi; in the
court records gerua bastar, red, or simply 'coloured clothes' described the *pahirāwa* (dress) of the Chauri Chaura volunteers.[165]
In fact the various volunteer corps, as they sprang up in the early
1920s, revealed a marked preference for coloured uniforms.[166] An
intelligence report noted that 'the yellow [gerua] shirt' was specially popular among the volunteers in UP. In North Bihar,
nationalist battalions were dressed in *khaddar* of 'yellow *rāmraj*
colour'. Rahul Sankrityayan, who raised one such unit of
'*rangīn vardi-dhāri swayam-sevaks*', also tried his hand at dyeing
by looking up the nationalist-chemist P.C. Ray's book on
colour.[167] The Bihar Sewak Dal, formed in late-1921 to foment
rebellion (*baghāwat*), had a wide range of coloured uniforms:
white for Hajipur, red for Muzaffarpur and green dhotis for those
enlisting in Sitamarhi district.[168] The UP Provincial Volunteer
Board, for its part, reserved these swaraj colours for shoulder
straps; it recommended kusumbi and *zāfrani* (safflower and saffron) as the preferred colours for khaddar uniforms.[169] All this was
in total disregard of Gandhi's express instructions on proper
nationalist attire.

    For Gandhi the satyagrahi had to wear white khaddar;
coloured clothes were out at least until swaraj was attained. The
Mahatma was willing to compromise on certain things: one's
bedding, for instance, could still be of 'foreign or mill-made cloth',
as there were 'difficulties in the way of immediate self-purification
to this extent'.[170] No such difficulty was countenanced for khaddar
as apparel. Those who could not afford to buy khaddar worth

Rs 5–10 for their clothes 'could certainly borrow this amount . . . and become volunteer(s)'.[171] It was not 'at all difficult', wrote Gandhi in late 1921, to 'use khadi for one's clothes'. A 'very poor man' could 'limit himself to a loin cloth, but this should be of khadi'.[172]

The importance of khadi consisted in three qualities: sparseness, coarseness and whiteness. Handloom silk and woollen clothes were to be abjured, except 'when . . . required by climatic or other urgent considerations . . . The fashion certainly should be . . . to wear coarse khaddar'.[173] The clothes of the Gandhian volunteer had to be coarse khaddar and white. 'India will lose nothing by wearing only white clothes for some time to come. Let them fill in colours after they have, clad in white, achieved their goal', Gandhi quoted approvingly from an unlikely source. He added: 'We wear white khaddar because we have no time to get it dyed. Moreover, many of us do not like colours, as they are of foreign make.'[174]

In early 1922, at the height of the volunteer movement (96,000 had signed up in UP alone), Gandhi's instructions on proper khaddar-wear were being ignored. 'Hardly 50 could be found dressed in hand-spun khaddar from top to toe' in Allahabad and Banaras. Others 'wore khaddar for outer covering, all the rest being foreign cloth'.[175] In Calcutta, Gandhi ruefully catalogued 'hundreds who have gone to jail know nothing about the pledge, are not dressed in khaddar, are not dressed even in Indian mill-made cloth but have gone to jail wearing foreign cloth, and . . . they have had no training in non-violence.'[176]

34

What the Otiyars Wore

The picture in Chauri Chaura was no different. For Naujadi it was Gandhi all right who had created volunteers, but she was clearer that the otiyars wore gerua than that it was khaddar.[177] In enquiries and testimonies khaddar and gerua often appear as exclusive categories. A report on the occurrence published in the *Pioneer* spoke of a 3000-strong 'procession . . . headed by *four or five volunteers in khaddar uniform*'.[178] The unofficial Congress Enquiry talked in turn about 'five or six hundred volunteers' all 'clad in gerua-coloured clothes . . . accompanied by a large crowd'.[179] In the first version it was texture, in the second colour, which marked a Chauri Chaura volunteer.

At innumerable places in the court records we get the equation gerua clothes = volunteers.[180] Bhagwan Ahir, himself a leading actor, stated: 'some [were] dressed in white and *some dressed as volunteers*'.[181] Nazar Ali was identified 'as a volunteer as he was in front of the crowd and *was wearing gerua cloth.*'[182] It was not as if no one wore khaddar. Dwarka Pandey of Barhampur mandal was in his khaddar dhoti-kurta when he was put up for identification in the district jail. The magistrate had to make special arrangements—two persons were asked to don khaddar clothes and stand beside Dwarka—to make the identification proceedings seem fair to the accused.[183] But even Dwarka, reminiscing fifty years later, talked about 'a 400-strong contingent of gerua-clad volunteers supervising the conduct of the 5000-strong crowd'.[184]

The distinction between colour and texture breaks down in several recollections in the courtroom. Meghu Tiwari, the chief villain involved in dishonouring the darogāin, was denounced as a volunteer who 'used to wear gerua-khaddar . . . before . . . [and] on Chaura riot day'.[185] Identifying eight men from his village, Mahatam of Kusmhi testified: 'They were all dressed in gerua khaddar. They told me they were going to Dumri sabha. *Volunteers wear gerua cloth*'.[186] We are back once again to gerua as the distinguishing marker.

Sarju Kahar, a domestic servant at the thana, was certain that 'the volunteers had on gerua cloth and were crying Mahatmaji's jai. The four men I identified had on gerua cloth'.[187] One of these, Bhagwan Ahir, the subaltern pensioner from the Mesopotamia campaign, was not wearing gerua. On 4 February Bhagwan was sporting, as usual, his 'khaki sarkari coat', appropriate attire for the drill-master of Chaura volunteers. Bhagwan, it seems, never took his jacket off, even while in hiding. Constable Jai Ram arrested him on 10 March in the northern jungle by the river Gandak 'because of his [khaki] uniform'.[188] Such was the metonymic connection gerua/otiyar that Sarju Kahar persisted in identifying Bhagwan-volunteer by his non-existent gerua clothes.

The association of otiyars with a particular colour was so strong that in the courtroom reconstruction of the riot those proved to be wearing white clothes were presumed to be spectators and not volunteers! The counsels for the accused spent considerable time getting the approvers to admit to this distinction between geru and white. 'I meant by "spectators" the people who were wearing white, not coloured clothes', Shikari stated at the beginning of his cross-examination. The Defence pushed him further:

I considered the persons wearing coloured clothes to be volunteers. And I thought the persons who were not wearing coloured clothes were not volunteers. Among those 4000 [outside the thana] were volunteers, non-volunteers and spectators.[189]

Thakur, the second approver, also stated under cross-examination: 'the volunteers had on ochre-coloured clothing [*gerua bastar*].'[190]

These were not abstract characterizations. What the approvers made of a man's attire was a matter of life and death for the person in the dock. Shikari had named Shahadat as 'taking part in the riot', but was unclear about his volunteer status. Under cross-examination Shikari replied that Shahadat of Dumri was 'not a volunteer *because* he wore white clothes'. The judge seemed to agree. Among other reasons, Shahadat's clothes were the reason why Holmes of Gorakhpur 'did not think it . . . safe to convict him'.[191] Clothes like Shahadat's testified to the presence of non-volunteers and spectators in the crowd. White, coarse khaddar was not a markedly nationalist sign in Chauri Chaura.

What significance do we ascribe to gerua then? How much 'reflexivity' was there in the wearing of these garments? Were the volunteers conscious that their clothes were different from those prescribed by the Mahatma?

The emphasis on gerua need not imply that the Gandhian creed was thereby divested of all meaning. Naujadi's heroes were clearly imbued with the idea of Gandhi. 'Otiyar' they conceived of as a novel category, a state requiring marked changes in living and attire: witness Nazar Ali, who had sold off his tailoring business ever since he became a volunteer-activist in early 1922.[192] Dyeing their clothes yellow—rather than wearing white and proper khaddar—and doing Gandhi's bidding were not incompatible practices for the Dumri nationalists.

So, for Naujadi and many others, chutki and gerua defined the volunteers.[193] True, these terms have histories of their own.[194] But the old woman has no urge to hurl her otiyars back into the enveloping fold of a context-free meaningful past. Naujadi remembers them in relation to a specific present: 'the time of Gandhi-raj and of the turmoil [*utpāt*] we [*hamman*] all created' on 4 February 1922. Naujadi's usage of hamman, the first person plural, embraces the otiyars and their families in a collective act of great national significance for which they still await adequate recompense.

35

Witness to a History

SITA: Chauri Chaura is really the first 'case' in connection with *swaraj*.

NAUJADI: No doubt about it, it is Chauri Chaura for sure—and Dumri is the place from where everything started . . . Everybody has got their raj, our raj never came. It's us [*hamman*] who created the turmoil [*utpāt*], and look what we got—nothing!

The old widow is of course complaining about Rameshar's political pension which, instead of coming to her, is intercepted by local politicos who parade relatives of the rioters in Lucknow and Delhi for their own ends. Naujadi no longer has her paper with 172 written on it. Rajbansi Sainthwar, a politician from Bansgaon tahsil has taken it away. Her poverty; the bully Rajbansi; the pension that never comes; the arrival of Gandhi; the sabha at Dumri—all are jumbled together into her poignant statement. Naujadi breaks down and the visiting historian hears himself mumble foolishly: 'What else do I ask you?'

Listen! In the month of Māgh chutki-gathering started, and this event also happened in the month of Māgh. This kānd took place after a year. After one year this, whatsitsname—the sabha—took place. Are you listening! 172 persons there are on my paper, and Rajbansi has taken it away. [Breaks down.] My son had died [and I had to go to Delhi with Rajbansi]. I said to Rajbansi, 'Oh neta', I said, 'I can't make it.' He replied, 'I'll beat your arse blue if you carry on like this.' Eh Babu! hearing this my daughter started crying. Rajbansi also took away a hundred rupees from me. Babua-lōg, give me something to keep me going.

Naujadi's story is not just about the event of 1922, it is equally about the iniquitous recognition of freedom fighters. Our long conversations somehow missed out on what it felt to be the wife or the son of a convicted rioter. Rather, the memory of privation, when the householder was locked up for eight to fifteen years, or indeed hanged, was enveloped by the quest for the political pension that was now due to the family. Recollections of the riot in Dumri are invariably interspersed with graphic accounts of a recent trip to New Delhi—to 'Rajiv's [Rajiv Gandhi's] house', to Jantar Mantar, or to the Rashtrapati Bhavan. The successful insertion of that infamous event into the life of the nation has both freed and framed familial memories.

36

Towards Conclusion

'Now Sir! Fathom it after your own heart! How much more can one narrate [*Babu! Apne dil se samajh leen! Ab kahwān le biyān kihal ja*].' So concludes Naujadi.

And so the time has come to stitch this narrative to a close and make an end of our story. In this book I have tried to do several things—some may feel too many. I have tried to raise certain questions about the ways of nationalist historiography. 'Chauri Chaura' is a tale of how the celebrated condemnation of a riot by Gandhi paradoxically entitles it to national importance. This outrage, this episode, this kānd, has until now been stereotypically forced into the narrative of the freedom struggle. This denotes the quiet confidence, indeed the supreme and not quite warranted confidence, that a dominant ideology has hitherto exuded over a colonial past. At a general level, the story of the riot suggests *how* a particular event is excised from a series in terms of its denouement and consequence, even though it belongs to a set of events similar in almost all respects. A close study of such an occurrence then discloses the tensions which such acts of excision hide within the body of an apparently homogeneous set of events: hours before the clash with the police, the Dumri volunteers were as Gandhian as most other peasant-volunteers in India in the winter of 1921–2. Hours after it, they were criminals.

It is the nationalist requirement to perceive Chauri Chaura differently that precludes a fuller understanding of all these tensions between the leaders and the led, authorized statements and popular understanding, organization and movement. Such tensions characterize all mass movements, nationalism included. The contrary tendency, the antithesis of nationalist historiography as exemplified in colonialist writings, is to see the riot in a common blur of rustic excesses fuelled by local political machinations. This again leaves us none the wiser, for it affords no space from where to write the history of such exceptional and revealing events.

Chauri Chaura is a metaphor both for nationalists and colonialists because it typifies violent police–peasant confrontations under the British Raj. Preparatory to the launch of his second all-India campaign of civil disobedience, Gandhi had in early 1930 'wished to discover a formula whereby sufficient provision can be made for avoiding suspension by reason of Chauri Chaura.' A singular event eight years in the past had by now come to inform an entire nationalist strategy. And in August 1942, when police and railway stations were targeted by student- and peasant-nationalists to force the British to 'Quit India', the governor of UP took recourse to the imagery of a past riot when characterizing the turmoil in the provinces of Uttar Pradesh and Bihar.

. . . there has been a second Chauri Chaura at a police station in Ghazipur, the police station burnt and the staff murdered.

It is not in its violence alone that 'Chauri Chaura' suggests other places, other events, other times. While paying particular heed to the riot outside the thana, I have also looked closely at the internal face of popular nationalism: the demiurgic presence of Gandhi, local elaborations on his teachings, the self-empowerment of volunteers. Chauri Chaura, this book implies, indicates peasant nationalism more generally. I have sought to show this by focusing on the deeds and lore of Nazar Ali, Bhagwan Ahir and Mir Shikari, all that went before the whistle for the volunteers to regroup, all that came prior to the first stone which was hurled at the police station. The escalation of such acts into a full-scale riot and its subsequent adjudication made a massive judicial archive available to the historian.

My other concern has been to follow closely the first historiographical exercises among the judges of the case. Here I have tried to overcome the historian's disappointment at the discovery of a mine of information—all the relevant facts about the peasant-accused—and yet not evidence enough for a telling of the full story.

This book has of necessity followed the making of the judicial archive, as well as the requirements and procedures for the production of penal truth, in some detail. Yet if peasant voices from the past are available to us in large measure through the medium of judicial records, we also know that peasants in court cannot be taken at their word. While the accused were evasive, it was the task of the approver to be persuasive and expansive. This is why I have paid so much attention to the testimony of Approver Shikari, and to the difference it made both to the judgment and to the lives of those on trial.

The retelling of this part of the story has been partly textual; at the same time I have sought to disrupt the self-sufficiency of judicial discourse. The prose of the judge, occasioned by his own proceedings, is internally consistent. But in my account of the trial I have attempted to go outside this field of judicial pronouncement into, for instance, the politics and religiosity of vegetarianism and picketing, in order to better analyse what the judgment itself reveals and obfuscates.

Although the difficulties with the actors' speech in the court and in the nationalist record pushes the possibility of narrating the event, historical fieldwork—i.e. interviews, conversations and the eliciting of contemporary recollections of a very old event—can feebly attempt to unify extant and emerging accounts. Testimony to the incompleteness of the existing record, familial memories are, however, themselves witness to *another* history, namely the recent nationalization of the event.

The enormous conceptual and narratological complications here are obvious by being on display. So, clearly, I am not suggesting that what we now have on record is the definitive voice and consciousness of the actors as it played itself out in early 1922. I simply note that the problems of capturing 1922 through interviews in 1990 are considerable, as are the pitfalls of a pragmatic reliance on contemporary evidence. Certainly, I have consciously shunned any attempt to use oral history as a seasoning to enliven documentary evidence. My effort has been to arrive at an enmeshed, intertwined and imbricated web of narratives from every available source. Without venturing into historical fieldwork I would have continued reconstructing the event through court records of 1922 without circumventing the problems that this procedure would have entailed. This, it seemed to me, would yield a somewhat barren archival book, a detailed textual analysis of the judicial archive which gratuitously failed to unearth exciting, alternative accounts which will soon be dead to the historian.

Given the negative charge attached to the event within Indian nationalism, competing contemporary narratives of the riot are largely absent. I have therefore tried to trace the event by teasing out local remembrances of things past. In my encounters with

Naujadi Pasin, Sita Ahir and others, processes and encounters external to 'Chauri Chaura', but not to its retellings, play their part. While according primacy to local speech, I have refrained from simple ethno-reportage. I have sought instead to reproduce specific, personalized and often eccentric accounts and have ranged, arranged, rearranged these against the authorized texts of historiography: court records, contemporary tracts, ethnological notices, even the dictionary. This is my own historiographical way of shaping events and their recall and their context into a far from final or authoritative text, yet nonetheless one which strives towards a complexity hitherto absent. The historian who seeks to garner memories of an event officially labelled 'crime', cannot escape marching outwards from the archives, for a refusal to recognize the prior presence of law, 'the state's emissary',[195] is unlikely to lead to a better dialogue at the present site of past action.

Writing history in this fashion leads one to constantly ask whether the really complex questions about the production of historical narratives have been answered, or indeed adequately posed. How does the passage of time affect the telling of stories? What structures existed prior to the event? What happens to a story-line in a village now freed from the constraints of law and national condemnation? What approaches to narrative were learned by informants in past listenings and in the telling of stories within other cultural constructions? In the hands of a master practitioner like Natalie Davis, such questions serve as starting points for a deft retelling of how peasants in sixteenth-century France fabricated the narratives of their crimes so as to invoke royal pardon. The telling of these stories lay in their effect, in creating a structure of feeling within readers by which the king's emissaries would be moved, literally, from a world of blood and gore to the domain of mercy.[196]

Important though such questions about narrative are, they were not the questions that animated my conversations in Chauri

Chaura. I was more interested in the way local people begin and close their retellings, and in the episodes with which such accounts are made to knit together into a story. In specialist phraseology, it was narrative detail rather than narrative performance that I was after. I was not primarily interested in the articulation of pre-existing codes within situated story-tellings. Must non-literates always exemplify a code when they speak—this is what I ask now that my account of such stories draws to a close. Is their way of speaking with elites not greatly affected by who they speak to, and indeed, by the subject and object of such a 'conversation'? Would not my writing have been different had I refused to approach the archive in the first place? Certainly: but the meaning of 'Chauri Chaura' lies in its ephemeral and metaphoric positioning within the colonial and the national archive in the first instance, and so it seems there was, in a sense, no escape from approaching the task in the way it was approached.

It is worth emphasizing that this book resists the temptation to structure Naujadi or Sita Ahir's recall along identifiably *Indian* or *peasant* patterns. I hope, rather, that this account throws some light on the ways in which many peasants in India relate stories from their public pasts. I have refrained from translating the terms used by these peasants back into pan-Indian cultural constructs, for semantically this would have resulted in a denial of agency to the actors of 1922, and to the present-day recollection of such actions. Ethnographic details which may have appeared as entanglements in the story were placed to prevent any simple or easy understanding of an overarching cultural context. Such unmediated descriptions allow, I feel, an appreciation of the ways in which an existing cultural repertoire is elaborated.

And so the peasantization of volunteers into the novel Bhojpuri term otiyar, and its association—both in Naujadi's and courtroom recalls of witnesses—with chutki and gerua appear as important markers of the ambiguous relationship between Mahatma Gandhi and his peasant followers. The Mahatma of his rustic protagonists was not as he really was, but as they had thought him up. Similarly, otiyars were not what the nationalist elite had willed them to be. The Dumri activists were tough wrestler-like characters who fed on alms, divested themselves of their normal clothing, moved about, and asserted their strength in markedly different attire—and all this in the name of Gandhi. Despite their similarities to Hindu sanyāsīs, which may even appear compelling, they were perceived then and are remembered now as otiyars, nothing more, nothing less.

Just as I have refused to call Naujadi's otiyars ascetics, so have I refrained from propping local accounts onto stories other than that of 'Chauri Chaura'. The significance of what Naujadi said lies in its validity as *an account* of 'Chauri Chaura', and not in its use as a typology of peasant recollection of upheavals and violent events. The Hindi word for interview, *sakshātkār*, has the sense of physical impression, and I have conceived of my presence in Dumri as a series of conversations, with all the attendant evils and possibilities of such an encounter.

Local and familial memories of the event, we see, are often at variance with, but seldom independent of, judicial and nationalist accounts. Subaltern recollections of historic events—historic because they are on record as infractions of the law which did not go unnoticed or unpunished—are also remembrances of the role of the police and the judge. Novel and emphatic recollections of nationalist activity in the villages similarly yield significant clues about the ways of peasant activists. Therefore the fieldwork in this book is not intended to supersede the colonial and the nationalist archive. Rather, it is placed in a complex relationship of variation to the official record.

Now that nearly all the rioters are dead, the voice of the peasant-actor emerges, both in the court records and in local recall, as an echo of other more powerful and persuasive voices. Exaggeration, conflation, repetition, redundancy, partial and idiosyncratic detail—all are present in this book. As I said, they are here not so much for colour but to delineate the ambiguities and tensions of an officious record.

Incongruence with known facts has not been construed as a lapse of memory, but rather as a necessary element in the stitching together of the story of Chauri Chaura.

37

Epilogue

As the last of the *puraniyās* (the old folk) die, familial recall will lose its intensity and facticity. But ironically, the investment made in 'Chauri Chaura' by local politicians will keep the stories alive. The stories of Gandhi's men, the beating of the volunteers, the firing on the crowd, the attack on the thana, the arrival of the avenging force, the circumstances that saved the locality, the punishment . . . and now the betrayal of these families by New Delhi and the Nation. Shikari's betrayal pales into insignificance against this.

Of course the nation has its own ways of memorializing the event. Now that the riot has been incorporated within the Great Freedom Struggle,[197] a space has been created for a monument so tall that lights flicker over it at night, warning away planes making their way to the airport in Gorakhpur. A marble column *enumerates* the nineteen hanged; it stands as an artifice of post-colonial history. An engraved stone tablet, situated across the railway track from the site of the burnt-down police station, similarly memorializes the event without mentioning a single person from Dumri or Chauri Chaura! Mahatma Gandhi, the progenitor of the Non-Co-operation Movement; Moti Lal Nehru, the impresario of satyagraha in the region(!); Indira Gandhi, the moving spirit behind the memorial—these are the three individuals who mark the beginning, the middle and the end of this 'Golden History of the Martyrs of Chauri Chaura'! The names of the Chauri Chaura accused are literally missing, even to this day, from every nationalist narrative.

Adjacent to the railway station stands the old Chauri Chaura memorial, inaugurated in February 1924 by the Lieutenant-Governor of that time. This monument, unveiled seventy years ago to honour the dead policemen, has also been nationalized. The legend the colonial masters engraved on it was gouged out by Baba Raghav Das, the prominent Gandhian of east UP, on 15 August 1947.[198] This noble worthy was followed by the post-colonial government, which did more than just smoothen the rough cutting edges of nationalist chisels. It chose to inscribe 'Jai Hind' on the police memorial, the slogan with which prime ministers of India end their Independence Day perorations from the Red Fort in Delhi. Both policemen and rioters, it now appears, laid down their lives for the Nation.

While embracing the colonial Indian policemen, this nationalist memorial manages nevertheless to underline one particular difference—that between Hindu and Muslim citizens of independent India. A close look at the names of the policemen killed, each given a niche where their relatives burn commemorative lamps, reveals that the Muslim names are written in Urdu and the Hindu names in Hindi! Further, while the names in Urdu are engraved, the lettering in Hindi is simply painted over. Clearly, the colonial government, which associated Hindi with subversive nationalism and found Urdu less threatening, had originally engraved all the names in Urdu, that being the vernacular most often used in administration. An influential post-colonial figure must have then ordered the plastering over of the Urdu-writing for the Hindu names! But the Hindu names were not re-engraved in

Devanagari. Re-engraving was passed over, perhaps because of budgetary constraints, for a shoddier painted inscription in Hindi.

This monument to the policemen killed at Chauri Chaura is testimony to the ways of the majoritarian nationalist discourse in India even today. All the policemen killed by nationalist peasants now belong to 'India's past'. But the 'essential' difference—Hindu and Muslim—surfaces surreptitiously through this notorious process of nationalist erasure and reinscription.

A few years ago the otiyars received yet another gift from the nation. A super-fast train named Shaheed Express in honour of the Chauri Chaura 'martyrs', was started between Delhi and Gorakhpur. Inaugurated on 2 October, Gandhi's birthday, it terminates ironically at the district headquarters, at a railway station which falls some fifteen miles short of Chauri Chaura.

And now, finally, even that irony has lost some of its poignancy. The train has in fact been extended. It now touches Chauri Chaura, but does not stop at that station. Another existing train, which once connected Gorakhpur and the smaller towns en route to the provincial High Court city of Allahabad, has been rechristened the Chauri Chaura Express. The memorialization of Chauri Chaura is far from over: it is now a routine, everyday affair.

Appendix A

प्रतिज्ञा-पत्र

23 नवम्बर के गर्वन्मैन्ट गज़ट के एलान गर्वनमैन्ट की ओर से वैलेन्टियरज़ के बारे में छपा है उसको समझ कर और उसके खिलाफ काम करने के नतीजों को पूरी तरह समझ कर मैं अपनी खुशी से ज़िला गोरखपुर के राष्ट्रीय वैलन्टियर (स्वयं सेवक) दल का मेम्बर होता हूँ और ईश्वर को साक्षी देकर प्रतिज्ञा करता हूँ कि

1. जब तक॰ मैं स्वयं सेवक दल का मेम्बर रहूँगा वचन और कर्म से अहिंसात्मक बना रहूँगा (करूंगा) और सच्चे दिल से इस बात का प्रयत्न करूंगा कि मैं मन से भी अहिंसात्मक बना रहूँ क्योंकि मेरा विश्वास है कि भारतवर्ष की वर्तमान स्थिति में केवल अहिंसा व्रत ही द्वारा खिलाफत और पंजाब की सहायता की जा सकती है और इसी के द्वारा स्वराज प्राप्त किया जा सकता है तथा भारतवर्ष के तमाम जातियों में चाहे वह हिन्दू, मुसलमान, सिक्ख, पारसी, इसाई अथवा यहूदी हों उनमें एकता स्थापित की जा सकती है।

2. मैं उक्त प्रकार की एकता में विश्वास करता हूँ और सर्वदा इस एकता को बढ़ाने का प्रयत्न करता रहूँगा।

3. मेरा विश्वास है कि स्वदेशी भारतवर्ष के आर्थिक, राजनैतिक तथा आत्मिक प्रश्न के हल करने के लिए परमावश्यक है और मैं हर प्रकार के वस्त्रों को छोड़ कर हाथ के कते तथा हाथ के बुने खद्दर का प्रयोग करूंगा।

4. बहैसियत एक हिन्दू के मेरा विश्वास है कि अछूतपन के दोष को दूर करना न्याययुक्त तथा परमावश्यक है और यथाशक्ति मैं हर मौके पर अछूतों से मिलने और उनकी सेवा करने के लिये प्रयत्न करूंगा।

5. मैं अपने आला अफसरों की आज्ञाओं का पालन करूंगा तथा उन तमाम नियमों को मानूंगा जो इस प्रतिज्ञा के प्रतिकूल नहीं होंगे और जो कि वौलन्टियर बोर्ड द्वारा अथवा कार्यकारिणी कमेटी द्वारा वा किसी और संस्था द्वारा जो कि कांग्रेस की ओर से स्थापित की गई हो—पास किए गए हों।

6. मैं कैद की सज़ा मार-पीट, तथा मौत के भी अपने धर्म और मुल्क के हेतु बिना किसी प्रकार के क्रोध के सहन करने के लिए तैयार हूँ।

7. जेल जाने की नौबत आने पर मैं अपने कुटुम्ब तथा आश्रितों की सहायता के लिये कांग्रेस से याचना नहीं करूंगा।

मटर केवट, भैंसा टोला दरशनवा
मोतीराम अड्डा

Notes

Abbreviations

CCR	Chauri Chaura Records, Gorakhpur (trial nos 44–45 of 1922).
CWMG	*Collected Works of Mahatma Gandhi* (Ahmedabad).
GRR	Gorakhpur Records Room.
IOL	India Office Library, London.
IOR	India Office Records, London.
NAI	National Archives of India, New Delhi.
NMML	Nehru Memorial Museum and Library, New Delhi.
NWP Gazetteer, vi	Statistical, Descriptive and Historical Accounts of the North-Western Provinces of India (Allahabad, 1881).
P.P.	Parliamentary Paper.
UPSA	Uttar Pradesh State Archives, Lucknow.

Notes to Prologue

1.   I am referring to such celebrated works of historical craftsmanship as Emmanuel Le Roy Ladurie, *Montaillou: The Promised Land of Error* (New York, 1979); Carlo Ginzburg, *The Cheese and the Worms: The Cosmos of a Sixteenth-century Miller* (London, 1980), Natalie Zemon Davis, *The Return of Martin Guerre* (Harvard, 1983), and Ranajit Guha, *Elementary Aspects of Peasant Insurgency in Colonial India* (Delhi, 1983).

2.   In a recent book, Alain Corbin has analysed the killing of a nobleman by a mob of three hundred to eight hundred people at Hautefaye in the Dordogne *département* on 16 August 1870 as 'the last outburst of peasant rage to result in murder' in France. His concern is 'to penetrate the psychological mechanisms that led to murder'. Alain Corbin, *The Village of Cannibals. Rage and Murder in France, 1870* (Cambridge, Massachusetts, 1992), pp. 1–2.

3.   Hayden White, 'The Question of Narrative in Contemporary Historical Theory', *History & Theory*, xxiii (1984), pp. 1–33.

4.   See in this connection, Ernest Renan, 'What is a Nation?', 1882, reprinted in Homi Bhabha, ed., *Nation and Narration* (London, 1990). See also Benedict Anderson, 'Narrating the Nation', *Times Literary Supplement*, 23 June 1986, for an interesting development of Renan's dialectic between remembrance and forgetting in the making of national pasts.

5.   For a general statement of these problems, see Dipesh Chakrabarty, 'Postcoloniality and the Artifice of History: Who Speaks for "Indian" Pasts?', *Representations*, 37 (Winter 1992), pp. 1–26.

Notes to Part One

1. 'The Crime of Chauri Chaura' (16.2.1922), 'Divine Warning' (19.2.1922), 'Gorakhpur's Crime' (12.2.1922), in *Collected Works of Mahatma Gandhi*, xxii, pp. 386–7; 415–21 (hereafter *CWMG.*) For a contemporary official version, see *United Provinces Gazette*, 25 March 1922 (pt. VIII), pp. 220–2.

2. *Gandhi-ki Larāi, urf Satyāgraha Itihās* (Bulandshahar, 1931), Proscribed Pamphlet, Hindi, B 247, IOL.

3. Rajendra Prasad, 'A Brief Sketch of the Non-Co-operation Movement', dated 31 August 1922, in *Young India, 1921–22* by Mahatma Gandhi, ed. by Rajendra Prasad (Madras, 1922), p. lxi.

4. In late January 1922, we read in an official Congress document, 'the country was all agog to witness the final triumph of soul force over physical might. But the gods had willed it otherwise. The crime of Chauri Chaura was perpetuated (sic!) on the 5th February 1922 and changed the whole outlook . . .'. See 'Report of the Congress Civil Disobedience Enquiry Committee' (1922), chapter III, para 39, in *The Indian Annual Register, 1922–23*. Following in the wake of this contemporary nationalist history, Professor Bipan Chandra also recounts the event in the passive voice, and, as in the Congress Report, gets the date wrong. 'On 5 February occurred the Chauri Chaura tragedy', Chandra writes in his Introduction to N.N. Mitra, ed., *The Indian Annual Register* (1920, reprinted Delhi, 1986), p. v.

5. Partha Chatterjee, 'Gandhi and the Critique of Civil Society', in Ranajit Guha, ed., *Subaltern Studies III* (Delhi,1984), p. 182. See also Ravinder Kumar, ed., *Essays on Gandhian Politics: The Rowlatt Satyagraha of 1919* (Oxford, 1971), and Ranajit Guha,'The Mahatma and the Mob', a review article in *South Asia*, no. 3, August 1973, pp. 107–11.

6. 'Democracy versus Mobocracy', 8 September 1920, *CWMG*, xviii, p. 240.

7. For a conceptualization of the problem, see Ranajit Guha, 'Discipline and Mobilize', in Partha Chatterjee and Gyanendra Pandey, eds, *Subaltern Studies VII* (Delhi, 1992).

8. *CWMG*, xviii, p. 244. Emphasis added.
9. 'Some Illustrations', *CWMG*, xviii, p. 275. See also Chatterjee's comments on this passage, in *Subaltern Studies III*, pp. 185–6.
10. Guha, 'Discipline and Mobilize', *Subaltern Studies VII*, p. 107.
11. *CWMG*, xviii, p. 240, cited in Guha, ibid.
12. For a specimen of the *pratigya patra* used in Gorakhpur, see Appendix A. For a slightly different pledge form (published at the Prayag Press), see Proscribed Pamphlet, Hindi F. 38, IOL. The standard English version, as drafted by Gandhi, is printed in *CWMG*, xxii, pp. 100–1.
13. The sketch of the event that follows is based on court records and fieldwork done in Chauri Chaura. It remains very much my own account. I have not tried to silence my voice from this brief history, which is meant to help the reader along.
14. Gail Minault, *The Khilafat Movement: Religious Symbolism and Political Mobilization in India* (New York, 1982), p. 1. I have not attempted to point out the linkages and the relative importance of these two movements in Gorakhpur or Chauri Chaura. My focus here and later in the book is on the volunteers of Dumri and the overlaps and displacements between these two 'movements' in the locality.
15. Maulvi Subhanullah, a leading Khilafatist, was also the President of the District Congress Committee. Pandit Dasrath Prasad Dwivedi, Secretary, District Congress, along with Hakeem Arif, was Vice President of the Gorakhpur Khilafat Committee.
16. Drawing on the root 'to possess', the term *mālik* has a wide range of connotations in popular Hindustani. Fallon's *Dictionary* gives the following: '1. owner; proprietor; 2. master; lord; 3. God; 4. husband; 5. *one empowered*; an employer (emphasis added)'. The 'maliks' of the crowd were those who had been clearly 'empowered' by the Dumri meeting.
17. Cf. Haidar chaukidar: 'The volunteers said the thanadar had no spirit left, *his rectum had split . . .*'. Evidence in the Session's Court, CCR, II, p. 217. The proceedings of the Committing Magistrate reproduce the abuse with its Bhojpuri inflection. Rameshar, chaukidar of Satrohanpur, is quoted: 'Some volunteers clapped their hands saying . . . "*Thana ki gānd phat gayil*" '. CCR, I, p. 318.
18. In all about 1000 'suspects' were listed and 225 put on trial. Not all of course had pledge forms pinned to their name. Many were arrested and tried on the basis of information supplied by local landlords or by the 'co-accused'.
19. See Report on this in *Aaj*, 13.2.1922.
20. 'The Gorakhpur Tragedy: Mr Devdas Gandhi's Account', *Leader*, 13.2.1922.

21. 'Letter to Members of Working Committee', 8 February 1922, *CWMG*, xxii, p. 350, pp. 377–81 ('Working Committee's Resolution at Bardoli').
22. *Abhyudaya,* 25.2.1922.
23. 'Swatantrata sangrām mein Gorakhpur-Deoria ka Yogdān', in *Swatantrata Sangrām ke Sainik*, vol. 35, Gorakhpur (Suchna Vibhag, Lucknow, 1972), p. 12.

Notes to Part Two

1. Assessment Notes Chaura, 1885, GRR. The figure of 132 given in *NWP Gazetteer*, vi, 1881, p. 476, seems to be an underestimate.
2. Assessment Notes, Chaura, 1885, GRR; *District Census Statistics, United Provinces: Gorakhpur District, 1891*; 'Returns Showing the Outwards and Inwards Traffic at each Station of Gorakhpur District, from Jan. 1885 to June 1889', Appx. IV/13, MS, Gorakhpur Settlement Report, 1889, Settlement Shelf, GRR.
3. *Gorakhpur Gazetteer*, 1909 (2nd edn, 1929), p. 219; Evidence of Sardar Harcharan Singh, supervisor Chaura bazaar, CCR, II, p. 134.
4. *Gorakhpur Gazetteer*, pp. 79, 219; CCR, II, pp. 132–4 (evidence of Sardar Harcharan Singh); interview with Sita Ahir, Chotki Dumri; Chandi Tiwari, Gaunar; Sardar Surinder Singh Majithia, Gorakhpur; B.C. Burt, *Description of the Working Sugar Factory exhibited in the Agricultural Court, United Provinces Exhibition, by Messrs. Blair, Campbell and Mac-Lean* (U.P. Agricultural Series, Bulletin no. 26, Allahabad, 1911).
5. *Report on the Industrial Survey of the United Provinces: Gorakhpur District*, by Mushtaq Mohammad (Allahabad, 1924), pp. 21–2, 43–4, 47; CCR, II, pp. 133, 385.
6. CCR, I, p. 75; 'Siwāi and Sāyar Āmadni', Wājib-ul-Arz mauza Dumri Khurd, tappa Keotali, Settlement Papers 1323 Fasli, GRR. See also Shahid Amin, *Sugarcane and Sugar in Gorakhpur: An Inquiry into Peasant Production for Capitalist Enterprise in Colonial India* (Delhi, 1984), esp. chs. 3 & 4.
7. CCR, I, pp. 75, 80, 132.

8.   'Cesses in Oudh', c. 1921, Report by D.M. Stewart, para 28, U.P.
     Revenue A Proceedings, May 1925, no. 21; Wajib-ul-Arz, Siwai aur Sāyar
     Āmadni, Settlement Papers, mauza Dumri Khurd and Chaura, 1323
     Fasli, GRR.
9.   CCR, II, p. 155.
10. Gorakhpur Gazetteer, p. 219; Gorakhpur Census Statistics, 1891; CCR, I,
     p. 110; II, pp. 92, 136, 112, 317.
11. Alan Swinton, Manual of the Statistics of Goruckpore (Allahabad, 1861),
     map; NWP Gazetteer, vi, map, pp. 290, 476; Gorakhpur Gazetteer, p. 259;
     Archaeological Survey of India: Report of a Tour in the Gorakhpur District
     in 1875–76 and 1876–77, xviii, by A.C.L. Carlleyle (Calcutta, 1883),
     pp. 53–5, plate ii; T.F. Downs, 'Civil Rebellion in the Banaras Division,
     1857–58', M.A. thesis, University of Canterbury, 1987, pp. 169–71.
12. CCR, II, p. 628.
13. CCR, II, pp. 104–5, 109, 112, 115, 134–5, 847–8.
14. Buchanan in his map of Northern Gorakhpur, c. 1813, locates 'Murera'
     on the wrong bank of the Majhna river; his tabular statement estimates
     the place to have twenty-five houses and a meagre complement of one
     moneychanger, two retailers of provisions and one potter. See Buchanan-
     Hamilton, 'An Account of the Northern Part of Gorakhpur', Map and
     Index to the Map, pp. 3–4, MSS Eur. D 93, IOL; see also 'List of
     Principal Markets in Gorakhpur District', Gorakhpur Settlement Report,
     1891 by A.W. Cruikshank, MS Appx IV/6, Settlement Shelf, GRR.
15. Assessment Notes, Mundera, 1885; Gorakhpur Census Statistics, 1891 &
     1921.
16. Industrial Survey Gorakhpur, 1924, pp. 12, 34–5. The rough estimate
     about the magnitude of profitability is based on the notional rental
     income of the two branches of the Majithia family who, between them,
     owned fifty-nine villages in the region. The notional rental income is
     arrived at by multiplying the revenue assessed on the Majithias by a factor
     of two, as revenue was assessed at 49 per cent of the rental assets. In 1917
     the Majithia brothers paid Rs 18,163 for their fifty-nine villages. Source:
     Rent Rate Report, Pargana Haveli, Tahsil and District Gorakhpur (1917),
     by D.C. Hunter, para 9; Gorakhpur Gazetteer, p. 119.
17. CCR, II, pp. 155–62, 447.
18. Ibid., pp. 98–9.
19. Ibid., p. 383.
20. Ibid., pp. 112, 135.
21. Gorakhpur Gazetteer, p. 81; Archaeological Survey, Report, xviii, p. 55;
     CCR, II, pp. 135, 140.
22. Khewat, village Chaura and Mundera, 1323 Fasli.

23. *Khewat* and *Dastur-dehi*, Mundera, 1323 Fasli; Interview with Mewa Lal Jaiswal, Mundera bazaar, Chandi Tiwari, village Gaunar. For a general discussion of weighing charges and the relationship between the official weighman and bazaar owners, see 'Cesses in Oudh', para 25.

24. *Khatyuni* mauza Mundera, 1323 Fasli.

25. Swinton, *Manual of Goruckpore Statistics*, 1861, p. 21; *Goruckpore-Basti Settlement Report*, 1871, i, pp. 199–200.

26. *NWP Gazetteer*, vi, pp. 399–400, 440–1; *Gorakhpur Gazetteer*, p.119; Map of Gorakhpur District, c. 1883; Survey of India, 1921, Map Sheets no. 63 N/9-10; Assessment Register of Villages in tappa Keotali, Gorakhpur district, 1836 and 1885 Settlements, GRR; S.A.A. Rizvi, ed., *Freedom Struggle in Uttar Pradesh*, iv (Lucknow, 1960), pp. 336, 341–5ff; interviews in Chotki Dumri and Mundera bazaar. '*Mukhtārnāma*' signed by O.N. Ganguli on behalf of Sant Baksh Singh, Settlement Papers, mauza Gaunar, ii, 1323 Fasli.

27. Commr. Gorakhpur to Sec. Govt. NWP, 4.1.1859, recommending that the 'confiscated Dumri estate be placed . . . in strong hands', NWP, Rev. Progs. 29.7.1859, no. 408. See also NWP Rev. Dept. Narrative of Progs. for 3rd Quarter of 1859, para 92, L/E/3/69, IOR, London.

28. 'Report on Pergunnah South Haveylee', in *Goruckpore-Basti, Settlement Report*, 1871, i, pp. 199–200; Buchanan-Hamilton, MSS Eur D 92, book IV, pp. 122–3, IOR, London.

29. *Goruckpore-Basti Settlement Report*, 1871, i, p. 200; *Gorakhpur Gazetteer*, pp. 119–21; fieldnotes; land grants (*Birt*) to Miyan Saheb Shah Roshan Ali from Sattasi Raj, dated 1 June 1795 and 1 December 1813, Imambara Files, Gorakhpur; interview with Mohamad Idris, *zillādār*, Mian Saheb estate (in 1923); N.H. Siddiqui, *The Landlords of Agra and Avadh* (Lucknow, 1950 ?), pp. 69–70; 'Deed of Partition of the Azmatgarh Estate', by M.M. Malaviya and Baldev Ram Dave, arbitrators, 30.1.1925, Sri Prakash Papers, Misc. File 10, NMML, New Delhi; C.A. Bayly, *Rulers, Townsmen and Bazaars: North Indian Society in the Age of British Expansion, 1770–1870* (Cambridge, 1988), p. 288; written communication from C.A. Bayly; Assessment Remarks on villages in tappa Keotali, 1885; Settlement Papers of individual villages, tappa Keotali, 1323 Fasli, GRR.

30. Assessment Remarks Dumri Khurd, 1885; Report of E.W. Ricketts, Special Manager, Dumri Estate (under Court of Wards) to Collr. Gorakhpur, 17.5.1892, D.T. Roberts, Collr. Gorakhpur to Commr. Banaras Division, 11.6.1887, File: I-13 (I), Court of Ward Bastas, GRR. For a general discussion of the cropping pattern in villages in Keotali tappa, where the alluvial heavy *bāngar* soil predominated, see *Rent Rate*

Report of Pargana Haveli, Tahsil and District Gorakhpur, 27 May 1917, pp. 3, 8–10, Rev. Dept. File 506/1913, UPSA, Lucknow.

31.   Assessment Remarks, Dumri Khurd, 1885; *Khewat, Khatyuni* and *Wājib-ul-arz,* Dumri Khurd, 1323 Fasli.

32.   This discussion is based on, *District Census Statistics, Gorakhpur, 1891 & 1921*; Assessment Remarks, Dumri Khurd, 1885, GRR.

33.   Memo of Examination of Duddhaie, s/o Debi Deen Chamar of Dumri Khurd, CCR, I, p. 576; testimony of Shikari, CCR, II, p. 5; interview with Ramji Chamar, s/o Puranmasi, Chamrauti, Chotki Dumri.

34.   *District Census Statistics, Gorakhpur, 1891 & 1921*; Assessment Remarks, Dumri Khurd, 1885; interview with Sita Ahir.

35.   CCR, I, pp. 109–10; II, p. 1; interview with Sita Ahir, Chotki Dumri.

36.   Interview with Sita Ahir; CCR, I, p. 658; II, p. 544.

37.   Interview with Sita, Sivcharan Ahir's grandson.

38.   CCR, II, pp. 463–74 (evidence of Jagat Narayan); *Tajwīz Angrezi Jild Awwal,* evidence, dated, 1.4.1922. For the Pandits of Malaon, see *Sankrityāyan Vansh (Saryupareen-shākha),* Appx. 2, in Rahul Sankritya-yan, *Meri Jeevan Yātra (1),* (Kalkutta, 1955), esp. pp. 452–3.

39.   Interview with Sita Ahir, Chotki Dumri.

40.   Register of Subscribers to *Swadesh,* 1921, Swadesh Bhawan, Gorakhpur; CCR, I, p. 575; II, pp. 543–5.

41.   The ¼ anna single postcard was first introduced in 1879; reply postcards, consisting of two detachable halves joined together, each with a ¼ anna impressed stamp, were put into circulation on 1 February 1884. See D.S. Virk, *Indian Postal History, 1873–1923: Gleanings from Post Office Records* (New Delhi, 1991), p. 39.

42.   Mannan Dwivedi Gajpuri, *Ram Lal (grameen jeevan ka ek sāmājik upanyas),* Prayag, 1917, p. 27, which contains the line: *Gānv mein pulis ke bād chitthirasa sāhab hi ka raub hai.*

43.   Revenue Administration Report, Azamgarh District, 1888–89, Commissioner Record Room, Gorakhpur. See also *Report on the Revenue Administration of the North-Western Provinces, 1887–88,* p. 24. I am much obliged to Sanjay Sharma for research help on the questions of rental money orders and postcards.

44.   Special rental money orders were printed, with separate columns for the name of the village, the estate, and of the *qist* or the particular period for which the payment related. The money order was then stamped with special rent payment, or qist stamps kept at the head and branch post offices. One such stamp for *Kharif Qist,* 1328 Fasli, is reproduced in Virk, *Indian Postal History,* p. 126. See also *Annual Report on the Operation of the Post Office of India, 1886–87,* Sec. V, para 32.

45. *Settlement Report, West Gorakhpur,* 1919, p. 21.

46. Interview with Sita Ahir and Naujadi Pasin, Chotki Dumri, August. 1988, February 1989; interview with Chandi Tiwari, village Gaunar; *Final Settlement Report of the Western Portion of the Gorakhpur District* (Allahabad, 1919), pp. 20–1.

47. CCR, II, pp. 476, 847. About 1915, Awadh Sainthwar sent his rent to Barki Dumri by money order. He was not sure, when asked in court, why he did so, except that this was what everybody else was doing: CCR, II, p. 483.

48. I am basing myself largely on *Jangi Novel, ya ek Sipāhi ki sarguzasht ka saccha photo; yāni fauj mein bharti hone ka aur sipahiyāna zindagi ke dilchasp hālāt* (Sitapur, 1918), by Maulvi Syed Najmuddin Ahmad Jafri, Deputy Collector, Sitapur.

49. Kapil Kumar, *Peasants in Revolt: Tenants, Landlords, Congress and the Raj in Oudh, 1886–1922* (New Delhi, 1984), pp. 148, 165–8.

50. Gorakhpur district, with a population of over 1.6 million, supplied a total of 7792 combatants and non-combatants to the First World War; the money contributed to 'the war effort' was considerably more: Rs 35 lakhs in war loans, equal to the entire revenue of the district, and a further contribution of Rs 2.5 lakhs to the various War Funds. See *Gorakhpur Gazetteer* (supplementary notes and statistics), 1921, pp. 20–1.

51. CCR, I, p. 279; II, p. 712.

52. CCR, I, p. 558.

Notes to Part Three

1. Extracts from the diaries of Supt. of Police from the various districts of UP, CID File on Chauri Chaura, UPSA, Lucknow.

2. *Azamgarh Glossary,* 1881 (J.R. Reid), s.v. 'uranghai'.

3. Police Abstracts of Intelligence, UP (hereafter PAI), 1922.

4. PAI, 25.2.1922.

5. Evidence, Dasrath Prasad Dube [Dwivedi], CCR, II, p. 568.

6. PAI, 11.3.1922.

7.   PAI, 18.3.1922.

8.   PAI, 4.3.1922.

9.   The phrase about the forceful advent of swaraj is taken from the testimony of Harbans Kurmi of village Mangapatti. Similar 'evidence' of public proclamations of swaraj on the evening of 4 February from the villages of Barhampur, Pokharbhinda and Mundera bazaar, was also provided in court. See CCR, II, pp. 525, 516, 522, 517.

10. 'At urgent request Civil Authorities 3 Platoons 2nd Rajputs proceeded to Gorakhpur on 5-2-1922. This detachment was relieved on 11-2-1922 by Dett: (Approx. 160 all ranks) 82nd Punjabis.' See Extract no. 4455/49-G, Survey of Intelligence 15 Jan.–1 Feb. 1922, Meerut 14.2.1922, in CID Chauri Chaura File, UPSA, Lucknow.

11. 'Bhīshan Upadrava', Aaj (Banaras), 9.2.1922.

12. Editorial Comment, Aaj, 12.2.1922.

13. This and the subsequent passages are from the editorial 'Bhīshan Upadrava', Aaj, 9.2.1922. Emphasis added.

14. 'The Crime of Chauri Chaura', 16.2.1922, CWMG, xxii, pp. 415–21.

15. Romain Rolland, Mahatma Gandhi: The Man Who Became One with the Universal Being (New York and London, 1924), pp. 200–1. I have taken small liberties with Rolland's syntax.

16. 'The Crime of Chauri Chaura', pp. 415–16.

17. Ibid., p. 416.

18. The sources for this paragraph include: Evidence of Maulvi Subhanullah, CCR, I, p. 477, II, p. 559; telegram to Devdas Gandhi by Bapu, 9.2.1922, CWMG, xxii, p. 376; statement by Dwarka Pandey, CCR, II, p. 841; statement by Raghubir Kewat, I, p. 679. Devdas Gandhi's detailed report, datelined Gorakhpur, 11 February, appeared in Leader, 13.2.1922. See also Devdas Gandhi to Jawaharlal Nehru, 14.2.1922, where Devdas accepts Nehru's 'chastisement' for comparing 'the thing' [i.e. the 'Chauri Chaura riot'] to Nankana . . . Not that the comparison is wrong but I had no business to go out of my way to give my opinion in that manner' (Jawaharlal Nehru Papers, pt I, vol. 21, NMML). Gandhi probably refers to this exchange when, in his famous letter to Nehru explaining the riot and his reaction, he writes: 'Let us not be obsessed by Devdas's youthful indiscretions. It is quite possible that the poor boy has been swept off his feet and that he has lost his balance . . . ', CWMG, xxii, p. 435.

19. 'The Crime of Chauri Chaura', 16.2.1922, CWMG, xxii, p. 416. Emphasis added. Quotations in the previous para are also from the same page of this article by Gandhi.

20. Gandhi undertook a five-day fast, both as 'a penance and as punishment . . . It is a penance for me and punishment for those whom I try

to serve . . . They have unintentionally sinned against the laws of the
Congress though they were sympathizers if not actually connected with
it.' 'The Crime of Chauri Chaura', pp. 419–20. These sentiments were
elaborated by an Uttar Pradesh nationalist in verse. Titled 'Prāyashchit',
the poem begins by describing the hopes aroused in early 1922 by
Karamvir Gandhi's campaign, which if successful would have 'forever rid
India of its woes and sorrows'. But inscrutable are the ways of the gods:

करने क्या थे चले, हो गया क्या, क्या है तेरी माया?
अस यमी उदण्ड जनों का कृत्य रंग लाया;
चौरी चौरा का भीषण नर-मेघ दृश्य दिखलाया ।

Chauri Chaura 'shook an ongoing struggle to its very foundations'.
Building on Gandhi's essay, this poet ends by making the 'ever peaceful
commander' utter the following rebuke with 'a heavy heart' to the
'cruel-hearted' rioters, for whose 'great sin' he himself has to expiate by
fasting:

हृदय थाम कर परम शान्त सेना अधिनायक बोला,—
"अरे! क्रूर निष्ठुर हृदया! भीषण प्रकाण्ड कर डाला,
सकल सभ्य जग के समक्ष हा! करवाया मुँह काला,
भूले शुचि उद्देश, प्रभो! क्या होगा और हमारा?
भँवर-ग्रसित भारत-नौका को कैसे मिले सहारा?
अनशन व्रत रहकर ही, यों निज व्यथा को हरता;
महापाप तुमने कर डाला, प्रायश्चित मैं करता ।"

See 'Prāyashchit', by Surendra Sharma, *Pratap*, 6.3.1922, p. 8. My thanks
to Sharmila Srivastava for going through the back issues of *Pratap* and
locating this poem. The last part of this poem is also reproduced in
Brahmanand, *Bhartīya Swatantrata Āndolan aur Uttar Pradesh ki
Patrakārita* (Delhi, 1986), p. 102.
21. 'The Crime of Chauri Chaura', p. 420.
22. The quotations in this paragraph are from *CWMG*, xxiii, p. 31; xxii,
     p. 436; xxii, p. 407; xlvii, p. 256. Emphasis added.
23. 'Letter to Konda Venkatappayya', 3 March 1922, *CWMG*, xxiii, p. 3.
     Emphasis added.
24. 'Interview to Bombay Chronicle', 18.2.1922, *CWMG*, xxii, p. 407.
     Emphasis added.

25.   The term *kānd*, which means a chapter or a part, is now colloquially used to characterize all incidents of police firing on crowds. What follows is largely based on a history of the 'Freedom Struggle' in Gorakhpur district appended to an official directory of accredited nationalists, compiled district-wise (in 1972) to commemorate the twenty-fifth anniversary of Indian independence. See 'Swatantrata Sangrām mein Gorakhpur-Deoria ka Yogdān', in *Swatantrata Sangrām ke Sainik (sankshipt parichay)*, vol. 35, Gorakhpur (Suchna Vibhag, Lucknow, 1972), hereafter *SSKS*.

26.   See 'The Crime of Chauri Chaura', *CWMG*, xxii, p. 416.

27.   'Bhīshan Upadrava', Editorial, *Aaj*, 9.2.1922.

28.   *SSKS*, p. 11.

29.   '*Risālon se ghore mangawāye* gaye, lekin ghoron ki *tāpon se kuchal jāne par bhi satyagrahiyon ne na to sāhas chora aur na hi ātankit hue.*' I am here using the more graphic description of the police–satyagrahi encounter now inscribed at the site of the new Chauri Chaura memorial. The 1972 District Account makes the same point in slightly different words.

30.   *SSKS*, p. 11.

31.   The whistle signal was meant to control the movement of the volunteers in large groups. A short whistle signalled 'march', a longer whistle was a command to 'stop'.

32.   *SSKS*, p. 12.

33.   Ibid.

34.   Ibid.

35.   Gandhi published one such account of the oppression carried on by sowars in the villages of central Gorakhpur. See Letter of Jang Bahadur Singh to the Editor, *Young India*, 28.2.1922, *CWMG*, xxiii, p. 28.

36.   *SSKS*, p. 10. In a non-nationalist pictorial account, it is the 'rioters' who 'fire . . . into the barracks until all the twenty-one [policemen] were dead or wounded . . .'! See Katherine Mayo, *The Face of Mother India* (London/New York, 1935), text accompanying photograph 335. My thanks to Ashwani Saith for drawing attention to this imagined sequence in Mayo's sensational account.

37.   *SSKS*, p. 11. On cloth shops in Chauri Chaura in 1922, see evidence of Harcharan Singh, 'supervisor' of the bazaar. CCR, II, p. 132–4, esp. p. 132.

38.   I have discussed this problem at greater length: see Shahid Amin, 'Gandhi as Mahatma: Gorakhpur District, Eastern UP, 1921–2', in Ranajit Guha, ed., *Subaltern Studies III* (Delhi, 1984), pp. 1–61; reprinted in Guha and G.C. Spivak, eds, *Selected Subaltern Studies* (New York, 1988), pp. 288–348.

39. See Shikari's Testimony, reproduced as Appx. B in Ranajit Guha ed., *Subaltern Studies V*, pp. 277–89.

40. Nazar Ali's sojourn in Rangoon was nothing exceptional for Gorakhpur district and Dumri village. At least two other residents of Dumri had worked in Burma. The information on Nazar Ali is from CCR, II, p. 544; I, p. 555; Judgment (Sessions), pp. 185–7, and interviews in Dumri village.

41. According to a demi-official *Life* of the prominent Gorakhpur nationalist, Moti Lal Nehru was approached to defend the Chauri Chaura convicts at the Allahabad High Court but expressed his inability because of pressing engagements. See '*Jeevan-Jhānki*', in *Baba Raghav Das Abhinandan Granth* (Varanasi, 1963), p. 31. The file on the Chauri Chaura Case kept at the Allahabad High Court makes no mention of Moti Lal Nehru. Similarly, there is no evidence that the elder Nehru was in any way connected with working out a strategy to wage satyagraha at the police station.

42. Evidence of Dr S. Mukerji, M.D. (Homeopathy), brother of Dr Vishvanath Mukerji, Sec. Sadr Congress Committee, Gorakhpur, CCR, I, pp. 616–19. The quotations are from p. 618.

43. *Abhyudaya* (Allahabad) and *Pratap* (Kanpur), cited in *Aaj* (Banaras), 23.1.1923. See also *Aaj*, 3.5.1923; also Note on UP Press, 12.5.1923, p. 7. All death sentences passed by the lower court had to be confirmed, or be commuted into lesser sentences by the provincial High Court.

44. Revision of Sentence (eight years) Sheet of Ganesh Kalwar, CCR.

45. M.M. Malaviya to Governor, UP, 20.8.1935, Jud. Criminal File 1453/1935, UPSA, Lucknow (hereafter File 1453/1935).

46. Note dated 26.9.1935 by L.S. White, Judicial Secretary, UP, in ibid.

47. Note by Sir Harry Haig, 11.1.1938, in ibid. The previous quotation is from a demi-official letter from the Commissioner of Gorakhpur, cited by the Governor.

48. The Congress ministries in the provinces of UP and Bihar had briefly resigned in protest at the governors' interference in the business of administration, including their stalling the release of political prisoners. See Haig Papers, MSS Eur. F. 115, vol. 22A, IOL; *CWMG*, lxvi, esp. pp. 376–9, 383–5, 464–5.

49. Note by G.B. P[ant], dated 12.7.1938, File 1453/1935. Emphasis added.

50. The United Provinces Criminal Tribes Enquiry (Tivary) Committee, appointed by the Pant Ministry, had railed against the category and sought its replacement by the term 'habitual offender'. See Sanjay Nigam, 'A Social History of a Colonial Stereotype: The Criminal Tribes and

Castes of Uttar Pradesh, 1871–1930' (unpublished Ph.D. thesis, London University, 1987).

51.   Note by Pant, 12.7.1938. Emphasis added.

52.   Note by Pant, 12.7.1938. Emphasis added.

53.   The release of other (i.e. non-Chauri Chaura) prisoners was considered by the UP cabinet as 'a political gesture and they did not want it to be accompanied by any indication of mistrust'—which is what 'demanding assurance of good behaviour' would have looked like to the nationalist public. The Bengal terrorists, Gandhi noted in a press statement, 'would not give any undertaking to the Government. The assurances given by them to me should, they said, be regarded as sufficient test of their *bona fides*. I told them that I would not be guilty of selling their honour or self-respect for the purchase of their liberty.' This discussion is based on G.B. Pant to Governor Haig, 14.8.1937; telegram of Governor, UP, to Viceroy, 4.8.1937, MSS Eur. F. 115, vol. 22A, IOL; Gandhi's statement on Bengal government's communiqué, 21.11. 1937, *CWMG*, lxvi, p. 304.

54.   Exh. 230, CCR; Note on Dwarka by DM Gorakhpur, 25.4.1938, File 1453/1938.

55.   Petition of Dwarka Prasad, *c.* April 1938, File 1435/1938. Emphasis added.

56.   Under the 1935 Government of India Act, the head of the cabinet of provincial ministers was called the prime minister. Soon after writing this letter, Dwarka Gosain went on hunger strike in jail, aimed at making the newly formed Congress government accede to three demands: (1) release of all political prisoners convicted of violent crimes; (2) failing which, keeping all such prisoners in one jail; (3) according all such prisoners 'B' Class status. Dwarka was persuaded to give up his hunger strike by Balwant Singh, the local Congress MLA, but was convicted for this misdemeanour under sec. 52 of the Prisons Act for four months' rigorous imprisonment.

57.   This and subsequent quotations are from Dwarka Prasad [Gosain] Giri's letter written from Farukhabad jail, dated 18.9.1937 to G.B. Pant, Prime Minister, UP, File 1453/1938.

58.   On the release of the Kakori political prisoners, see Haig Papers, vol. 22A, MSS Eur F 115, IOL; *CWMG*, lxvi (1938).

59.   Note by Governor Hallett, 5.7.1938, File 1453/1938.

60.   *SSKS*, p. 58.

Notes to Part Four

1. I take the idea about discriminatory and total violence from Ranajit Guha's *Elementary Aspects of Peasant Insurgency in Colonial India* (New Delhi, 1983).
2. Testimony of Shikari, CCR, II , p. 9.
3. Evidence of Jagat Narayan, zamindar of Malaon, CCR, II, pp. 465–6.
4. Evidence of Circle Inspector Piare Lal, CCR, II, p. 796; cf. Report by Ajodhya Das et al., *Mashriq* (Gorakhpur), 16.2.1922, p. 3.
5. Evidence of Harhangi Kahar, domestic servant of the thanedar, CCR, II, p. 118.
6. Evidence of DSP, Mr Kher, CCR, I, pp. 2, 6, 11.
7. Population figures for Dumri are from *District Census Statistics (United Provinces): Gorakhpur District, 1921*, p. 6; the description of the deserted village is that of Sita Ahir. Sita's father was a village policeman who was killed in the riot.
8. Evidence of Stanley Ray Mayers, Supt. of Police, Gorakhpur, CCR, II, pp. 657–8.
9. Evidence of Circle Inspector, Piare Lal, CCR, II, p. 828.
10. Evidence of Sub-Inspector Sukhdeo Rai, CCR, II, p. 747.
11. Evidence of Jaddu Chamar, CCR, II, p. 852.
12. On Jaddu, see CCR, I, pp. 10–11; II, pp. 715, 747; Exhibits 9, 20; Judgment of Sessions Judge, p. 142 (accused no. 67, Jaddu).
13. CCR, I, p. 535.
14. CCR, I, pp. 555, 556, 557, 759, 639.
15. Judgment of the High Court, cited in Theodore Piggott, *Outlaws I Have Known and Other Reminiscences of an Indian Judge* (Edinburgh & London, 1930), chapter VI: Chauri Chaura, p. 259.
16. Evidence of Khan Bahadur Saiyid Ashfaq Husain, Deputy Superintendent of Police, CCR, II, p. 682.
17. *Woodroffe and Ameer Ali's Law of Evidence* (14th edition), edited and revised by B.R.P. Singhal and Narayan Das (Allahabad, 1981), iv, p. 338. Unless otherwise stated, Ameer Ali, *Law of Evidence*, refers to the fourth edition of this classic work compiled by the original authors.

18. Committal Proceedings, 5 April 1922, CCR.
19. See 'Rules for the Working of the Thagi and Dakaiti Department', Chapter X: Approvers and Confessing Prisoners, UP, Police Progs. Oct. 1893, no. 17, UPSA. See also Sanjay Nigam, 'A Social History of a Colonial Stereotype: The Criminal Tribes and Castes of Uttar Pradesh, 1871–1930', esp. pp. 19–28, 65–83, and Sandria B Freitag, 'Crime in the Social Order of Colonial North India', *Modern Asian Studies*, 25, no. 2 (1991), esp. pp. 236–8.
20. Cf. William Crooke: 'As to [judicial procedure], the same eccentricity prevailed. Approvers were not recognized, nor was the evidence of one witness, under any circumstances, sufficient'. *The North Western Provinces of India: their History, Ethnology and Administration* (1897; reprint Karachi, 1972), p. 126.
21. Gutherie v. Commonwealth, 198, SE. 481, 482, 171, Va 461 (South Eastern Reporter, Virginia), cited in *Words and Phrases 1658 to Date (All Judicial Constructions of Words and Phrases by the State and Federal Courts etc.)* (Minneapolis, 1964), vol. 3A, p. 517. See also State v. Graham, 41 New Jersey Law (12 Vroom), 15, 16, 32m, Am. Rep. 174, also cited on the same page.
22. The technical position was that 'the trial of an approver whose pardon is withdrawn . . . should not be merely a continuation of the trial at which he gave false evidence, but a trial so far as he is concerned, *de novo*'. Q.E. vs. Brij Narain, *Allahabad High Court Weekly Notes*, 1898, p. 153, citing Q.E. vs. Mulua, *Indian Law Reports*, 14 (Allahabad), p. 502. Where a conditional pardon had not been given, the confession of a prisoner could obviously be held against him, as happened with at least two of the accused, Ramrup Barai and Bhagwan Ahir, in the Chauri Chaura case.
23. 'List of Volunteers Chaura P.S.', sd./Gupteshar Singh, 27.1.1922, entry no. 228, Exh. 80, CCR.
24. CCR, II, pp. 422, 668.
25. CCR, II, p. 13.
26. Ibid., p. 41.
27. Evidence of Thakur Mahendra Pal Singh, Dy. Magt., CCR, II, pp. 624–5. The magistrate was here following the instructions laid down by the UP government for the recording of confessions. See United Provinces Manual of Government Orders: no. 852, in *Correspondence Relating to the Procedure in Regard to Confessions of Persons Accused of Criminal Offences*, P.P. Cmd. 7234, 1914, pp. 27–8. The legal position is that such confessions are considered 'voluntary' statements if recorded with procedural safeguards by a competent magistrate, and are inadmissible as evidence in court *only* if 'the making of the confession appears to the

court to have been caused by any inducement, threat or promise, having reference to the charges against the accused person in authority [e.g. the police]'. If, for example, the confession were extracted by the police holding out the promise or hope of obtaining pardon for the accused (from the magistrate), such a confession would be inadmissible in court. There is nothing apart from a possible retraction in court to prevent the police from inducing such confessions and extracting vital pieces of evidence at the preliminary stages of the investigation. Failed approvers regularly retracted their confessions in the courts. In colonial sociology this was often portrayed as a 'weakness of native character'.

28. The descriptions of Shikari are taken from the marginal note of the Sessions Judge's proceedings, dated 29 June 1922, and from the recollections of Shikari in Chotki Dumri today.

29. Statement under sec. 164 of the Criminal Procedure Code of Shikari, s/o Mir Qurban, age twenty-five years, resident of Dumri Khurd, P.S. Chaura, 16 March 1922, exh. 138, CCR.

30. The quotation is taken from Sir Cecil Walsh, *Indian Village Crimes: with an Introduction on Police Investigations and Confessions* (1929; reprint, Delhi, 1977), pp. 23, 25. Emphasis added. Walsh was basing himself on his experiences as a High Court judge in the United Provinces.

31. Statement under section 164 Cr.R.P.C. of Ramrup s/o Ram Tihal, caste Barai, resident of Mundera, P.S. Chaura, dated 6 March 1922, Exh. 225, CCR.

32. Ibid. Emphasis added.

33. Memo of examination of Dwarka Gosain, 28 May 1922, CCR.

34. CCR, II, p. 682.

35. CCR, II, p. 906.

36. CCR, II, pp. 898–906; Judgment of the High Court, pp. 41, 70.

37. Statement of Bhagwan Ahir, 13 March 1922, exh. 226, CCR.

38. This paragraph is based on the testimony of Thakur approver: CCR, II, pp. 21–30, 48–61, esp., pp. 21, 48, CCR, I, pp. 210–19, esp. p. 212; CCR, Exh. no. 523 (Petition by M.R.B. Kadri, dt. 21.4.1922 praying for the grant of a conditional pardon to Thakur to function as an approver), and the Testimony of Shikari, CCR, II, p. 12.

39. Evidence of G.S. Kher, DSP, Police, 21 April 1922, CCR.

40. Indian Evidence Act, section 27.

41. M.R.B. Kadri, Petition, 21 April 1922 to the Committing Magistrate, exh. 523, CCR. In this discussion I shall concentrate on Shikari's testimony as he was clearly the chief approver in this case.

42. CCR, II, pp. 22, 23. Emphasis added.

43. CCR, II, p. 28.

44. CCR, II, pp. 51, 55. After the conclusion of the testimony and cross-

examinations of the two approvers, the Sessions Judge noted in the margin of his record for 26 June 1922: 'Thakur appears dull, heavy-witted, and stupid; a great contrast to . . . Shikari, who appears active, quickwitted and intelligent.'

45.   CCR, II, p. 47. The quotations from Shikari in the previous para are from CCR, II, p. 40.

46.   The Sadr Kotwāl raided the Congress and Khilafat offices the next day and carried a cartload of papers (forty files, nine bundles of pledge forms, both signed and unsigned, a dictionary and even a one-maund weight!) to the kotwali. These papers were gone through by the Deputy Superintendent of Police to extract lists of volunteers of the Chaura thana. See, CCR, II, pp. 791–4, and exhibit nos. 17–122, CCR.

47.   See for instance the evidence of Sadhai, the syce of the daroga, Autar, the washerman of the thana, and of Siddiq, the only surviving constable from the thana, CCR, II, pp. 61–75, 222–37.

48.   See, *inter alia*, the statement of Nazar Ali and Lal Mohammad, Committal Proceedings, 6 June 1922, CCR.

49   Cf. Ricoeur, 'Testimony is that on which we rely to *think that . . . to estimate that . . . in short to judge.* Testimony wants to justify, to prove the good basis of an assertion which, beyond the fact, claims to attain its meaning.

The eyewitness character of testimony, therefore, never suffices to constitute its meaning. It is necessary that there be not only a statement but an account of a fact serving to prove an opinion or truth'. Paul Ricoeur, 'The Hermeneutics of Testimony', in *Essays in Biblical Interpretation* (Philadelphia, 1980), pp. 129, 124–4. Emphasis in original.

50.   The 225 committed to the sessions were charged with the following offences:

1.   That they, on the fourth day of February 1922, at Dumri agreed among themselves to do illegal acts, to wit, to overawe the police with force or show of force, or to beat them, in consequence of what the sub-inspector and his subordinates had done in the discharge of their duty as public servants in preventing 'volunteers' from committing a breach of peace. (Section 120B of the Penal Code.)

2.   That they on the said date, at Chaura, were members of an unlawful assembly, the common object of which was to challenge the Chaura police, to intimidate them by force, or show of force, to beat, burn and kill them, to burn and destroy their property and other property belonging to government, and to loot the same. (Section 47.)

3.   That they . . . assembly in prosecution of the common object of which all or some of the members of the said assembly intentionally

caused the death of 23 police officials. (Section 302 . . . , with reference to section 149.)

4. That they . . . assembly committed mischief by fire intending or knowing it to be likely that they would thereby cause destruction of the buildings of the police station. (Section 436, with reference to section 149.)

5. That they . . . assembly in prosecution of the common object of which some of the members of the said assembly committed the offence of dacoity. (Section 395 . . . , with reference to section 149.)

6. That they . . . assembly in prosecution of the common object of which hurt was voluntarily caused to various police officials, including chaukidars, in the discharge of their duty (i.e. the dispersing of the unlawful assembly) as such public servants, or in consequence of the Sub-Inspector and constables stopping an unlawful procession for forcible picketing at Mundera Bazaar. (Section 322, with reference to section 149.)

Besides these, twenty-six accused were charged with 'railway and telegraph offences'.

51. Michael Foucault, *Discipline and Punish: The Birth of the Prison* (Harmondsworth, 1977), p. 38.

52. See Shikari-Approver's Testimony in the court of the Sessions Judge, Gorakhpur, reproduced in *Subaltern Studies V*, Appx. B, pp. 277–89.

53. CCR, II, p. 12. Emphasis added.

54. From Shikari's Testimony in the Court of the Sessions Judge, CCR, II, pp. 4–9. Emphasis added.

55. Cf. 'On Saturday, the market day, eight days before the occurrence of Chaura, Nazar Ali went to Mundera Bazaar with the volunteers to stop the sale of toddy, wine, fish and meat. Raghubir Dayal said to them "Go away from the market as the Babu saheb does not permit it." So all of them went away. After this we went to Hata on Tuesday. Nazar Ali and I went to Hata with 50 volunteers. A meeting was held there. A Pandit of Gorakhpur had gone to join the meeting. He in his lecture said that Muhammad Ali and Shaukat Ali had been sentenced to two years' each and their mother had sent a message to them to give their lives in the cause of Khilafat. From Hata we came back to Mundera . . . ' Exhibit 138 (Shikari's Confession), Committal Proceedings, CCR.

56. Statement of Shikari in the court of the Committing Magistrate, 29 March 1922, CCR.

57. CCR, II, p. 47.

58. See Roland Barthes, 'Introduction to the Structural Analysis of Narratives', in his *Image-Music-Text* (Glasgow, 1979), p. 93 and *passim.*

59. 'Order' of the Committing Magistrate, M.B. Dikshit, 18 June 1922, p. 1 and *passim*, CRR.

60. Ibid., pp. 4–5. Emphasis added.

61. Paul Ricoeur, 'The Narrative Function', in his *Hermeneutics and the Human Sciences: Essays on Language, Action and Interpretation* (Cambridge, Paris, 1981), esp. p. 278.

62. I am here following some of the suggestions made by Upendra Baxi on my earlier paper on Approver's Testimony and Judicial Discourse. See Upendra Baxi, '"The State's Emissary": the Place of Law in Subaltern Studies', in Chatterjee and Pandey eds, *Subaltern Studies VII*, esp. pp. 258–60. The notion of popular illegalities is Foucault's.

63. This discussion is based on a reading of the cross-examination of Shikari, conducted both by the prosecution and the defence, between 26 and 28 June 1922.

64. Memo of Examination, Gobardhan, s/o Ram Baksh, *Pasi*, 31 May 1922, CCR.

65. Memo, Dudhaiee, s/o Debi Deen, *Chamar*, 27 May 1922, CRR.

66. Judgment, (High Court), p. 33.

67. Memo, Bikram, s/o Sheocharan, *Ahir*, 25 May 1922, CRR.

68. Memo, Kauleshwar, s/o Janki, *Kurmi*, 2 June 1922, CRR.

69. Memo, Abdulla, alias Sukhi, s/o Gobar of Rajdhani, *Churihar*, 23 May 1922, CRR.

70. Amir Ali, *Law of Evidence* (4th edn), p. 838.

71. Judgment of H.E. Holmes (Gorakhpur), 9.1.1923, p. 17 of the printed copy.

72. Theodore Piggott, *Outlaws I Have Known and Other Reminiscences of an Indian Judge*, chapter VI: Chauri Chaura, esp. p. 286, from which the quotation at the end of the previous paragraph is also taken.

73. *Law of Evidence* (14th edn), commentary on section 133, *passim.*

74. Ibid., pp. 841–2.

75. Piggott, *Outlaws I Have Known*, chapter VI: Chauri Chaura, pp. 258–9. Emphasis added.

76. See Judgment (High Court), p. 28.

77. Ibid.

78. Ibid., p. 29.

79. Judgment (High Court), pp. 35–6.

80. Judgment (High Court), pp. 17–19.

81. Ibid., pp. 10–11.

82. For a development of this argument about the relationship between religiosity and politics, see my 'Gandhi as Mahatma: Gorakhpur District, Eastern UP, 1921–2'.

83. I am here relying on the prominent local ethnographer, Ram Gharib Chaube's note on 'Eating Meat', William Crooke Papers, MS 131, Museum of Mankind, London; 'Maori' (pseud. James Inglis), *Sport and Work on the Nepaul Frontier, or twelve years reminiscences of an indigo planter* (London, 1878), p. 55; and Satinath Bhaduri's evocative fiction, *Dhorāi Charit Mānas* (original in Bengali; Hindi tr. by Madhukar Gangadhar, Ilahabad, 1981), p. 47. Dhorai, the eponymous tribal protagonist of Bhaduri's novel, becomes a vegetarian *bhagat* in response to the miraculous appearance of 'Ganhi-Baba' in the village.

84. *NWP Gazetteer*, vi, 1881, p. 321; *Sport & Work on Nepaul Frontier*, p. 55; Bhartendu Harishchandra, 'Saryupār ki Yātrā', *c.* 1879, in *Bhartendu Samagra* (Varanasi, 1989), p. 1041. For a general discussion on food (including meat and fish-eating) in Gorakhpur in the nineteenth century, see Buchanan-Hamilton's account, *c.* 1813, in Montgomery Martin, ed., *The History, Antiquities, Topography, and Statistics of Eastern India*, ii (London, 1838), pp. 472–3; Reply by Mr Speeding, Collr., Gorakhpur to question no. 9, *Report of the Indian Famine Commission, 1874–75*, Appx. iii, *P.P.* Cmd. 3086 (1881), pp. 280–1

85. *Swadesh*, 6 Feb. 1921.

86. Reported in *Swadesh*, 1 May 1921, p. 7 and 27 Feb. 1921, p. 11. For a fuller discussion of these and similar stories and the popular constructions of Mahatma Gandhi, see my 'Gandhi as Mahatma', *Subaltern Studies III*, pp. 1–60.

87. This is not to undervalue the ideological, organizational and demotic aspects of the *khaddar* campaign in the region as a whole. The campaign ranged from the commissioning of carpenters to fabricate spinning wheels (and nothing else); the intelligentsia, including the novelist Premchand, investing in nationalist handloom 'factories'; and village panchayats imposing the purchase of spinning wheels (*charkhās*) or the production of a certain length of yarn as punishments for transgressions. Contemporary demotic poetry was full of earthy appeals to abstain from the use of foreign cloth: several such poems asked women to forsake the finely woven (and therefore diaphanous) *phariā* or skirts of foreign cloth for the denser and more becoming *khaddar phariās*. There even was a special injunction for prostitutes to ply *charkha*: 'Hukm Gandhi ka sir-ānkhon se bajāna hoga; randiyon tumko bhi ab charkha chalāna hoga'! See 'Randion ke nām Hukmnāma', in *Dumkati Sarkar* (Prakashak, Ramgovind Misr, Phīlkhāna, Kanpur, 7 Farwari 1922), P.P. HIN. B 209, IOL, from where the couplet is taken. The rest of this discussion is based on a survey of Proscribed Pamphlets for this period, the Gorakhpur newspaper, *Swadesh*, 1920–22, and Premchand, *Chitthi-patri*, ii (Ilahabad, 1962), pp. 112–13.

88. The preceding discussion on Bandhu Singh and the Tarkulha fair is based on interviews in Dumri and Mundera bazaar; the information about attendance and taxation is derived from 'List of Fairs in the Gorakhpur District' and Bazaar Collections, File I-A13/1917, GRR.

89. On the activities of Dwarka Pandey in Rampur Raqba, see CCR, II, pp. 259, 263–4.

90. Testimony of Shikari, CCR, II, p. 3; the earlier quotation is from p. 47 of these records.

91. Police Report of S.I., Hata, 1 February 1922, exh. 370, CRR.

92. Judgment (High Court), pp. 26–28, 3–8.

93. Ibid., pp. 28–9. Emphasis added.

94. Two reasons were given by the High Court for their view. First, 'that the crime had not been the work of the National volunteers alone, and it could be proved by figures that somewhere about a thousand enrolled Volunteers, residing within marching distance of Chaura Police Station' had not come to the Dumri meeting at the thana. Second, 'disorderly characters and riff-raff' must have swelled the ranks of the volunteer crowd marching 'against the local police, and promising moreover opportunities for looting the Mundera bazar'. See Piggott, Outlaws, p. 296; Judgment (High Court), pp. 29–30.

95. The quotations in this paragraph are from Piggott, Outlaws I Have Known, p. 296.

96. The first tally was as follows: 132 convicted; 19 hanged; 14 sentenced to life imprisonment; 19 for 8 years' rigorous imprisonment (RI); 57 for 5 years' RI; 20 for 3 years' RI, and 3 for 2 years' RI;. Source: DM Gorakhpur to Sec. Jud. Criminal, Jud. Cr. File 1483/1935 UPSA.

97. Judgment (Sessions Court), p. 268.

98. Judgment (High Court), p. 29.

99. Ibid., pp. 28–9.

100. Evidence of Dasrath Dwivedi, 19 May 1922, CRR.

101. 'Order' of M.B. Dikshit, 18 June 1922, (p. 10), CCR. Emphasis added.

102. Editorial Note, Aaj, 18 February 1922.

103. Piggott, Outlaws, pp. 279–80.

104. Outlaws, pp. 280–1. Emphasis added.

105. Ibid., pp. 281–2. Emphasis added.

106. The notion of 'the rule of colonial difference' is borrowed from Partha Chatterjee. It 'marks the points and the instances where the colony had to become an exception precisely to vindicate the universal truth of the theory.' See Chatterjee, The Nation and Its Fragments: Colonial and Postcolonial Histories (Princeton, 1994), p. 22, and below.

107. Note by TCP [Theodore C. Piggott], 15.4.1923. Emphasis added. File on Chauri Chaura Case, Museum of the High Court, Allahabad.

108. Revision of Sentence Sheet of Kamla Kewat of Kusmhi, present age 27, at Central Prison, Bareilly , 31 August 1926, CCR.

109. Evidence of Parmeshwar Lal, Patwari of Kusmhi, CCR, II, p. 540.

110. Evidence against Commitment Order, Kamla, s/o Bakkas, caste Kewat, resident of Simrahaiatola of Kusmhi, appendix to Committal Proceedings, CCR.

111. Mike Hepworth and Bryan S. Turner, *Confession: Studies in Deviance and Religion* (London, 1982), p. 159.

112. OSD Political Pensions to DM, Gorakhpur, 19 August 1957, CCR. Emphasis added.

113. I got this idea from Ranajit Guha. See his 'Chandra's Death', in Guha, ed., *Subaltern Studies V* (Delhi, 1987), p. 141. The two meanings of the word 'case' are taken from *The Concise Oxford English Dictionary*, also cited by Guha.

Notes to Part Five

1. I am here borrowing Veena Das' characterization of Shikari's testimony. See her 'Subaltern as Perspective', in Guha, ed., *Subaltern Studies VI*, pp. 315–16. See also Renato Rosaldo, 'From the door of his Tent: The Field-worker and the Inquisitor', in J. Clifford & G.E. Marcus eds, *Writing Cultures: The Poetics and Politics of Ethnography* (University of California Press, Berkeley, 1986).

2. One such document in possession of Ramdihal Kewat's son reads as follows:

प्रमाण पत्र – थाना चौरी चौरा, गोरखपुर

प्रमाणित किया जाता है कि रूदली पुत्र रामदीहल केवट, त० लक्ष्मणपुर थाना चौरी चौरा, गोरखपुर सन् 1922 के असहयोग आन्दोलन (चौरी चौरा काण्ड) में भाग

लिये थे। इनके विरूद्ध धारा 147/148/149/332/302 आई० पी० सी० का मुकदमा चला है और हाई कोर्ट अदालत से फांसी की सजा पाए थे।

पी० एस० चौरा

10.2.73

निशान अंगूठा

3. See the section *'Chauri Chaura kand'* in *Swatantrata Sangrām ke Sainik (sankshipt parichay)*, xxxv , Gorakhpur (Suchna Vibhag, Lucknow, 1972), pp. 10–12.

4. While chitthiāon (lit. lettering) was undertaken by Nazar Ali for the *bator* of 4 February, the news of the forthcoming gathering was spread in neighbouring villages and bazaars by word of mouth. See the testimonies of Ugra, Nazir, Raghubir and Bahadur, Committal Proceedings of 7.2.22, 8.2.22, 1.3.22, 20.3.22, CCR. For the importance of oral and unauthored speech, and the metaphoric uses of writing by peasants, see Ranajit Guha, *Elementary Aspects*, chapter 6.

5. These letters now figure as Exhibits 93, 94 and 95 of the Chauri Chaura Records.

6. Eighty of these pledge forms were produced in the court as incriminating evidence.

7. Testimony of Shikari, CCR, II, p. 2. On Nackched, see CRR, II, pp. 543–55. The letters sent out from Dumri, inviting nearby volunteer units to gather at the village (so as to go and demand an explanation from the thanedar) were dictated by Nazar Ali and written by Nackched.

8. For a complete list, see *'Fehrist barāmdagi māl baqabza Ahmad Husain wald Hafiz Abdul Rahim wa Nur Baksh chaprāsi, Khilafat Committee, Gorakhpur'*, and *'Fehrist ashiyay Congress Committee, Gorakhpur*, 5 February 1922', Exhs. 121 and 122, CCR.

9. See *'Fard talāshi mandal fehrist kagzāt jo barāmad hue, mauza Burha Dih, be tārīkh, 19 farwari 1922, rūbru Ali Hasan wa Gobind ki bamaujūdgi sahib sub-inspector'*, Exh. 114, CCR.

10. Exhs. 115, 117, CCR.

11. The search list from Burha Dih mentions two bundles of *raddi kaghzāt* and *kāghaz sāda.*

12. For the police officer the twin Dumri leaders had become one composite figure!

13. Ranajit Guha, *Elementary Aspects*, pp. 146ff.

14. 'Imposition of Collective Fines', SDM, Padrauna, 26.1.1943, xx-35-1942, GRR. The Committing Magistrate had this angry outburst on the destruction of the police turbans at the thana: 'The red turban was particularly offensive to the non-co-operation lamb. Minute strips of these turbans, two or three inches long and a quarter inch broad, were lying all over the place, as if the police force had been dispersed to the four quarters by that token. It appeared as if some men had been detailed for that attractive job'. 'Order' by M.B. Dikshit, 18 June 1922, p. 13, CCR.

15. 'Pledge [Form] of Bhagirathi Pasi of Dumri', Exh. 150, CCR.

16. CCR, I, p. 658; interview with Sita Ahir.

17. Cf. *Najar Ali ke akhāra rahal inhān. Hamār chachera bhāi Neur o laren. Bahut dūr-dūr se pahalwān āwen. Bahut lāmbe-lāmbe se. Baki sab ke Neur mār dein: dekhe mein chōt rahlān—asl mein unkar Durga dhail rahal—kahin pachaurlan nāhin.* Interview with Sita Ahir, Neur's cousin.

18. I am here following Ranajit Guha's discussion of bodily manifestation of subordination among the peasantry. See his *Elementary Aspects*, esp. pp. 55–6.

19. In urban setlements, where the exercise of dominance was parcellized, the formation of such akhārās had a more localized and individualistic significance. From the late-nineteenth century, wrestling and physical culture were increasingly propagated in numerous towns as a sort of corporal stirring up of an enervated body polity of India! But as Rosselli acutely observes, 'In the myth of physical downfall and resurgence the educated elite appeared as sole actors', and peasant wrestler-rebels like Titu Mir of the 1832 Barasat revolt were largely relegated to the margin. See John Rosselli, 'The Self-image of Effeteness: Physical Education and Nationalism in Nineteenth-Century Bengal', *Past & Present*, no. 86 (February 1980), pp. 121–48, esp. pp. 148, 135. Within nationalist arenas, e.g. the Hindu Mela organized by the Bengali elite in the 1860s, indigenous styles of wrestling were put on display so as to contrast favourably with the European culture of physical exercise. Akhārās, like the one run by Nazar Ali in Dumri, were not construed as a sign for regenerate India, these existed within a traditional and more stable domain of physical culture. For a recent discussion of elite concern for physical prowess, see Indira Chowdhury Sengupta, 'Colonialism & Cultural Identity: The Making of a Hindu Discourse, Bengal 1867–1905' (Ph.D. thesis, London University, 1993), esp. pp. 72–5. For a valuable discussion of the urban culture of wrestling, see Nita Kumar, *The Artisans of Banaras: Popular Culture and Identity, 1880–1986* (Princeton, 1988), chapter 5. Kumar (p. 119) also reports that the preponderance of Ahirs/Yadavs among the Banaras wrestlers is attributed to the cowherds' longer leisure hours and the easy availability of milk and fruit.

20.   CCR, I, p. 211.
21.   On Gandhi's notion of the sacrificing-volunteer, see Partha Chatterjee, *Subaltern Studies III*, pp. 188–9.
22.   General Note on Police Administration Report of Gorakhpur Division for the year 1923, 4–5 March 1924, xx-5–1923–24, GRR.
23.   Commissioner Gorakhpur to I.G. Police, 10 March 1925, xx-20–1924–25, GRR.
24.   Interview with Sita Ahir.
25.   See *Swadesh*, 27.2.1922, p. 12; 13.1.1924, p. 9; 2.3.1924, p. 7; 6.4.1924, p. 11. A considerable sum in those days, Rs 800 was distributed as reward to the three police officers principally responsible for Komal's arrest in 1924.
26.   Interview with Mewa Lal Jaiswal and Ram Awadh 'Bookseller', Mundera bazaar, 22.2.1989.
27.   Evidence of Audhu, CCR, II. p. 498.
28.   The High Court judge's comment is instructive. 'Before the next morning's sun arose . . . each man felt himself marked out for the vengeance of the irresistible power which, in a moment of madness, he had challenged'. Theodore Piggott, *Outlaws I Have Known*, p. 281.
29.   Evidence of Audhu Tiwari, CCR, II, pp. 498, 500; I, p. 507.
30.   Awadhu when asked to comment on the oppressive nature of his master, had proffered a diplomatic reply: 'I cannot say about B[abu] Sant Baksh Singh being *zabardast*, he is considered to be a zamindar', he told the Counsel for the Defence. CCR, II, p. 500.
31.   '*Babu-saheb koi "police station" apne gāon ke pās nahīn banne dete the— "administration" par asar parega. Gāon Gaunar rakkha—dekhiye thana [wahān] nahīn banne diya! Inki "monopoly" thi, jo man mein āta tha karte the*'. Interview with Shiv Shankar Tiwari, village Gaunar, 24 February 1989.
32.   Evidence of Hasnu chaukidar of Mundera, CCR, II, p. 313.
33.   Pirthi Rai, a peon of Mundera bázaar, testified in court: 'In the Chaura case, by order of the estate (of Babu Sant Baksh Singh) I arrested [several suspects] . . . I arrested . . . [them] in Mundera bazaar. After arresting them I took them to the police Dy. Sahib in Chaura with their faces covered, because the Manager [of the estate] had ordered that after arrest they were to be taken to the thana with their faces covered [a technical requirement for the subsequent identification to be legally tenable]'. CCR, II, p. 719.
34.   Interview with Raghvendra Sharma 'Vaid', Mundera bazaar, 22 February 1989.
35.   The terms 'sufferers' and 'back-mein' are Mewa Lal Jaiswal's.

36. The statement about the composition of the Dumri crowd is based on lists of volunteers (both police and Congress), volunteer pledge forms and court records. The Committing Magistrate's description is taken from his 'Order', p. 10. For a suggestive discussion of the age and caste composition of the Chauri Chaura accused, see Lal Bahadur Varma, 'Kshetriya Itihās ka Pariprekshya: Seemāin aur Sambhāvanāin', in *Uttar-Pradesh ka Itihās* (mimeo: Gorakhpur University Conference, March 2–3 1984), pp. 238–9.

37. 'Index to the Map', Buchanan-Hamilton's Account of Gorakhpur, MSS Eur D 93, pp. 3–4, IOL; Survey of India, 1921, Map nos. 63/N and 63/N 11; 'List of Principal Markets in Gorakhpur District', MS Appx. IV/6, Gorakhpur Sett. Report, 1891, GRR.

38. Narrative of Janab Mohram Sheikh of Madanpur, 28 February 1989.

39. The Pathan traders of Madanpur make a parenthetic appearance in the confession of Ramrup Barai of Mundera: 'There was much smoke and so they [the policemen] all came out of the thana. Nazar Ali and Shikari and *four or five Pathans of Madanpur who were there* said: 'You all should keep watch so that no one may run away. *Tum kya māroge ham mārenge*'. Exh. 225, CCR. Circle inspector Piare Lal and party raided Madanpur on the night of 23 February and arrested Ali Husain, Nawab and Shubrati. All three were acquitted for want of evidence. *'Thana jalāne mein Madanpur ke Pathanon ka bahut hāth tha—wahi sab "trader" the'*, so said Mewa Lal who had heard it from his father.

40. The full Hindi version goes as follows: *'Pahchanon mat! Azādi ka sawāl hai! Yeh sab ke liye kiya gaya hai. [Pahchān] karoge to phānsi pa jaenge yeh log. Desh ke sāth ghaddari hogi. Desh ko āzād karāna hai, kam-se-kam itna to karo!'*

41. A significant index of nationalism in the village is the fact that one Sheikh Amman from Madanpur was a subscriber to the Gorakhpur weekly *Swadesh* in 1921. See Register of Subscribers, Swadesh Bhavan, Gorakhpur.

42. CCR, II, pp. 785ff.

43. The lawyers were Pandit K.N. Malaviya, N.K. Sanyal, K.C. Srivastava and A.P. Dube. Chauri Chaura Case, Museum of High Court, Allahabad.

44. Judgment (High Court), pp. 6–8.

45. This fact earned the veteran nationalist the following entry in an official directory: 'in 1922 [he] specially resumed practice to plead on behalf of the famous Chouri Choura conspiracy case.' *Fighters for Freedom: 2: Varanasi Division* (UP, Information Dept., Lucknow, 1964), p. 512.

46. C.J. Wingfield, Commr. Gorakhpur to Sec. Govt. NWP., 4.1.1859, NWP Rev. Progs. 29 July 1859, no. 408A; Aug. 1859, no. 296; NWP,

Rev. Dept. Narrative of Progs. for the 3rd Quarter of 1859, paras 92–95, L/E/3/69, IOL. Apart from one village, Bilari, which bordered on Gaunar, the home village of Sant Baksh Singh's family, where the Dumri Sardars were joint owners, in every other village granted to them they were the sole proprietors. See Bandobast papers for villages in Tappa Keotali, Pargana Haveli, Tahsil Sadr (*Khewat* & *Dastur dehi*), 1323 Fasli, GRR.

47. Both Shikari and Thakur Ahir went to Harcharan Singh's *kothi* in Chaura bazaar before offering themselves (and their stories) to the police. See Judgment of H.E. Holmes, Sessions Judge, Gorakhpur, pp. 23, 25, in Criminal Appeal no. 51/1923, Museum, Allahabad High Court.

48. Shikari is described in the Court records as, 'son of Mir Qurban, Saiyid, 24 . . . cultivator and hideseller'.

49. Shikari's wife had died; his father was also dead. His mother, who had married a second time, lived in a separate house in Dumri. Shikari's sister, who lived with him, presumably took care of the brother's household. CCR, II, pp. 31-2; evidence of Bikram Ahir, 25.5.1922.

50. Interview with Ramji Chamar, s/o Puranmasi Chamar, Chamrauti, Chotki Dumri, 28.1.1992. The last two sentences grieving the loss of Shikari 'Kāka' were uttered by Ramji's wife and mother-in-law in agreement.

51. This was just one of the stratagems for getting even with high rates of infant mortality. The other custom, 'when a family happen[ed] to lose several children in succession', was to get the nose of the 'next born bored on the right' nostril. The surviving child then bore the name Nackched. Chotki Dumri had its own Nackched Kahar, the schoolboy who functioned as 'writer' to Nazar Ali and Shikari. On nose-piercing as a survival strategy, see *North Indian Notes & Queries*, Sept. 1894, no. 247.

52. In Mundera the same phrase, in chaste Hindi, was used to describe the power of Bansu Singh, the manager of the bazaar. According to Fallon's *Dictionary* (s.v. peshāb), the phrase is: '*unke peshāb mein chirāg jalta hai*: the water he discharges reflects a burning light (said of the well-to-do)'.

53. Interview with Sita Ahir. *Pace* Gandhi: 'I would advise those who feel guilty and repentant to hand themselves voluntarily to the Government for punishment and make a clear confession'. Gandhi also exhorted the Gorakhpur Congress 'workers . . . to find out the evil-doers and urge them to deliver themselves into custody'. *CWMG*, xxii, p. 420.

54. '*Tāp-ki-kham-kham*' is the standard phonetic rendering of the sound of horses' hooves in Hindustani. See Vidyanivas Misr, *Hindi ki Shabd Sampada* (Rajkamal Prakashan, Nai Dilli, 1982), p. 22.

55. Interview with Ramji Chamar, Puranmasi's son, Chotki Dumri, 28.8.1991.

56. Memo of Examination, Abdulla alias Sukhi, s/o Gobar of Rajdhani, *Churihar*, 23 May 1922, CCR.

57. See above, pp. 97, 107–9.

58. The quotations in this paragraph are taken from Theodore Piggott, *Outlaws I Have Known*, pp. 287–9. Piggott was one of the two judges of the High Court who passed the final sentence in the Chauri Chaura case.

59. Ibid., pp. 288–90.

60. Douglas Hay, 'Property, Authority and Criminal Law', in Hay et al., eds., *Albion's Fatal Tree: Crime and Society in Eighteenth Century England* (Harmondsworth, 1975), esp. pp. 40–9.

61. Piggott, p. 288. See also above, p. 107–9.

62. In answer to the question about the location of the trial, Sita also mentioned 172, but in a garbled way. Here there were 372 who were sentenced to death at Gorakhpur, and this number was reduced to 172 at Allahabad due to the efforts of Madan Mohan Malaviya. To quote Sita:

मोकदमा जेहल में चले, इहाँ के जज जेहलिया में जा और "केस" करे चौरी चौरा के त ओकरे बाद ई फैसला कर दिहलां—अ 372 अदमी के सजा-ए-फाँसी दे देहलां, मदन मालवीजी—इत्थी—"अपील" कर दिहलां—हाई कोर्ट। हाई कोर्ट से 172 आदमी के सजा-ए-फाँसी भईल, और अदमी छूट गइलां, हर एतवार जेहलवा में भेंट कीहल जा।

63. '*Hān rahlān!*', Sita replied to a question, '*pahila phānsi Abdullah ke hai*'. The Criminal Appeal no. 51, decided on 30th April 1923, from the Order of Special Sessions Judge, Gorakhpur was titled *Abdullah and Others* versus *King Emperor*.

64. 'A whole lot were punished; we, (their family members) have got (copies of) the judgment'. Sita Ahir then dwells on the three orders of punishment: '*jail*', '*dāmul*' (transportation for life, in effect fourteen years' rigorous imprisonment in the Andaman Islands) and '*phānsi*' (death by hanging).

जजमेंट हम्मन लिहल बानी. . . जे जेहल रहल तौनो छूट गइल—कांग्रेस के राज भईल त—अ जे "डामल" रहल तौनो छूट गइल, बाकि जे-के फाँसी हो गइल ऊ ना आईल. . . ऊ लोग अइलां—फाँसी हो गइल त ऊ नाई आइल।

'Damul', the popular term for transportation for life used by Sita, is a
peasantized abridgment of the Persian legal term '*Dāyam-ul-habs*', lit.
enclosed/imprisoned forever. Interestingly, Sita uses the technical term
'saza-i-phānsi' for death by hanging in the passage cited in note 62 above.

65.   Report on the Goraits of Gorakhpur, by E.J. Mardon, Police Progs.
(NWP), June 1894, no. 103, para 9. In a fictionalized account of police
work in UP, 'Suarghenta Pasi', the 'swine' gorait, is spat upon by a
fellow-gorait under order of a police official so as to induce(?) him to
produce the culprit! See *Constablevrittāntmāla va Pulisvrittāntmāla ka
dūsra bhāg jise 'Bhārat Jīvan' sampādak Babu Ram Krishan Varma ne
sarvsādhāran upkārārth saral bhasha mein anuvād kar prakāshit kiya*
(Kashi, 1901), p. 63.

66.   Of the 7543 goraits in 1894, 83 per cent belonged to the Chamar-
Dusadh-Bhar lower-caste cluster, with the Chamars accounting for a high
60 per cent. Among the chaukidars, Ahirs (the caste to which Sita's family
belonged), 26 per cent and Musalmans, 22 per cent were the largest
groups; Chamars and Dusadhs, by contrast, accounted for no more than
7 per cent of the 2302 chaukidars. Statistics from Report on the Goraits
of Gorakhpur, cited above.

67.   After a protracted debate, the 'office' of gorait was merged with that of
the chaukidar . Under this scheme many goraits lost their post. Provisions
were made to prevent the dispossession of rent-free allotments of these
ex-goraits. See Gorakhpur Goraits Act, 1919 (UP Act 1 of 1919), in Rev.
A Progs., March 1919, nos. 6–41.

68.   On the status of the Chauri Chaura thana, see *NWP Gazetteer*, vi (1881),
p. 476; File xx-69 (II)-1896, Gorakhpur Records; NWP Police Progs, A
Dec. 18983, no. 41, Dec. 1902, no. 3.

69.   The tasks expected of the chaukidars were truly fantastic. Under section 8
of the NWP Village & Road Police Act, 1873, 'Every Village Policeman
and every Road Policeman [was to] perform the following duties:
(a)   He shall give immediate information to the officer in charge of the
police station appointed for his village or beat,
(i) of every unnatural, suspicious or sudden death occurring in the
village . . .
(ii) of each of the following offences occurring in such village . . .
(that is to say), murder, culpable homicide, rape, dacoity, theft,
robbery, mischief by fire, house-breaking, counterfeiting coin, causing grievous hurt, riot, harbouring a proclaimed offender, exposure
of a child, concealment of birth, administering stupefying drugs,
kidnapping, lurking, house trespass, and
(iii) of all attempts and preparations to commit, and abatement of,
any of the said offences.

(b) He shall keep the police informed of all disputes which are likely to lead to any riot or serious affray.

(c) He shall arrest all proclaimed offenders, and all persons whom he may find in the act of committing any offence specified in para (a) clause 2 of this section.

(d) He shall observe, and from time to time report to the officer in charge of the police station . . . the movement of all bad characters.

(e) He shall report to the officer-in-charge of such police station the arrival of suspicious characters in the neighbourhood.

(f) He shall supply to the best of his ability any local information which a Magistrate or an Officer may require, and shall promptly execute all orders issued to him by a competent authority.'

Though the chaukidar had the right to arrest, he was to take the arrested person to the police station as soon as possible. Source: 'Agra Village and Road Police Act and Related Papers', Leg. A Progs. Nov. 1873, nos. 31–53, NAI.

70. NWP Police Circular no. 3 of 1875: IG Police to all Distt. Supdts. of Police, NWP. Police Circulars (1875–6) Register, GRR.

71. Evidence of Sheoraj Kahar, chaukidar of Bhauwapar, CCR, II, p. 278; I: Appx. pp. 131ff.

72. See 'Maori' (James Inglis), *Sport & Work on the Nepaul Frontier*, (London, 1878), p. 156.

73. I.G. Police to Sec. Govt., NWP & O, 25.3. 1890, no. 2, Police Progs., May 1890, no. 2.

74. Sec. NWP & O to IG Police, 23.5.1890, Police Progs., May 1890, no. 3.

75. Sec. GUP to all Heads of Depts. (except police), Order no. 1597/viii-506H-I of 1902. For detailed rules controlling the distribution of uniforms within police lines, see, Police Progs, Aug. 1893, nos. 52–71.

76. I am here following the remarks of Ranajit Guha in his *Elementary Aspects*, p. 66.

77. 'Order' by M.B. Dikshit, 18 June 1922, p. 13, CCR.

78. CCR, II, p. 274.

79. The evidence of the chaukidars from CCR, II, pp. 274; I, pp. 281, 39; II, pp. 257, 448.

80. *Seven Photographs of the Results of the Chauri Chaura Massacre showing the Police Station and Bodies of the Victims* (Government Press, Allahabad: Published for Private Circulation Only), CID File on Chauri Chaura, UPSA.

81. Note by C. Sands, Deputy Inspector of Police, 8.3.1922, in ibid, and the CID photographer's response, in ibid.

82. Notings dated 23.3.22 and 20.4.22 in JP File 2153/1922, L/PJ/6/1789, IOR, London.

83. See the evidence of Harpal, chaukidar of Dumri, CCR, II, pp. 244–8.

84. List of volunteers in Hata and Sadr Tahsils, 27 Jan. 1922; see Exh. 80, CCR.

85. The proverb is reproduced in *Indian Notes & Queries*, iv, 1886, no. 116. For a poetical attack on *darogas*, see the poem '*Naghmāt Pulis Naseh*', in *Report of the Committee to Enquire into Police Administration of the NWP & Oudh* (Allahabad, 1891), para 53. Constable Ram Saran Singh of Chaura thana had been set upon by volunteers in January and beaten with lathis. See CCR, II, pp. 729–31.

86. For a brief account of Bikram Ahir/Yadav in the narrative of his grandson, see pp. 124–5.

87. Memo of Bikram Ahir, 25 May 1922, CCR. See also above, p. 147.

88. On Neur Ahir, Sita's cousin and Bikram's son, see CCR, I, p. 506; Judgment, Sessions Court, p. 187.

89. Cf. 'Accused [Bikram] was a chaukidar . . . I heard that when the accused had been convicted Suraj Bali, his brother, was appointed in his place'. Evidence of Kumar, chaukidar of Mundera, CCR, I, p. 344.

90. Entry no. 782, Register of Volunteers of Gorakhpur, Unnumbered Exh. CCR.

91. CCR, II, 245.

92. Judgment of Sessions Judge, p. 120, CCR.

93. Interview with Raghvendra Sharma 'Vaid', Mundera Bazaar, 22 February 1989.

94. Committal Order by M.B. Dikshit, p. 12; Judgment of Sessions Judge, pp. 176-7.

95. Musammat Rajmani Kaur, 'Answers to Interrogatories', CCR, II, p. 379b. Emphasis added. Under the Evidence Act there was a special procedure for taking the evidence of women in purdah.

96. Committal Order, p. 12.

97. CCR, II, p. 379a.

98. For the full text of the darogain's testimony, see CCR, II, pp. 379a–379c.

99. The *buzurg*, glowingly described as '*qaddāwār jawān, first-class-ki-dārhi, amāma pahine-hue*', prayed successfully for the Madanpur undertrials. In addition, it was because of his 'powers' that the police raiding party had difficulty locating the village on the night of 18 March. Interview with Moharam Sheikh.

100. Judgment, High Court, pp. 16–17.

101. Extract from the District Khilafat Committee's [confiscated] Papers: '*Āmad-ke kāgzāt ka Ragister*', Exh. no. 95, CCR. I have modified the translation from the one given in the High Court Judgment, p. 16.

102. Judgment, High Court, p. 16.
103. Exh. 95, CCR.
104. Judgment, Sessions Judge, p. 9.
105. For Gandhi's reception at Chauri Chaura, see Shahid Amin, 'Gandhi as Mahatma', *Subaltern Studies III*, pp. 19–20.
106. Interview with Sita Ahir, Chotki Dumri.
107. The quotations in this para and the estimate of the crowd at Chauri Chaura are from 'Mahamtamji ki Aguāni', Report by Pandit Shyamdhar Mishra, in *Swadesh*, 13.2.1921, p. 3.
108. 'Some Illustrations', 22.9.1920, *CWMG*, xviii, p. 273.
109. See the chapter Dumri-Chauri Chaura-Mundera above.
110. 'Necessity of Discipline', 20.10.1920, *CWMG*, xviii, p. 361. The next quotation in this paragraph is also from the same source.
111. For an account of Gandhi's Gorakhpur meeting, see Shahid Amin, 'Gandhi as Mahatma', in R. Guha, ed., *Subaltern Studies III*, pp. 21ff.
112. *Swadesh*, 13.2.1921, p. 3.
113. 'What to do when one loses one's temper', 20.2.1922, *CWMG*, xviii, pp. 373-5; Mahadev Desai, *Day-to-day with Gandhi* (Secretary's Diary), iii (Varanasi, 1965), p. 264.
114. 'Democracy "versus" Mobocracy', 8.9.1920, *CWMG*, xviii, pp. 242–4. For an analysis of Gandhi's attempt at 'mob control', see Ranajit Guha, 'Discipline and Mobilize', in Chatterjee and Pandey, eds, *Subaltern Studies VII* (Delhi, 1992).
115. This rumour was reported by Sri Murlidhar Gupt from Majhauli in *Swadesh*, 16.3.1921, p. 5. I discuss this and several other rumours about the 'powers' of Mahatma Gandhi in 'Gandhi as Mahatma', *Subaltern Studies III*, pp. 1–61.
116. *CWMG*, xviii, p. 374.
117. For a brief discussion of these two themes, see Shahid Amin, 'Gandhi as Mahatma', *Subaltern Studies III*, pp. 52–3.
118. The statement about the singing of songs at the Dumri sabha is taken from Shikari's Testimony, CCR, II, p. 9. While describing a non-co-operation meeting at the tahsil town of Hata on 31 January 1921, Shikari had earlier recalled: 'A Panditji standing on a [stool] . . . recit[ed] Mohammad Ali's mother says "son die for the Khilafat"', CCR, I, p. 165; see also above p. 88. For similar singings by itinerant minstrels (and the text of the second song), see Qazi Mohammad Adil Abbasi, *Tārīkh-i-Khilāfat* (New Delhi, 1978), p. 190. I am emboldened by family ethnography and fieldwork into hazarding the guess that many more Muslim urban dwellers than peasants had committed these two songs to heart.
119. CCR, I, p. 919.

120. Testimony of Shikari, CCR, II, p. 1. Emphasis added.
121. *Gyan Shatki*, Feb. 1921, p. 404.
122. See for instance the official handbill 'Khabardār' issued by the Dy. Commr. of Rae Bareli, encl. in Jawaharlal Nehru Papers, pt II, File 120, NMML.
123. See 'Some Instances of the highhanded methods of Non-Cooperation Volunteers', encl. to Bihar Govt. letter dated, 5 Dec. 1921, Home Pol. File 327/I/1922, NAI.
124. *Tajwiz Awwal,* p. 358, CCR.
125. Judgment, High Court, p. 9.
126. CCR, I, p. 712.
127. CCR, II, p. 21.
128. Judgment, High Court, p. 9. The evidence about Lal Mohammad in the next sentence comes from the testimony of Shikari before the Sessions Judge, p.1.
129. Evidence of Mindhai, cultivator of Mahadeva, and Birda, cultivator of Bale, CCR, II, pp. 512–13.
130. CCR, II, pp. 250, 337, 348, 349.
131. CCR, II, p. 525.
132. CCR, p. 516.
133. See Majid Hayat Siddiqi, *Agrarian Unrest in North India: The United Provinces, 1918–1922* (Delhi, 1981); Kapil Kumar, *Peasants in Revolt: Tenants, Landlords, Congress and the Raj in Oudh, 1886–1922* (Delhi, 1984); Stephen Henningham, *Peasant Movements in Colonial India, North Bihar, 1917–42* (Canberra, 1982); Sumit Sarkar, *'Popular' Movements and 'Middle Class' Leadership: Perspectives and Problems of a 'History from Below'* (Calcutta, 1983). See also the evidence contained in my 'Gandhi as Mahatma', *Subaltern Studies III,* esp. pp. 53–4.
134. The phrase equating volunteer activity with 'Gandhi Mahatma's work' was actually used by a rural policeman in his testimony in the court. See evidence of Jagannath, chaukidar of Awadhpur, CCR, II, p. 362.
135. *Dāda* (grandfather in Hindustani) stands for 'father' in the kinship terminology of rural east UP. The Bhojpuri exclamation, *'Ahi-ho-Dāda!'* is the exact equivalent of the Hindustani, *'Bāp-re-Bāp!'* Both correspond to the English 'Oh my God!'
136. Naujadi offered this clarification in answer to my question. *Khariyāni,* from *khalihān,* harvest floor: dues collected at the threshing floor. District Congress records mention *khaliyāni* dues which were to be collected in the villages.
137. CCR, II, p. 2.
138. CCR, I, pp. 161ff; II, pp. 245, 705, 707.

139. *S.V. Chutki*, in *A New Hindustani Dictionary, with illustrations from Hindustani literature and folklore*, by S.W. Fallon (Banaras/London, 1879).

140. The full statement on 'chutki' runs as follows:

अमीन	:	त ओटियर लोग का करत रहलां?
नौजादी	:	ओटियर! ऐसे बता देईं—ओही! चुटकिया मांगें।
अमीन	:	का कह कर मांगें?
नौजादी	:	मांगे भिखिया जैसे मांगल जा-ला—सब के जाहिल न रहे! चाहे दाल-ए-बनावे, चाहे भात बनावे, चाहे पिसान बनावे, उनके खातिर काढ़-के धरा जा।
अमीन	:	त काहे लोग उनकर बतिया मानत रहलां भाई?
नौजादी	:	बतिया ई मानत रहलां—सरकार के हुकुम दीहल रहल, सरकार के हुकुम रहल, सरकार के ओर से मांगत रहलां।
अमीन	:	सरकार के, कि गान्ही-बाबा के?
नौजादी	:	उहे! गान्ही-ए-बाबा के—त उहे दिया जाए।
अमीन	:	त का कह के मांगत रहलां?
नौजादी	:	रोज नाहिं न कहें! . . . नाहिं दुसरे तिसरे दिन चुटकी दियात रहल . . . उनके नियुति से तीन दिन रसोई बनावल जा—चाहे बढ़े चाहे घटे, उनकी चुटकी धइल रहे - त जेहिया आवें भीख मांगे, त उनके दिया जाए।

141. To quote Sita Ahir, '*Olantiyar bhīk māngat rahlan. Olantiyar—koi kharcha de nāhīn—din-bhar ghoomen, aur khāe-khātir mānge—khāeke*'. The chaukidar of Bishembharpur named Buddhu and Iddan as volunteers in the Court. He ' . . . found out [that] they were volunteers when Budhu *went hither and thither asking for chutki*'. Emphasis added. CCR, II, p. 423.

142. Cf. 'According to the stated rule, they must not approach a house to beg until the regular meal-time is passed; what remains over is the portion of the mendicant'. Article on 'Asceticism (Hindu)', by A.S. Gedden, in J. Hastings ed., *Encyclopedia of Religion and Ethics* (New York, 1910), II, p. 92.

143. Gen. [Admn.] Dept. Resolution of NWP Govt., dt. 29 Aug 1893, para 3(a), xvi–37/1898–1900, Commissioner's Records, Gorakhpur.

144. *Swadesh*, 10 April 1921.

145. 'Notice by Raghupati Sahai', *Swadesh*, 1 May 1921, p. 8.

146. Exhs. 114, 121, CCR; Trials of Volunteers in Padrauna tahsil, 1922, Defence of India Rules Bastas, GRR.

147. Chutki, a pinch, had become *muthia*, a fistful. See 'Budget 1921–22 of the District Congress Committee, Part B', Exh. 82, CCR.

148. CCR, II, p. 593.

149. See for instance the Report on Non-co-operation in Hata Tahsil, *Swadesh*, 16.10.1921, p. 11.

150. Account of Income, dt. 4.5.1921, Budget 1921–22 of the District Congress Committee, Gorakhpur, Exh. 81, CCR.

151. See Exh. 82, CCR.

152. Testimony of Shikari, CCR, II, p. 2.

153. Judgment, Sessions Judge, p. 18.

154. There was the further problem of the distribution of this collection between the Tilak Fund and the Khilafat Fund. A meeting of the Gorakhpur Committee had agreed in early January to divide the muthia collection in a 'fixed proportion'. In some other UP districts the ratio was 25 per cent for the Khilafat collection with 75 per cent reserved for the Tilak Fund. See Evidence of Maulvi Subhanullah and Hakeem Arif, CCR, II, pp. 562, 687; Jawaharlal Nehru to Sec. AICC, 19 Oct. 1921, *Selected Works of Jawahar Lal Nehru*, vol. I (Delhi, 1972), p. 200.

155. On public levy, see Ranajit Guha, *Elementary Aspects*, pp. 113–15.

156. Testimony of Shikari, CCR, II, p. 8, also pp. 125, 514, 515.

157. *'Dholak baja rahe the aur jhande uthāe hue the'*: Evidence of Sarju Kahar, *Tajwiz Awwal*, p. 358 CCR.

158. *Sattu*, or *satua*, flour of parched barley and gram, is a common *kaccha* food in eastern UP and Bihar. Sattu is mixed with water and kneaded into a dough and garnished with chillies and onions. A few pounds of sattu is enough for a peasant to subsist on for a couple of days.

159. *S.V. Bhandara*, in Fallon, *New Hindustani Dictionary*.

160. The 'luckless peasant' in Ram Kumar Upadhyay Vaid's lament goes hungry because of all manner of imposts, including chutki demanded by babas:

हाकिम इनसे पोत मांगे, मेम्बर इनसे ओट मांगे
बाबा दुआरे मांगे दाल-ओ-पिसान हो!
देवता कराही मांगे, लकड़ी सिपाही मांगे
गंगा के तीर मांगे, पण्डा इनसे दान हो!

गुरू बाबा पूजा मांगे, लाला इनसे भूसा मांगे
माता-भवानी मांगे, चुरकी-ओ कान हो!
खसी-भेड़ा दुर्गा मांगे, गाजी मियाँ मुर्गा मांगे.

— राम कुमार उपाध्याय, "वैध", *वैध की लचारी* (जौनपुर, 1942)

161. Gandhi regarded alms-seeking as a part of 'the beggar problem', a 'social
nuisance', especially in the cities. In August 1921 he wrote strongly
against the 'hundreds and thousands of people [who] do not work and
live on alms, thereby putting their ochre robes to shame . . . Today we
simply have no work of a kind which we could offer to a beggar.' The
answer lay with the handloom and the spinning wheel. With village
industry revived, 'only Brahmins and fakirs who disseminated knowledge
among the people will continue to live on alms . . . Rogues will no longer
be able to roam around in the garb of sadhus and beg for alms'. In his
speech in January 1925, however, Gandhi employed the metaphor of
alms and begging to help enlist volunteers at the Petlad Cultivator's
Conference in Gujarat. The sources for the above quotations are, *CWMG*,
lxxii, pp. 136–7; xxii, p. 471; xxv, p. 599.

162. That mārkīn, the mill-cloth, was primarily white is attested by Sita Ahir's
remark, '*mārkīn jyada chale; rangīn kam chale*'. See also Appx. B: 'On
Cloth and the Clothes of the Natives of Eastern United Provinces' by
Ram Gharib Chaube, in William Crooke, *A Glossary of North Indian
Peasant Life*, ed. by Shahid Amin (Delhi, 1989), para 726.

163. Evidence of Abdul Karim, CCR, I, p. 109. Emphasis added.

164. Montgomery Martin, ed., *The History, Antiquities, Topography and Statistics of Eastern India*, II (London, 1838), pp. 267–8. *Kusum* or safflower
in fact formed the basis of as many as 19 different colours, ranging from
saffron-yellow, orange to green, light blue, dark blue and even black. In
the preparation of most of the darker colours it was used in conjunction
with indigo. The riddle '*Bāp rahal pete, pūt gel bariyāt*': While the father,
i.e. the seed was still in the womb (i.e., pod), the son (safflower dye) went
to a wedding party, indicates 'the comprehensive range of colours em-
braced by safflower'. Marriages, of course, were the occasion for a riot of
colour. See George A. Grierson, *Bihar Peasant Life* (Calcutta, 1885), para
1043.

165. CCR, II, pp. 38, 39, 49, 76, 115, 460. The organic dyes used in
Gorakhpur to colour the white *nān-gilāt* (long cloth) *dhotis* were: *kusum*
(safflower), *haldi* (turmeric), the bark of the *tun* tree (*Cedrela toona*) and

the flowers of *tesu* and *harsingār* (*Nyctanthes arbortristis*). Turmeric, an essential condiment, was used by those too poor to afford the fees of a professional dyer. Written communication, Habib Ahmad, Gorakhpur. See also 'List of Trees and Shrubs in the Gorakhpur Forest Division', *Working Plan for the Forests of the Gorakhpur Division*, by R.G. Marriott (Allahabad, 1915), Appx. iv.

166. 'The pathetic anxiety of all volunteer bodies to model themselves on the pattern of the military and police uniforms . . . ', as noticed by the Intelligence Bureau in 1939, belonged to a later period. In August 1940, with the war in full swing, 'the wearing of unofficial uniforms bearing a colourful resemblance to military or official uniforms' was prohibited in India. See, Note on Volunteer Movement in India, Pt. III by IB, June 1939, and copy of despatch by Reuters, Simla, 5 August 1940, in L/PJ/8/678, IOL.

167. Note, dated May 27 1922 by UP CID on Volunteer Movement, GAD File 658/1920, UPSA, Lucknow; Rahul Sankrityayan, *Meri Jeevan Yatra*, pp. 355, 358–9.

168. Bihar & Orissa Secret Abstracts, 17.2. 1921, para 2071, cited in Police Abstracts of Intelligence, UP, 7.1. 1922, p. 41.

169. Instructions issued after the Dec. 3 1921 meeting of the (UP) *Prantiya Swayam Sevak Dal*, Exh. 118, CCR.

170. *CWMG*, xxii, p. 152.

171. Ibid., xxii, p. 273.

172. Ibid., xxii, p. 152.

173. Ibid., xxii, p. 323.

174. Ibid., xx, p. 451. The source of Gandhi's quotation was Mr Pickthall, editor of *The Bombay Chronicle*.

175. Cf. Hakeem Arif, 'founder' of Dumri mandal : 'I wear khaddar still as I did before. My upper garment is not khaddar, nor are my trousers'. Evidence dated, 12.9.1922, CCR, II, p. 685.

176. *CWMG*, xxii, pp. 463–4.

177. When the Pandit of Malaon stated that he 'remember[ed] the condition that *gārha* was not to be worn and *khaddar* was', he was implying that the rough handloom cloth (gārha) of the locality was fabricated from mill-made yarn. CCR, II, p. 469.

178. *The Pioneer*, 9 February 1922, cited in Sir C. Sankaran Nair, *Gandhi and Anarchy* (Madras, 1922), Appx. xii: Gorakhpur Tragedy, p. 164.

179. Report by H.N. Kunzru, Maulvi Subhanullah and C.K. Malaviya, *Leader*, 23.2.1922.

180. See CCR, I, pp. 161, 115, 76, 49; II, 38, 49, 76, 115, 245, 705, 707.

181. CCR, I, p. 267. Emphasis added.

182. CCR, I, p. 145. Emphasis added.

183. Evidence of Pandit Mahesh Bal Dixit, Dy. Magistrate, CCR, II, p. 807. See also, 'Instructions re: Identification of undertrial prisoners in jails', UP Police A Progs., Sept. 1910 no. 4(a).

184. Interview with Dwarka Pandey, cited in Ram Murat Upadhyay, 'Gorakhpur janpad mein Swatantrata Sangharsh, 1857–1947' (Gorakhpur University, Ph.D. thesis, 1975), pp. 152–3.

185. Evidence of Thag Chamar, chaukidar, Gaunar, CCR, I, p. 303.

186. Evidence of Mahatam Sukul, CCR, I, p. 287. Emphasis added.

187. CCR, I, pp. 273–4.

188. On Bhagwan Ahir's uniform, see testimonies of Bhagwan Ahir, Harcharan Singh, the Pandit of Malaon and Constable Jai Ram, CCR, I, pp. 82, 264ff, 366, 491; II, p. 473.

189. Testimony of Shikari, Chauri Chaura Trials, II, pp. 38–9.

190. Testimony of Thakur Ahir, CCR, II, p. 49.

191. The quotations are taken from the Judgment of Sessions Judge H.E. Holmes, pp. 234–5. Emphasis added.

192. CCR, I, pp. 338, 422.

193. There seems to have been general agreement about this in Dumri. 'I understand what volunteers are', stated Subhag of Chotki Dumri in court. 'Shikari, Nazar Ali, Nageshar and Awadhi Pasi. These 4 are volunteers', he told the Sessions Judge. 'I considered them to be volunteers because they *wore ochre-coloured clothes and demanded chutki*'. CCR, II, p. 481, Emphasis added.

194. 'Gerua' from the Sanskrit 'gairika', that is, the colour of 'giri' or hills, is used by many Hindu sects as a prescriptive colour for garments worn by those of their members who have renounced the world. As such it came to symbolize the spirit of world-renunciation in Hindu religious thought and practice. Adopted by Hindu nationalist discourse of both literary and political genres since the middle of the last century, 'gerua' has been operating in north-Indian culture as an index of Hindu-nationalist sentiment with various idealist connotations, such as religiosity, patriotism, self-sacrifice etc. A well-known Bengali (Hindu) patriotic play, based on a fictionalized version of Shivaji's conflict with the Mughals, was called *Gairik Patāka* (The Saffron Flag). As with so many other things, Bankimchandra Chattopadhyay's writings did much to promote the Hindu-nationalist symbolism of this particular colour. The armed band of sanyasis whose exploits are celebrated in his novel, *Anandmath*, were all clad in saffron robes. They called themselves *santāns*, i.e. children of The Mother (= Motherland), and stepped out of fiction into real life during the Swadeshi Movement when many of its nationalist volunteers adopted

the appellation and the dress. The arrival of such a band at the house of the liberal-landlord hero of Tagore's novel *Ghare Baire* acts as a cue in the development of its plot. Written Communication from Ranajit Guha.

195. The phrase is Ranajit Guha's. See his 'Chandra's Death', in Guha, ed., *Subaltern Studies VI.*

196. See Natalie Zemon Davis, *Fiction in the Archives: Pardon Tales and their Tellers in Sixteenth-century France* (Stanford, 1987), esp. p. 4 from where the bulk of the questions and quotation in this paragraph have been taken. My argument is in partial response to Professor Davis' comments on an earlier draft of this manuscript.

197. The official directory of accredited nationalists published by the Information Department of the UP Government in 1972 not only gives pride of place to the twenty 'martyrs' hanged for their part in the 'Chauri Chaura *kānd*', it also affords an honorable mention to the five undertrials who expired (*divangat*) in jail. See *Swatantrata sangrām ke sainik (sankshipt parichay)*, vol. 35, Gorakhpur (Suchna Vibhag, Lucknow, 1972), pp. 1–2.

198. Amodnath Tripathi, 'Poorvi Uttar-Pradesh ke jan-jeevan mein Baba Raghav Das ka Yogdān' (Ph.D thesis, Allahabad University, 1981), p. 135; Interview with Raghvendra Sharma 'Vaid', Mundera Bazaar, 22 February 1989.

Bibliography

UNPUBLISHED RECORDS

Gorakhpur Records Room

Files in Revenue, Political, Police, General Administration, Judicial
   Criminal & Criminal Investigation Departments, 1858–1943.
Gorakhpur Settlement Report (1889–91), MS Appendices.
Assessment Notes on individual villages in *tappa* Keotali, 1885.
Khewat, Khatyuni, Dastur dehi and *Wajib-ul-arz* of individual villages
   in *tappa* Keotali for 1323 *Fasli.*
Defence of India Rules *Bastas,* 1921–1942.
Papers connected with Trial nos. 44–45 of 1922 [Chauri Chaura
   Records].

Museum of the High Court, Allahabad

File on the Chauri Chaura Case.

UP Criminal Investigations Department (CID), Lucknow

Police Abstracts of Intelligence, UP, 1922–23.

UP State Archives, Lucknow

Files in Revenue, General Administration, CID Departments, 1870–
   1940.

National Archives of India

Files in the Political, Home Political, Revenue and Legislative Departments, 1870–1922.

India Office Records, London

Proceedings in the Revenue, Political and Police Departments of NWP and UP, *c.* 1857–1923.

Survey of India, 1921, Map Sheets.

Private Papers

Buchanan-Hamilton, 'An Account of the Northern Portion of Gorakhpur', MS Eur. D-92, D-93, IOL.

Haig Papers MSS Eurp. F. 115, IOL.

Jawahar Lal Nehru Papers, Pt. I and Pt. II, NMML.

Sri Prakash Papers, Misc., NMML.

Miyan Sahab Estate, Imambara, Gorakhpur.

William Crooke Papers, Museum of Mankind, London.

Newspapers

Aaj
Abhyuday
Gyan Shakti
Leader
Mashriq
Pioneer
Pratap
Swadesh

Hindi and Urdu Sources

ABBASI, Qazi Mohammad Adil, *Tārīkh-i-Khilāfat* (New Delhi, 1978).

Baba Raghav Das Abhinandan Granth (Varanasi, 1963).

BHADURI, Satinath, *Dhorāi Charit Mānas*, (original in Bengali; Hindi translation by Madhukar Gangadhar, Ilahabad, 1981).

Bhartendu Samagra (Varanasi, 1989).

BRAHMANAND, *Bhartiya Swatantrata Āndolan aur Uttar Pradesh ki Patra-kārita* (Delhi, 1986).

Dumkati Sarkar (Kanpur, 1922) Proscribed Pamphlet, India Office Library, London.

Gandhi-ki Larāi, urf Satyāgraha Itihās (Bulandshahar, 1931), Proscribed Pamphlet, India Office Library, London.

GAJPURI, Mannan Dwivedi, *Ram Lal (grameen jeevan ka ek sāmājik upanyās* (Prayag, 1917).

JAFRI, Maulvi Syed Najmuddin Ahmad, *Jangi Novel, ya ek Sipāhi ki sarguzasht ka saccha photo; yāni fauj mein bharti hone ka aur sipāhiyāna zindagi ke dilchasp hālāt* (Sitapur, 1918).

MISR, Vidyanivas, *Hindi ki Shabd-sampada* (Nai Dilli, 1982).

PREMCHAND, Munshi, *Chitthi-patri*, i (Ilahabad, 1962).

SANKRITYAYAN, Rahul, *Meri Jeevan Yatra* (1), (Kalkutta, 1955).

Swatantrata sangrām ke sainik (sankshipt parichay), vol. 35: Gorakhpur (Suchna Vibhag, Lucknow, 1972).

TRIPATHI, Amodnath, 'Poorvi Uttar Pradesh ke jan-jeevan mein Baba Raghav Das ka Yogdān.' (Ph.D. thesis, Allahabad University, 1981).

UPADHYAY, Ram Murat, 'Gorakhpur janpad mein Swatantrata Sangharsh 1857–1947' (Ph.D. thesis, Gorakhpur University, 1975).

'VAID', Ram Kumar Upadhyay, *Vaid ki Lachāri* (Jaunpur, 1942).

VARMA, Babu Ram Krishan, *Constablevrittāntmala va Pulisvritāntmala ka dūsra bhāg* (Kashi, 1901).

VARMA, Lal Bahadur, 'Kshetrīya Itihās ka Pariprekshya: Seemāin aur Sambhāvanāin', in *Uttar Pradesh ka Itihas* (mimeo: Gorakhpur University Conference, March 2–3, 1984).

European Language Sources

Allahabad High Court Weekly Notes, 1889 (Allahabad).

AMIN, Shahid, 'Gandhi as Mahatma: Gorakhpur District, Eastern UP, 1921–22', in Ranajit Guha ed., *Subaltern Studies, III* (Delhi, 1984).

—— *Sugarcane and Sugar in Gorakhpur: An Inquiry into Peasant Production for Capitalist Enterprise in Colonial India* (Delhi, 1984).

ANDERSON, Benedict, 'Narrating the Nation', *Times Literary Supplement*, 23 June 1986.

Annual Report on the Operation of the Post Office of India, 1886–87 (Calcutta).

Archaeological Survey of India: *Report of a Tour in the Gorakhpur District in 1875–76 and 1876–77*, xviii by A.C.L. Carlyle (Calcutta, 1883).

BARTHES, Roland, *Image-Music-Text* (Glasgow, 1979).

BAXI, Upendra, ' "The State's Emissary" the Place of Law in Subaltern Studies', in Partha Chatterjee and Gyanendra Pandey eds, *Subaltern Studies, VII* (Delhi, 1992).

BAYLY, C.A., *Rulers, Townsmen and Bazaars: North Indian Society in the Age of British Expansion, 1770–1870* (Cambridge, 1988).

BURT, B.C., *Description of the Working Sugar Factory exhibited in the Agricultural Court, United Provinces Exhibition, by Mesrs. Blair, Campbell and Maclean* (U.P. Agricultural Series, Bulletin no. 26, Allahabad, 1911).

CHAKRABARTY, Dipesh, 'Postcoloniality and the Artifice of History: Who speaks for "Indian" Pasts?' *Representations*, 37 (Winter, 1992), pp. 1–26.

CHATTERJEE, Partha, 'Gandhi and the Critique of Civil Society', in Ranajit Guha ed., *Subaltern Studies III* (Delhi, 1984).

—— The *Nation and its Fragments: Colonial and Postcolonial Histories* (Princeton, 1993).

CORBIN, Alain, *The Village of Cannibals. Rage and Murder in France* (Cambridge: Mass., 1992).

Correspondence relating to the Procedure in regard to Confession of persons accused of criminal offences, P.P. Cmd. 7234 (London, 1914).

CROOKE, William, *The North Western Provinces of India: Their History, Ethnology and Administration* (London, 1897, reprint Karachi 1972).

—— *A Glossary of North Indian Peasant Life*, Shahid Amin ed. (Delhi, 1989).

DAS, Veena, 'Subaltern as Perspective' in Guha ed., *Subaltern Studies, VI* (Delhi, 1989), pp. 310–24.

DAVIS, Natalie Zemon, *The Return of Martin Guerre* (Cambridge: Mass., 1983).

—— *Fiction in the Archives: Pardon Tales and their Teller in Sixteenth Century France* (Stanford, 1987).

District Census Statistics (United Provinces): Gorakhpur District, 1891 (Allahabad).

District Census Statistics (United Provinces): Gorakhpur District, 1921 (Allahabad).

DOWNS, T.F., 'Civil Rebellion in the Banaras Division, 1857–58' (M.A. thesis, University of Centerbury, 1987).

FALLON, S.W., *A New Hindustani Dictionary, with Illustrations from Hindustani Literature and Folklore* (Banaras/London, 1879).

Final Settlement Report of the Western Portion of the Gorakhpur District, 1919 by D.M. Stewart (Allahabad).

FOUCAULT, Michel, *Discipline and Punish: The Birth of the Prison* (Harmondsworth, 1977).

FREITAG, Sandria B., 'Crime in the Social Order of Colonial North India', *Modern Asian Studies*, 25, no. 2 (1991), pp. 227–61.

GANDHI, M.K., *The Collected Works of Mahatma Gandhi* (Ahmedabad, 1958–), xviii, xxii, xxiii, xxv, lxvi, lxxii.

GEDDEN, A.S., 'Asceticism (Hindu)' in J. Hastings ed., *Encyclopedia of Religion and Ethics* (New York, 1910), vol. II.

GINZBURG, Carlo, *The Cheese and the Worms: The Cosmos of a Sixteenth Century Miller* (London, 1980).

Gorakhpur: A Gazetteer, being volume xxxi of the District Gazetteers of the United Provinces of Agra and Oudh, ed. H.R. Nevill (Allahabad 909, 2nd edn., 1929).; *Supplementary notes and Statistics*, 1916, 1925 (Allahabad).

GRIERSON, George A., *Bihar Peasant Life* (Calcutta, 1885).

GUHA, Ranajit, 'The Mahatma and the Mob', *South Asia*, no. 3 (August, 1973), pp. 107–11.

—— *Elementary Aspects of Peasant Insurgency in Colonial India* (Delhi, 1983).

—— 'Chandra's Death', in Guha ed., *Subaltern Studies, V* (Delhi, 1987).

—— 'Discipline and Mobilize', in Partha Chatterjee and Gyanendra Pandey eds, *Subaltern Studies VII* (Delhi, 1992).

HAY, Douglas, 'Property, Authority and Criminal Law', in Hay et al.

eds, *Albion's Fatal Tree: Crime and Society in Eighteenth Century England* (Harmondsworth, 1977).

HENNINGHAM, Stephen, *Peasant Movements in Colonial India, North Bihar, 1917–42* (Canberra, 1982).

HEPWORTH, Mike and Bryan S. Turner, *Confession: Studies in Deviance and Religion* (London, 1982).

Indian Notes and Queries, iv., 1886.

KUMAR, Kapil, *Peasants in Revolt: Tenants, Landlords, Congress and the Raj in Oudh, 1886–1922* (New Delhi, 1984).

KUMAR, Nita, *The Artisans of Banaras: Popular Culture and Identity, 1880–1986* (Princeton, 1988).

KUMAR, Ravinder ed., *Essays on Gandhian Politics: The Rowlatt Satyagraha of 1919* (Oxford, 1971).

LE ROY LADURIE, Emmanuel, *Montaillou: The Promised Land of Error* (New York, 1979).

"MAORI" (pseud. James Inglis), *Sport and Work on the Nepaul Frontier, or twelve years' reminiscences of an indigo planter* (London, 1878).

MARTIN, Montgomery ed., *The History, Antiquities, Topography, and Statistics of Eastern India*, ii (London, 1839).

MAYNE, J.W., *Hints on Confessions and Approvers for the Use of the Police* (Madras, 1906).

MAYO, Katherine, *The Face of Mother India* (London/New York, 1935).

MINAULT, Gail, *The Khilafat Movement: Religious Symbolism and Political Mobilization in India* (New York, 1982).

MITRA, N.N. ed., *The Indian Annual Register, 1920* (reprint, Delhi, 1986).

NAIR, C. Sankaran, *Gandhi and Anarchy* (Madras, 1922).

NIGAM, Sanjay, 'A Social History of a Colonial Stereotype: The Criminal Tribes and Castes of Uttar Pradesh, 1871–1930' (Ph.D. thesis, London University, 1987).

PIGGOTT, Theodore, *Outlaws I Have Known and Other Reminiscences of an Indian Judge* (Edinburg & London, 1930).

PRASAD, Rajendra ed., *Young India, 1921–22 by Mahatma Gandhi* (Madras, 1922).

REID, J.R., *Azamgarh Glossary*, being Appendix III to *Azamgarh Settlement Report* (Allahabad, 1881).

RENAN, Ernest, 'What is a Nation?' (1882), in Homi K. Bhabha ed., *Nation and Narration* (London, 1990).

Rent Rate Report, Pargana Haveli, Tahsil and District Gorakhpur (1917) by D.C. Hunter (Allahabad).

Report on the Settlement of the Gorakhpur-Bustee District, i and ii (Allahabad 1871).

Report of the Indian Famine Commission, 1874–75, Appendix iii, P.P. Cmd. 3086 (London, 1881).

Report on the Revenue Administration of the North-Western Provinces, 1887–88 (Allahabad).

'Report of the Congress Civil Disobedience Enquiry Committee' (1922), in N.N. Mitra ed., *The Indian Annual Register, 1922–23* (Calcutta, 1924).

Report of the Committee to Enquire into Police Administration of the NWP and Oudh (Allahabad, 1891).

Report on the Industrial Survey of the United Provinces: Gorakhpur District, by Mushtaq Mohammad (Allahabad, 1924).

RICOEUR, Paul, 'The Hermeneutics of Testimony', in *Essays in Biblical Interpretation* (Philadelphia, 1980).

—— *Hermeneutics and the Human Sciences: Essays on Language, Action and Interpretation* (Cambridge/Paris, 1981).

RIZVI, S.A.A. ed., *Freedom Struggle in Uttar Pradesh*, iv (Lucknow, 1960).

ROLLAND, Romain, *Mahatma Gandhi: The man who became one with the Universal Being* (New York and London, 1924).

ROSALDO, Renato, 'From the door of his Tent: The Field-worker and the Inquisitor', in J. Clifford and G.E. Marcus eds, *Writing Cultures: The Poetics and Politics of Ethnography* (Berkeley, 1986).

ROSSELLI, John, 'The Self-image of Effeteness: Physical Education and Nationalism in Nineteenth-century Bengal', *Past & Present*, no. 86 (February, 1980), pp. 121–48.

SARKAR, Sumit, *'Popular' Movements and 'Middle Class' Leadership: Perspectives and Problems of a 'History from Below'* (Calcutta, 1983).

SENGUPTA, Indira Chowdhury, 'Colonialism and Cultural Identity: The Making of a Hindu Discourse, Bengal, 1867–1905' (Ph.D. thesis, London University, 1993).

SIDDIQI, Majid Hayat, *Agrarian Unrest in North India: The United Provinces, 1918–1922* (Delhi, 1981).

SIDDIQI, N.H. *The Landlords of Agra and Avadh* (Lucknow, 1950?).

SINGHAL, B.R.P. and Narayan Das eds, *Woodroffe and Ameer Ali's Law of Evidence* (14th edn, Allahabad, 1981).

Statistical, Descriptive and Historical Account of the North-Western Provinces of India, vi (Allahabad, 1881).

SWINTON, Alan, *Manual of the Statistics of Goruckpore* (Allahabad, 1861).

United Provinces Gazette, 25 March 1922.

VIRK, D.S., *Indian Postal History, 1873–1923 Gleanings from Post Office Records* (New Delhi, 1991).

WALSH, *Indian Village Crimes: With an Introduction on Police Investigations and Confessions* (London, 1929, reprint, Delhi, 1977).

WHITE, Hayden, 'The Question of Narrative in Contemporary Historical Theory', *History & Theory*, xxiii (1984), pp. 1–33.

Words and Phrases 1658 to Date (All Judicial Constructions of Words and Phrases by the State and Federal Courts etc.) (Minneapolis, 1964).

Working Plan for the Forests of the Gorakhpur Division, by R.G. Marriott (Allahabad, 1915).

Index

DATE DUE